AF083211

Being at Home
Race, Institutional Culture and Transformation at South African Higher Education Institutions

Edited by Pedro Tabensky and Sally Matthews

UNIVERSITY OF KWAZULU-NATAL PRESS

Published in 2015 by University of KwaZulu-Natal Press
Private Bag X01
Scottsville, 3209
Pietermaritzburg
South Africa
Email: books@ukzn.ac.za
Website: www.ukznpress.co.za

© 2015 University of KwaZulu-Natal

Reprinted 2016

All rights reserved. No part of this publication may be reproduced or transmitted in any form or by any means, electronic or mechanical, including photocopying, recording or any information storage and retrieval system, without prior permission in writing from University of KwaZulu-Natal Press.

ISBN: 978 1 86914 290 2

Managing editor: Sally Hines
Editor: Alison Lockhart
Typesetter: Patricia Comrie
Indexer: Ethné Clarke
Cover design: MDesign
Cover image: Antony Kaminju/Independent Contributors/Africa Media Online

Print administration by DJE Print Solutions, Cape Town

Contents

Acknowledgements · vii

Introduction · 1
  Sally Matthews and *Pedro Tabensky*

PART I: THE BASIC QUESTIONS · 19

1 'Tell Us a New Story': A Proposal for the Transformatory Potential of Collective Memory Projects · 21
  Louise Vincent

2 'Feeling at Home': Institutional Culture and the Idea of a University · 45
  Samantha Vice

3 White Privilege and Institutional Culture at South African Higher Education Institutions · 72
  Sally Matthews

PART II: RHODES UNIVERSITY: A CASE STUDY · 97

4 Making Room for the Unexpected: The University and the Ethical Imperative of Unconditional Hospitality · 99
  Minesh Dass

5 The Violence beneath the Veil of Politeness: Reflections on Race and Power in the Academy · 116
  Thando Njovane

6   What about the Queers? The Institutional Culture of
    Heteronormativity and Its Implications for Queer Staff
    and Students   130
        Natalie Donaldson

7   Employing Safe Bets: Reflections on Attracting,
    Developing and Retaining the Next Generation of
    Academics   147
        Amanda Hlengwa

PART III: PATHWAYS   155

8   Race and Justice in Higher Education: Some Global
    Challenges, with Attention to the South African Context   157
        Lewis R. Gordon

9   Thinking Outside the Ivory Tower: Towards a Radical
    Humanities in South Africa   184
        Nigel C. Gibson

10 Towards a Decolonial Analytic Philosophy: Institutional
    Corruption and Epistemic Culture   203
        Paul C. Taylor

11 The Countercultural University   221
        Pedro Tabensky

12 Africanising Institutional Culture: What is Possible
    and Plausible   242
        Thaddeus Metz

13 Instrumentalisation in Universities and the Creative
    Potential of Race   273
        Bruce B. Janz

Postscript   297
    Pedro Tabensky and *Sally Matthews*

Contributors   302
Index   305

Acknowledgements

This book went through a very difficult and painful gestation period and we hope that our struggles to give birth to it will help to inform future debates on South African higher education. Our struggle, in many ways, mirrors the struggle of the South African academy to reckon with itself, indeed to start to understand what this reckoning amounts to. But we would not be satisfied if all we did here was to enrich a debate. It is also our wish that this book will help to inform, even if only in a small way, the future trajectory of higher education in South Africa.

Many midwives were necessary for this painful delivery and we can only mention some here. In addition to thanking contributors other than ourselves – for it would be very odd to thank ourselves – for their rich work, we would like to thank Tshidi Hashatse – Rhodes University's first Director of Equity and Institutional Culture – for her unwavering support and faith in this project. It is likely that without her support, this project would have foundered. This book would never have got off the ground without the generous financial support of the Ford Foundation, which has been funding the Centre for Higher Education, Research, Teaching and Learning (CHERTL) Roundtable Series on Critical Issues in Higher Education since 2009. This forum has encouraged us, the editors of this collection, and academics around the country (and internationally as well) to put our heads together and to reflect in depth on the nature of university life, particularly university life in the context we find ourselves in today. We would also like to thank Debra Primo from UKZN Press for believing in the project and for her patience. Despite the shifts in deadlines and slight changes in focus, she never lost faith in the project. We ought also to thank the anonymous reviewers of an earlier manuscript. Their useful feedback has helped us to improve what we are now offering to the reader. Finally, we are grateful to Alison Lockhart for her superb editing skills.

Introduction

SALLY MATTHEWS and PEDRO TABENSKY

There is a building on Rhodes University's campus called the Stephen Bantu Biko Building. It was given this name in 2008 as part of the slow process through which Rhodes University has been attempting to recognise its own commission of, and complicity in, past injustices. The renaming of buildings is one of the typical ways in which formerly white South African universities have been trying to carve out a new post-apartheid identity. In this building is a seminar room used by the Student Representative Council (SRC). Its walls are lined with photos of previous SRCs, from the early 1900s to the present. The students in the early photos are all white and mostly male. Gradually, the proportion of women increases in the photos, but until the 1990s there are only white faces. During the 1990s, a rapid change happens and in 1997 the SRC consists exclusively of black students. Since then, each photo features a 'rainbow nation' of students from various backgrounds, with women generally well represented.

The name of the building and the pictures hanging on the walls suggest a transformed institution, one that has moved from being the preserve of white men to one that celebrates diversity. Yet, when one of the editors of this collection – Sally Matthews – was asked recently to lead a discussion on institutional culture in this very room, the incompleteness and complexity of institutional transformation at South African universities was helpfully and, to some extent, disturbingly revealed as the SRC members spoke about their experiences. One SRC member spoke about how it is mainly black students he finds himself having to assist in making appeals against financial and academic exclusion. An SRC residence representative talked about the 'whiteness' of residence cultures and related an incident where a warden shouted at a group of black students animatedly watching a soccer game on television, telling them to 'stop acting like monkeys'. Others told of the difficulties of navigating 'black-on-black' racism (where being relatively light-skinned and speaking with a 'white' accent is valued by some black students) and of negotiating identity in a country where race and class remain aligned, but in more complex and ambiguous ways than before.

This renamed building, these changing photographs and this stimulating discussion all point to the complexity of transformation in South African higher education institutions. In particular, they reveal how superficial changes (renamed buildings and deracialised student bodies) sometimes disguise continuities in terms of the institutional cultures of formerly white universities. While the particular example used here is taken from Rhodes University, other formerly white South African institutions have very similar trajectories and very similar issues. Indeed, we suspect that the questions about transformation raised by the case discussed above are relevant to many universities further abroad, which are also struggling to transform their institutions to be more welcoming and accommodating for students who were previously excluded.

This book emerges out of discussions held at Rhodes University about transformation in higher education. These discussions formed part of the Centre for Higher Education, Research, Teaching and Learning's roundtable series on critical issues in higher education, which was sponsored by the Ford Foundation. While these origins mean that the book draws particularly on the Rhodes University context, this context is, as stressed above, similar to many other universities. Many, if not all, South African universities (and many universities elsewhere) are struggling to transform. In particular, many institutions are struggling to shift their institutional cultures. While policies aimed at transformation have been implemented, there is growing awareness that these policies will not succeed if they are undermined by untransformed institutional cultures. While this means that it is very important to try to change institutional cultures, they are highly nebulous things that are extremely difficult to pin down.

While this nebulousness makes it very difficult to clearly define 'institutional culture' and the various other terms usually discussed alongside it, such as 'transformation', it is necessary to try to provide some clarity about how these terms are used in this book and exactly which aspects of institutional culture and transformation are its focus.

It is difficult to find any commentary on the South African higher education sector post-1994 that does not, at some point, use the term 'transformation'. Indeed, a keyword search of the *South African Journal of Higher Education* reveals that 771 articles published in the journal since 2000 include 'transformation' as a keyword. However, what exactly 'transformation' entails is often, and perhaps understandably, rather unclear. In its most basic form, to transform means to change and it suggests deep and meaningful change for the better. In the South African higher education context, 'transformation' could be said to typically refer to attempts to change higher education institutions such that they no longer reflect the values promoted by apartheid and rather reflect the values embodied in South Africa's 1996 Constitution. Given the centrality of racial discrimination to the apartheid era, 'transformation' inevitably refers particularly to attempts to increase the proportion of black staff and students and to eliminate racism, but it also refers to attempts to address sexism, class discrimination, homophobia, xenophobia and other forms of discrimination made illegal by our 1996 Constitution, as well as to attempts to make universities more responsive to their local, national and continental contexts. Consider the goals of transformation as given in South Africa's 1997 'Education White Paper 3: A Programme for the Transformation of Higher Education': 'to redress past inequalities, to serve a new social order, to meet pressing national needs and to respond to new realities and opportunities' (cited in Govinder, Zondo and Makgoba 2013: 86). These are clearly very broad and general goals. Furthermore, 'transformation' is sometimes also referenced in discussions about the need to increase transparency, accountability and professionalism at higher education institutions. Given the broadness of the term 'transformation', it is perhaps more manageable to focus on one aspect of transformation than to try to tackle the topic as a whole. For this reason, and because institutional culture is often raised as a key impediment to transformation, we have decided to make institutional culture the focus point of this book, even while we also seek to contribute to broader discussions about higher education transformation as a whole.

While 'institutional culture' is a more specific term than 'transformation', it is also fairly broad and nebulous. As John Higgins (2007a) points out, the term 'institutional culture' has become something of a 'buzzword' in discussions of higher education in South Africa. Furthermore, his impression is that while the term apparently refers to a broad range of institutional features, it is typically used in South Africa to refer to the way in which formerly white universities continue to embody a culture perceived as being white. Thus, while the term is in many ways the equivalent of a term such as 'organisational culture' – which has been defined as the 'basic assumptions and beliefs that are shared by members of an organization that operate unconsciously, and that define in a basic "taken-forgranted" fashion an organization's view of itself and its environment' (Schein 1985 cited in Higgins 2007b: 111) – 'institutional culture' is used in South African discussions on higher education in a very specific and far narrower way, focused particularly on race. Higgins argues that an unfortunate consequence of this narrower approach is that other aspects of institutional culture, such as tensions between academic and managerial cultures, have been marginalised. Rather than trying, as does Higgins, to shift the way in which institutional culture is discussed in South Africa, this collection reflects the priorities of current debates on institutional culture in its foregrounding of race, in particular, as a key issue that needs addressing as we try to change South African higher education institutions. As a result, while many contributions touch on issues other than race, all include some reference to race in their engagements with institutional culture. The strength of this approach is that it reflects and engages with dominant debates on institutional culture in South Africa. However, a negative consequence is that the collection is far more relevant to thinking about institutional cultures at formerly white higher education institutions than it is to questions of institutional culture at formerly black institutions. We hope that subsequent discussions might pick up on some of the ways in which institutional cultures block transformation of the latter institutions.

Introduction

The first part of this book consists of three chapters that put forward some fairly broad and general reflections on institutional culture. The first two, by Louise Vincent and Samantha Vice, complement each other well and serve as a good starting point for the debates embodied in this collection as they tackle some of the basics. Both contributors recognise the difficulty of defining institutional culture and neither seeks to pin the term down definitively, although Vice favours a narrower approach to institutional culture than that advocated by Vincent. Both present some thoughts on how we can best understand and talk about institutional culture.

Vincent proposes that we need to think of institutional culture with reference to both the discursive and the material and, importantly, that we need to think of the discursive and the material together. The discursive dimension of institutional culture includes the beliefs and practices that define institutions – the 'worldview' of institutions, as Vincent puts it. The material dimension, on the other hand, relates to the actual physical features of institutions (buildings, furniture, artworks, lecture theatre design, the use of colour, security and so on) and how they affect how we experience institutions. In addition to arguing that we ought to include both the discursive and the material in our discussions of institutional culture, Vincent argues that we can best understand institutional culture in general, and the interaction of its discursive and material aspects in particular, through narrative; it is through telling stories that we make sense of our situations, personal and collective. Vincent emphasises that it is not only individuals who shape their identities through the telling of stories, but institutions also have stories that help to construct and perpetuate their institutional cultures. However, as Vincent makes clear, stories not only do the work of social reproduction; they can also interrupt social reproduction by 'making the normal strange'. Thus, she argues, the telling of narratives about our institutions can be used to change institutional cultures. Narratives can best have this effect if they are told and analysed collectively and if those in leadership positions in the institution provide legitimate spaces for new stories to be told and heard.

Vice's chapter further explores what we mean by the term 'institutional culture'. She makes use of two metaphors: being 'at home' and being 'in one's element' and argues that institutional cultures, like cultures generally, are places where some feel at home and others do not. One feels at home when one is in one's element. 'Being in one's element,' Vice argues, 'means one can both *do* what one has to do and *be* who one authentically is.' Like fish, who are in their element in water, academics should ideally be in their element at universities. Furthermore, the metaphor of being in one's element helps us, normatively speaking, better to understand the metaphor of being at home and, indeed, may be a better metaphor for thinking about institutional cultures. For, as Vice puts it, 'home can be a restrictive and overly secure space, in which one is protected from any strangeness or discomfort'. 'Being in one's element', on the other hand, 'need not entail the uncritical comfort that many are suspicious of when thinking about the notion of home.'

The third chapter in the first part, authored by Sally Matthews, has a slightly narrower focus, exploring the 'whiteness' of the institutional culture of formerly white higher education institutions in South Africa. The chapter draws on literature on white privilege, particularly the work of Shannon Sullivan (2006), to explore how racism operates in post-segregationist settings and, in particular, how it operates in formerly white higher education institutions in South Africa, such as Rhodes University. Matthews argues that the transformation of institutional cultures may require some quite creative strategies since much contemporary racism operates 'under the radar', thus making it difficult to root out.

Following on from these three chapters, which deal with the issue of institutional culture in a fairly broad way, Part II focuses on particular aspects of institutional culture. Each chapter in this section engages in some way with Rhodes University. Engagement with a particular context is helpful as it facilitates the telling of narratives, which, as Vincent points out, provide rich detail about how institutional culture functions and how it can be transformed. By engaging with their particular university's culture(s), the various authors manage to go beyond what could be rather general and vague claims in order to show specifically how institutional cultures function and how universities manage to remain untransformed despite apparently sound policies, indeed, even despite (often misguided) good intentions. However, the critical focus on Rhodes University is not meant to suggest that this institution is particularly problematic. Our experience has been that the vice chancellor and other key figures have been very welcoming of our attempts to think critically about the university's institutional culture and this welcoming attitude suggests a willingness, at least on the part of some, to drive transformation forward at Rhodes University. Furthermore, and as mentioned above, we suspect that many other institutions, in South Africa and abroad, share many of the features of Rhodes University's institutional culture described here and are thus confident that our discussion will resonate with many who are thinking through the same issues at other institutions.

The first of these chapters, by Minesh Dass, reflects on Dass's experiences as a new staff member at Rhodes University. Dass relates Stefan Collini's (2012) reflections on what universities are for to Jacques Derrida's (2000) discussion of unconditional hospitality. Collini argues that open-endedness and limitlessness must be core to the character of universities, while Derrida argues that the only kind of hospitality worthy of the name is one that is limitless and deeply inclusive, in the sense that strangers must be invited in as strangers. In this regard, Derrida's views are closely related to those of Emmanuel Levinas (1979). For Levinas, the primary ethical moment is the face-to-face encounter with the other. Such an encounter involves not subsuming the other into the category of the familiar, but rather openness to the other *as other*; openness, one could say, to the possibility of surprise and, crucially, from an epistemic point of view, to being changed by the other. This fundamental ethical moment contrasts markedly with the assimilationist approach which, Dass suggests, is characteristic of institutions such as Rhodes University. Drawing Collini and Derrida's ideas together, and illustrating them with reference to his own sense of the incompleteness or ambivalence of the hospitality offered to him on arrival at Rhodes University, Dass argues that in order for a university to be truly hospitable, those who form the university community have to open themselves to what is not known and cannot be anticipated.

Dass's chapter is followed by Thando Njovane's reflections on race and power in the academy. Njovane presents us with several intimate narratives that reveal ways in which institutions such as Rhodes University remain untransformed. As she puts it, she seeks to find out how 'covert racism [can] thrive, despite national and institutional policies that forbid it'. She argues strongly that tolerance of black people and a kind of reciprocal politeness between blacks and whites stands in the way of a deeper, more meaningful kind of transformation – transformation that will impact upon the university's 'way of being', rather than resulting only in changed clauses in policy documents.

Natalie Donaldson continues the engagement with Rhodes University in her discussion of gender and sexuality. Echoing Njovane, but in relation to sexuality rather than race, she stresses that inclusion and tolerance are insufficient to bring about transformation. Her analysis of Rhodes University's parental leave policy (an expression of misguided good intentions) and her discussion of some of the shortcomings of the university's responses to homophobic incidents add to the arguments of previous chapters about the limitations of changes in policy and procedure in transforming universities.

Part II ends with Amanda Hlengwa's reflections on the use of accelerated development programmes to attract and facilitate the flourishing of young women and black academics. Hlengwa argues that people who qualify as 'safe bets' (in that they are culturally similar to those already at the institution) are often employed in such programmes, while those who are considered more radically other are excluded. This limits the extent to which such programmes can be transformative, Hlengwa concludes. Her perspective is deeply personal, for she thinks of herself as a 'safe bet' and is deeply troubled by this.

Part III focuses on providing some thoughts on how to move forward. This section turns from Rhodes University in order to bring perspectives from other contexts to the discussion. The aim here is to provide some creative and thought-provoking ideas about how we can move beyond critique towards transforming our institutions.

In the opening chapter, Lewis Gordon pushes us to think about how best our institutions can overcome the exclusions of the past in such a way that they are able to identify and promote the flourishing of excellent black staff and students. His discussion of debates on affirmative action relates the South African situation to other contexts, most particularly to that of his home, the United States. Gordon rebuts many of the arguments presented against affirmative action, showing that we continue to live in a context that fails to recognise and develop the ability and potential of so many black people. He argues, interestingly, that affirmative action not only does not undermine excellence – a view defended by many who are generally happy with the status quo – and also suggests that excellence feeds on diversity.

Like Gordon, Nigel Gibson is profoundly critical of the extent to which the post-apartheid landscape has not resulted in a just social order. He brings some of Frantz Fanon's arguments to bear upon the idea of the postcolonial university, arguing in favour of a 'radical humanities', which will take seriously those who have thus far been excluded. He offers us what could be characterised as the Fanonian university as an alternative to our present tendencies to subsume all learning to the needs of capital.

In his contribution, Paul Taylor argues that universities are shaped in part 'by the "epistemic cultures" (Knorr-Cetina 1999) of the wider institutions that sustain professional scholarly communities'. Academics do not only engage with their specific academic institutions, but also, and possibly primarily, participate in – and are shaped by – broader specialist communities. Taylor puts flesh on the bones of this idea by discussing the epistemic culture of analytic philosophy, showing why it has failed to engage with central themes in postcolonial thinking and how this failure has adversely shaped its global trajectory. A central consequence of blindness to postcolonial concerns is the inability of analytic philosophy to properly reflect on itself, on why, for instance, certain epistemic biases continually replicate themselves.

Taking his lead from Taylor's contribution in particular, Pedro Tabensky argues that epistemic cultures, which flow from broad social modes of being and perceiving, delimit the contours of understanding in the academy. If these cultures are corrupt, so too is the academic project as a whole. He is concerned with racist styles of being and perceiving in South African universities and with the global trend, embodied, as one would expect, in a substantial proportion of the student body, of subsuming the value of understanding to the self-serving desire for social status and affluence. He argues that rather than being a means by which the status quo is perpetuated, universities should act as countercultural points of resistance. This is not merely an ethical responsibility for universities; it is also an epistemic responsibility. He offers examples of how universities could take the lead by describing two initiatives that he has tested among students at Rhodes University. The aim of universities should not merely be to equip students with tools that they can sell in the marketplace but, rather, to play a leading role in the formation of the consciousness of the future. This would only seem to be a responsibility that is not directly related to the academic project if one ignores the role that epistemic cultures play in shaping our understandings.

Thaddeus Metz's chapter also focuses on epistemic culture, but in a way that is significantly different to Taylor's and Tabensky's contributions. Metz explores the idea that institutional culture in the South African tertiary sector should be Africanised, which is to say that 'curriculum, research, language, aesthetics and governance' ought to be transformed – without ignoring the importance of non-African perspectives (Western and Asian, for instance) – in the light of modes of understanding that are typically associated with sub-Saharan Africa. He calls this form of Africanisation the 'moderate' form and distinguishes it from strong forms (which consider Africanisation to be imperative and allow little space for alternative perspectives) and weak forms (which regard Africanisation as optional). Metz argues that the most convincing reasons for Africanisation pertain to issues of facilitating redress, contributing to civilisation and fostering identity. He endorses Joseph Ki-Zerbo's view that to Africanise is to promote the value of self-understanding and self-development. He maintains that Africanisation is important, in part, because it promotes a certain kind of personhood, one that avoids fragmentation. Metz concludes that 'given a largely African context, public institutions have some substantial obligation to enable people to become Africans' in a manner that is not exclusionary of difference or of other values typically associated with the academic project.

The final chapter in Part III, by Bruce Janz, reflects on what struggles against racial injustice can teach us about how to respond to the increased instrumentalisation being experienced by universities. He argues that the 'cramped spaces' created by oppression result in new forms of creativity and, rather than trying to oppose and defeat instrumentalisation at universities, which is, following Gilles Deleuze, to 'attempt to meet one molar system with another', we should learn how to respond with creativity to situations of oppression, to discover unanticipated 'lines of flight'. Janz suggests that creative resistance is one of the key forms of transformative work and that real creativity occurs in the interstices, rather than as a result of attempts to bring about another master narrative or 'molar system'.

* * *

The remainder of this introduction discusses some common themes that emerge from the diverse contributions to this collection. Firstly, several of the authors argue that we cannot properly think about how to transform our universities without relating our attempts at transformation to the very idea of what a university is and, relatedly, what its ideal aims are. Vice, for example, stresses that when trying to think about how to adjudicate between the very different needs and interests of the various members of a university, we may be helped if we can identify the 'core value or function of a university, to which other functions and values ought to be subordinated' and which can and ought to constitute the 'essence of an institution's culture'. She puts forward Gordon Graham's account of the idea of a university as one that provides a helpful guiding ideal. According to Graham (2008: 165), one way to understand the idea of a university is to say that it is 'a place in which the pursuit of truth and understanding are given special protection, not to the exclusion of useful or socially relevant subjects, but not principally in their service either'.

Dass also turns to debates about the idea of a university in his discussion of the ethical imperative of unconditional hospitality. The conception of a university that Dass, using Collini, outlines bears much in common with the one discussed by Vice: the university, Collini (2012: 55) argues, must be an institution where 'the quest for understanding has primacy' and in which research is undertaken 'under the sign of limitlessness'. Like Graham, Collini also insists that knowledge cannot be subjected to the requirement of 'usefulness'. But Vice and Dass take up these rather similar conceptions of a university in quite different ways. Vice suggests that this way of understanding a university is helpful partly because it 'offer[s] even recalcitrant members of an institution . . . a way to engage on their own terms'. By placing the pursuit of truth and understanding at the centre, those who are most resistant to transformation might, Vice proposes, feel less threatened by transformation and be less likely to oppose it. Dass, on the other hand, argues that if we are to understand the pursuit of knowledge as ideally open-ended and limitless, we must be radically open to the other because we cannot know what we might learn from the other. This latter implication of the view that universities should, first and foremost, be places that prioritise the pursuit of knowledge, is far more discomforting to those recalcitrant academics whose pursuit of knowledge has not thus far involved openness to the other.

A second theme that emerges is the idea that narratives can help us to understand what we mean by institutional culture and in sketching out how it functions. Contributors agree that the concept of institutional culture is difficult to understand and that it needs to be fleshed out in various creative ways. Vincent provides both an argument for and some examples of the use of narrative to improve our understanding of institutional culture. Other contributors, most notably Dass, Njovane, Donaldson and Hlengwa, provide us with narratives that help us to see just how institutional cultures can make people feel alienated from their institutional environments. Indeed, this book presents us with a rich variety of narrativeses: about tall chairs making people feel diminished, about teatime rituals being experienced as foreign and awkward, about disturbing comments on essays and about homophobic insults being overlooked on the grounds of academic freedom.

One of the topics that kept emerging in the discussion at one of the roundtable conversations that resulted in this collection was the question of whether or not it is acceptable to use anecdotes to help us to understand concepts such as institutional culture. Some might say that the stories some contributors tell are only anecdotes that reveal the experiences of only a few individuals. This means, such critics may think, that we do not know if these anecdotes are representative and, therefore, such anecdotes are of little scholarly value. We disagree. As Vincent, with reference to Pat Sikes and Ken Gale (2006), points out, human beings are storying creatures: stories help us to explain our world to others and listening to the stories of others allows for a more vivid and profound grasp of what is under discussion.

Several of the chapters emphasise an important point that we could say constitutes a third common theme in these contributions: we cannot transform our universities without transforming the broader cultures of which they are a part. In some ways, this might seem like a trite point, but as Taylor points out, almost all discussions of higher education transformation relate to 'the specific constellations of objects and relations that answers to a name such as "Rhodes University"', even though members of such institutions are also part of other scholarly communities, which stretch across different institutions and, often, across countries and continents. Can we really think of transforming our institutions without transforming the disciplinary communities to which we belong? Furthermore, as Gibson's and Gordon's chapters show, the lack of transformation of South African universities (as well as universities elsewhere) is partly the result of a general lack of transformation. Our partial and, in many ways, inadequate and ambivalent transition from apartheid hampers the complete transformation of our universities in all kinds of ways. Metz relates discussions of the transformation of universities' institutional cultures to larger discussions about Africanisation of formerly colonial societies in Africa, asking to what extent it is necessary for universities to become more 'African' and what this Africanisation would entail.

Related to this third theme is a general concern about how contemporary moves towards the instrumentalisation of higher education affect our ability to transform our institutions. As Janz and Gibson both note, higher education institutions around the world are being pushed to conform to goals that are outside the traditional idea of a university discussed above. Janz and Gibson (and I am sure many other contributors to this volume, although they do not discuss this issue explicitly here) share a concern that universities are being 'corporatised', 'bureaucratised' and 'marketised'. However, Janz and Gibson suggest quite different responses to this instrumentalisation of higher education. Gibson wants to confront the instrumentalised university – and, in particular, the humanities – with the 'radical humanities' model that places the pursuit of human freedom at its centre. Janz, on the other hand, resists the idea that we ought to confront this vision of an instrumentalised university with another totalising opposing vision, with another 'molar system'. Rather, in Janz's view, we should find ways of transgressing this oppressive vision of a university by flourishing in creative and disruptive ways in the 'cramped spaces' created by the instrumentalised university. A transformed university, according to Gibson, would be one operating under an entirely different set of assumptions to those dominant today and would necessarily be rooted in and made possible by a transformed social context. Janz's transformed university, on the other hand, would, he implies, be one that has been slowly and creatively brought into being through the erosion and subversion of oppressive structures.

Another theme that comes up in more than one contribution concerns the limits of tolerance and inclusion. Njovane suggests that politeness and tolerance are a veneer that disguises the violence that many institutions enact upon black bodies, while Donaldson shows that attempts to be 'inclusive' of queer staff and students do not sufficiently challenge heteronormativity. These two chapters, as well as Dass's, show how an institutional culture that prioritises polite, smooth, non-conflictual interactions can prevent the development of a deeper, more engaged, more passionate and open attitude that welcomes and embraces difference.

While none of the chapters here aims to provide explicit policy guidelines for the use of those in leadership positions in higher education, several make suggestions that would be helpful for policy-makers, but also show how typical attempts at transforming institutions by changing policy fall short of their goals. Matthews, for example, argues that policies aimed directly at addressing racism and other forms of exclusion are likely to have limited effects; more creative and roundabout strategies are required since contemporary forms of racism operate in subtle and complex ways. Writing about heteronormativity, Donaldson shows how policies aimed at being more inclusive and addressing discrimination often end up reinforcing exclusion and discrimination, even though this is the opposite of their intent. And Hlengwa reveals how policies aimed at bringing in those who are different to the norm may actually be undermined when the least different others are appointed. None of the contributors would, however, argue that this means that we should not put policies in place that aim to address discrimination and exclusion, but rather they argue that more creative policies, expressive of subtle and caring thinking, are needed, instead of the standard wooden policies, and also that policy alone is insufficient. Gordon takes up an important aspect of policy aimed at transformation: affirmative action. Writing generally, rather than specifically about the South African higher education context, Gordon shows the flaws in many arguments against affirmative action and provides us with good reasons for thinking that current affirmative action policies do not go far enough in creating opportunities for black academics and students. Furthermore, he pushes us to recognise how, rather than resulting in mediocrity, affirmative action policies actually work to decrease the mediocrity that results from continued white supremacy.

In addition to providing some pointers for policy-makers, contributors to this collection comment on the question of *who* should be responsible for driving the transformation of our institutions. If our institutions are to be transformed, who will be the agents of this transformation? Vice argues that all members of the institutions, and particularly those 'for whom its purpose and values matter personally as much as professionally', need to be committed to creating a culture that is 'distinctive, fair and generous'. She does not assign a particular role to university leadership and, indeed, implies that if anyone has a special responsibility to transform institutional cultures, it is academics since their personal and professional lives are typically tied so closely to the idea of a university. Vice's suggestion that the responsibility does not lie principally with university leadership is supported, at least implicitly, by Janz. He argues that we will best subvert the instrumentalised university not by confronting its 'totalising picture' with 'an equal and opposing vision', but rather by flourishing in the 'cracks' that will always exist, no matter how totalising an oppressive system may be. His argument suggests that it is not so much those in positions of power that can be expected to transform universities, but rather those who are marginalised who can, through responding creatively to oppression, begin to find ways to flourish and, surely, this flourishing will be transformative.

However, other contributors suggest a greater responsibility for those in positions of leadership. For example, Donaldson concludes that the role academics can play 'means nothing if those in positions of leadership cannot even acknowledge that there is a problem'. While 'ordinary' members of an institution certainly have responsibility to transform it, she suggests that transformation is unlikely to occur without a responsive and committed university leadership. Vincent's chapter also suggests a bigger role for university authorities. Changing institutions requires changing their 'story stock', which requires that new stories must be told, she argues. However, this telling of new stories must involve something more than only individual storytelling – spaces needs to be created for the telling of these new stories and, importantly, for those who occupy hegemonic positions to hear them and be unsettled by them. Vincent quotes Charlotte Linde (2009: 45), who warns that new stories cannot enter into the 'story stock' if there is 'no time, event, place, object, or practice' that allows for these new stories to be told, heard and validated. While all members of a university can be charged with the responsibility of telling and listening to new stories, those in positions of leadership have a greater ability to provide the occasions for such stories to be told and legitimated.

In closing, it is important to be clear about the intentions of this book: we do not purport to be providing a comprehensive overview of all the key issues relating to transformation in South African higher education institutions. Nor do we claim to be providing a conclusive 'way forward'. Rather, what we have gathered together here are some thought-provoking pieces that reflect on a range – and, most certainly, an incomplete range – of questions relating to race, institutional culture and transformation at South African universities and beyond. Rather than attempting to elicit contributions covering a specific range of topics (perhaps race, gender, sexualities, disabilities and so on), we have selected these contributions on the basis of their ability to bring to the discussion of transformation something different, something that gives pause or pushes us to consider things afresh. The contributions are thus varied, both in terms of *what* they discuss and in terms of *how* they approach their topic. While the book is certainly not a 'handbook' that could be used to get an overview of all the key questions relating to the transformation of the South African higher education sector, its key strength is, we believe, the way in which the contributions invite us to consider well-worn, even somewhat tired and frustrating, questions about transformation in new, inventive and often deeply personal ways.

References

Collini, S. 2012. *What Are Universities For?* London: Penguin Books.

Derrida, J. 2000. *Of Hospitality: Anne Dufourmantelle Invites Jacques Derrida to Respond*. Translated by Rachel Bowlby. Stanford: Stanford University Press.

Govinder, K.S., N.P. Zondo and M.W. Makgoba. 2013. 'A New Look at Demographic Transformation for Universities in South Africa'. *South African Journal of Science* 109 (11/12): 86–96.

Graham, G. 2008. *Universities: The Recovery of an Idea*. Exeter: Imprint Academic.

Higgins, J. 2007a. 'Institutional Culture as Keyword'. *Review of Higher Education in South Africa*, 97–122. Pretoria: Council on Higher Education.

———. 2007b. 'Managing Meaning: The Constitutive Contradictions of Institutional Culture'. *Social Dynamics* 33 (1): 107–29.

Knorr-Cetina, K. 1999. *Epistemic Cultures: How the Sciences Make Knowledge*. Cambridge: Harvard University Press.

Levinas, E. 1979. *Totality and Infinity*. Dordrecht: Kluwer Academic Publishers.

Linde, C. 2009. *Working the Past: Narrative and Institutional Memory*. New York: Oxford University Press.

Schein, E.H. 1985. *Organizational Culture and Leadership: A Dynamic View*. San Francisco: Iossey-Bass.

Sikes, P. and K. Gale. 2006. 'Narrative Approaches to Education Research'. Faculty of Education, University of Plymouth. http://www.edu.plymouth.ac.uk/resined/narrative/narrativehome.htm.

Sullivan, S. 2006. *Revealing Whiteness: The Unconscious Habits of Racial Privilege*. Bloomington: Indiana University Press.

PART I

THE BASIC QUESTIONS

1

'Tell Us a New Story'
A Proposal for the Transformatory Potential of Collective Memory Projects

LOUISE VINCENT

John Higgins has argued that 'it is simply the massive fact and bulk of institutional culture that may be the main obstacle in the way of the successful transformation of South Africa's higher education system . . .' (2007: 97). But, as many contemporary commentators have pointed out, for all its apparent significance and ubiquity, the idea of institutional culture is difficult to pin down (Higgins 2007; Jansen 2004; Ensor 2002).

Many of our institutions have bravely offered attempts at defining 'institutional culture', but such attempts have often immediately given rise to contestation across the spectrum of opinion (see, for example, Goga 2008: 15). Institutional culture is said to be the '"way things are done" within an organisation, specifically the traditions, customs, values, and shared understandings that underpin the decisions taken, the practices engaged in and those practices that are rewarded and supported' (Rhodes University 2004: 4). Institutional culture is defined as the lived experience of the university by all those who inhabit it, including students, academic staff, management, support staff, workers and members of the public who come into contact with the institution. Institutional culture, it is argued, should be understood 'to encompass the policies and practices (tangible and intangible) that mark the daily and long-term experiences of those who share and pass through the university's spaces' (University of the Witwatersrand 2013). Moreover, it is frequently argued that institutional culture needs to change in order to achieve what is sometimes referred to as a 'culture of inclusivity'. There is a need for 'change in the culture, values and practices of the University' and for us to 'interrogate our ways of being, customs and practices and reshape the entire social ambience of th[e] University' (Botman 2008). These 'ways of being', as they stand now, are said to be the 'result of Apartheid practices' and are 'experienced by some staff and students as alienating'.

But what exactly these 'cultures, values and traditions' are – these ways of being – is seldom spelled out. Concrete practices are seldom named and described. There is mention of the under-representation of 'women, black people and people with disabilities' and the desire for an institutional culture that 'values diversity' (University of Cape Town 2013). There is mention of how current institutional cultures have 'been shaped by a very specific historical cultural grouping' and how 'the worldview which informs this position has been normalised' in our contemporary institutional environments (Steyn and Van Zyl 2001). Sometimes it is specified that the cultural milieus of our institutions have been characterised by 'whiteness', although exactly what it is that inheres in the practices of whiteness, other than the obvious fact of the mere existence of white people, is much more difficult to portray. Occasionally it is acknowledged that institutions do not have 'a culture' or perhaps never did have a singular, homogenous culture that is fixed, static or clearly delineable; rather there are 'cultures which are constantly created and recreated, with some cultures being expressed more dominantly or privileged more' (Waghid 2008).

While it is common to insist that changing institutional culture should not be about 'lip service' and 'definitely not about yet another document that we can frame and hang up in our offices and then ignore', but should rather entail 'a serious and sincere individual and collective acknowledgement that . . . we need to transform . . . prevailing mindsets' (Makhanya 2011), what exactly these prevailing mindsets are remains subterranean. I am reminded of the giant mushroom that occupies 965 hectares of soil in Oregon's Blue Mountains – a fungus so huge that its extent would cover 1 665 football fields or nearly 10 square kilometres of turf, yet all that one is able to describe at the surface is a small outcrop of trivial-looking honey mushrooms. When it comes to describing in concrete terms the mass and bulk of what we mean by institutional culture and its power in our lives we flounder, managing to point only to anecdotes and passing incidents.

Higgins (2007: 98) makes the important point that our response to the conceptual slipperiness of the term 'institutional culture' should not be an impulse to settle on an exact, objective or scientific 'definition'. Rather, we should accept that what this term tries to name is a contested social reality and our interest ought, precisely, to be in the nature and terms of that dispute. In an attempt to say something about how we can 'get at' institutional culture without having to arrive at a settled 'definition', in this chapter I identify two levels at which we can understand institutional culture: the discursive and the material. But instead of compartmentalising the two, I want to suggest, using the framing of what has been termed 'new materialism' – here I have in mind mainly the work of Karen Barad (2007), but also Gilles Deleuze and Felix Guattari (2000) and the idea of the 'machine' – that the discursive and the material need to be thought of together. This work, I argue, offers us a more concrete way of thinking about institutional culture because it brings together the material and the discursive and gives us a way of understanding the entanglements of the two in relation to agency and subjectivity. New materialism eschews the distinction between the discursive and the material and offers instead the idea of 'material-discursive'. This idea is not about interaction, but about how our sense of being emerges in intra-action – in the spaces between bodies, chairs, floors, discourses and narratives that pervade an institutional setting. Institutional culture, I shall argue, has seemed intangible because it operates at this nexus of intra-action (in)between discourse, subjectivity and materiality and has seemed complicated precisely because agency in this nexus is very complex.

Narrating institutional culture

One level at which we can understand institutional culture is at the level of the discursive. Discourses are conjoined statements that suggest ways of seeing the world. Discourses are also truth statements in the sense that they tell us something about what is to be regarded as normal and right. Discourses say something about how 'we' are and by implication suggest ways in which we are not and 'they' are. At any given moment in any given social milieu, there will be discourses that are dominant, hegemonic, powerful and influential and there will be those that are marginalised, subordinated and suppressed. One way of understanding institutional culture at this discursive level is to understand the culture of an institution through the stories we tell about it and ourselves and ourselves in relation to it – and indeed the stories that the institution itself, *qua* institution, tells, authorises, negates, suppresses, circulates and propagates. Institutional culture, in short, can be understood as something that is 'narrated'. Essentially here I am suggesting that if you want to understand something about institutional culture at the discursive level, it is useful to listen to the stories that the institution tells about itself and its members and to listen to the stories told by those who people its halls and corridors, its offices and theatres and playing fields. If you want to know something tangible about how institutional culture is working at any given time, what its dominant and subordinated discourses are, listen to the way in which the institution narrates its identity. This will also tell you something about how forms of dominance are being reproduced and will suggest ways in which dominance is being or can be interrupted or unsettled.

Why take a 'narrative' approach to understanding institutional culture? Roland Barthes (1977: 79) famously observed that 'narrative is present in every age, in every place, in every society' (see also Barthes and Duisit 1975). Human beings, Pat Sikes and Ken Gale (2006) point out, are 'storying creatures'. We construct narratives in order to help us to explain and interpret events both to ourselves and to other people. While narrative research typically focuses on narration as an individual identity-constructing mechanism, important for the purposes of the present chapter is that stories are also mechanisms for the construction of institutional identities. Here I draw in particular from the work of Charlotte Linde on how 'institutions use narratives in their practices of remembering' (2009: 4). Thus narratives are sense-making tools and instruments for the construction not only of individual, but also of social and institutional identities. We use stories to make sense of social action. To understand their own lives (and those of others), people put them into narrative form – thus actions acquire meaning by gaining a place in a narrative of life or some aspect of life. 'Narrative descriptions,' Donald Polkinghorne (1995: 5) says, 'exhibit human activity as purposeful engagement in the world', drawing together the diverse events, happenings and actions of human lives to make a meaningfully interpreted whole.

Stories are not, importantly for our purposes, only individual sense-making and identity-constructing tools. They also do this work at the level of institutions. Institutional stories, Linde (2009) contends, are used to induct people into institutional membership. And part of this process of induction has to do with individuals learning to 'shape their stories to harmonise with the events and values of the main institutional values' (4). Those who people institutions narrate these stories, but are also 'narrated by' prevailing institutional stories. In this sense, it is in and through narrative that we negotiate our collective and individual identities within institutions. Every institution has what Linde calls a 'story stock'. For the most part the story stock of an institution does not reveal itself as a 'stock' at all, but rather as random narrations that are not connected in any way. But taken together, these stories do constitute an anthology, a gathered repository of knowing, which means that by gathering and interpreting them, we are able to gain powerful and concrete insights into the subterranean workings of what we refer to as 'institutional culture'. A little later in this chapter I suggest a politicised and potentially transformatory version of this work of gathering and interpreting in the form of 'collective memory projects'.

Stories do the work of social reproduction
One of the central conundrums associated with institutional culture at South African universities has been the surprising ways in which changes at the level of policy, leadership and demographics have not seemed to coincide with change to an equivalent extent in the way the institutions 'feel'. Somehow the past, with its ways of violence, discrimination, exclusion and inequality, is being reproduced in the present, these other levels of change notwithstanding. Social reproduction refers to how prevailing ways of seeing and doing things,

understanding things and 'being' in the world often seem resilient against change. Laws, policies and institutional frameworks may change, but 'social and cultural structures, practices, habits of mind and heart, remain stable over time' (Linde 2009: 8). But continuity is a phenomenon to be explained, rather than taken as a given. Continuity, as Linde puts it, is an 'accomplishment' and the question then becomes about what work is constantly and invisibly performed in order for continuity to be accomplished. To be able to lay bare the workings of this accomplishment requires attention to the details of what have been called 'micro cultures' – the minutiae of experience, the everyday, the ordinary and the apparently mundane. And these can be accessed in multiple ways in the stories that circulate in institutions.

What, historically, has been the content of our common stock of institutional stories at South African higher education institutions? To illustrate: at some institutions the idea of 'excellence' has come to sum up a deeply contested sense that we have of ourselves. Part of what is meant by this idea seems to have embedded in it a longing to be associated with the pedigree of universities with medieval roots, such as Oxford. If we unravel this notion of excellence, we can immediately begin to see how it is sustained through various stories we tell every day. A history of excellence in scholarship is narrated and compared and contrasted with current purported slippages. The narrative of excellence in turn creates the space for a conversation that frames transformation in relation to something called 'standards'. The stock story about excellence is intimately tied up with the ways in which anxieties about change are articulated. The spectre of a black candidate for the top post immediately evokes the mantra of potentially compromised standards. Importantly, while not everyone is involved directly with questioning the credentials of black candidates, what we need to understand is the way in which the stock story of excellence, which we contribute to perpetuating, acts as a dominant framing and sense-making mechanism, which provides a kind of substratum for the perpetuation of prejudice. While counternarratives ask whether it is possible to conceive of excellence under circumstances of exclusion and discrimination, and the narrowing of possibilities of knowledge and exchange that has characterised the bulk of our institutional histories, these counternarratives are up against the stock stories. And the pernicious thing about stock stories is that they often have a taken-for-grantedness about them, so that we often end up colluding in countless day-to-day interactions with the telling of small stories that continually recreate and revitalise the dominant narratives. In this way, we come to shape our own and others' identity: through telling and retelling we make the dominant narratives our own, sometimes even in spite of ourselves. It is much harder to tell the kinds of stories that do the work of interrupting the dominant narratives and by implication the relations of injustice, discrimination and inequality that those narratives sustain.

The stock story of excellence is, of course, not one of the dominant or most important ones at every institution. The point here is merely to illustrate how this kind of analysis might proceed – through the identification of what the dominant tropes in our stock stories are, we can come closer to understanding the content of our institutional cultures and the microcultures of the present that sustain them.

Stories can do the work of interrupting the reproduction of injustice by making the normal strange

As Higgins (2007) has noted, institutional culture is often a shorthand reference to 'race' and, in particular, to whiteness. Richard Dyer (1997), in his powerful discussion of whiteness, writes of the enormous privilege that is associated with being the invisible norm against which all others are measured. Part of what it means for there to exist a 'culture of whiteness' is for there to be multiple ways in which whiteness continues to be privileged as 'normal'. To say, for instance, that one 'never thinks of race', as many white people do, is not an indicator of enlightened thinking; it is rather an indicator of a profound and hurtful blindness to one of the most important privileges of whiteness – the privilege of 'race' 'not mattering'. But there are many other dimensions to what counts as the somatically 'normal' – whether those are to do with gender or sexuality, with body size and shape or various dispositions of the body that are rooted in class, such as accent, posture and dress. To realise that there is a somatic norm in operation in institutions – a very particular embodied subject that 'masquerade[s] as the universal' (Puwar 2004: 8) – is to realise that institutional transformation is not only or even perhaps most importantly about getting different types of bodies (black, female, etc.) into the institution and into its structures of power, but it is about unsettling what counts as normal and by implication what is privileged and what is rendered illicit, strange, abnormal. Instead of taking for granted the world as we see it through our own eyes, it has to do with making room for the partialness of our own view, whoever we may be and wherever we may be situated – what might be referred to as making our own particular version of normal strange. Making the normal strange means being able to see that practices that have become so familiar that they are naturalised and do not seem to require an explanation are in fact social productions serving particular interests and perpetuating particular value systems while excluding others. Making the normal strange is a deliberate attempt to see old and familiar things with new eyes. Normality is difficult to resist and strangeness is discomforting, but as Julia Kristeva (cited in Elliot 2002: 21) has argued, there is something emancipatory about opening ourselves up to the possibility of astonishment.

Kristeva argues that a repressed strangeness is 'the hidden face of our identity' and that emotional contact with this sense of strangeness is central to the enlargement of both psychic space and political imagination. According to Kristeva, we have to be prepared to go all the way through the complex interplay of identity and difference and see, in a working through of the impact of astonishment, whether we can emerge somewhere on the other side. Anthony Elliot (2002: 21) has argued that the emancipatory significance of emotional astonishment and shock has to do with undoing the fantasy of omnipotence that dominant social actors would otherwise have. Kristeva thus proposes an alternative basis of identity, founded upon 'an openness to the dimensions of uncanniness, of strangeness, and of Otherness'. However, this imperative suggests also the limitation of storytelling processes that remain at the level of the individual and that are merely told, rather than being seen as part of a broader process of critical interpretation. Encounters with the other require a process that goes beyond individual storytelling – not so much to encounter the strangeness of others, but to gain a sense of estrangement from our own normalcy.

Narratives provide us with a way not only of observing what is taken for granted as normal, but also with interrupting cosy assumptions about what is normal. If we understand stories, in the way that I have proposed, as potent sense-making, identity-producing mechanisms, we can begin to see how one powerful way of truly encountering one another, seeing one another and making the normalcy of our own particular stories strange is through encountering different stories. For those who occupy hegemonic positions, encountering new stories can be about recognising that their experience is not everyone's experience. The telling of marginalised or subjugated stories, the production of counternarratives that interrupt the stock stories in our institutional anthologies may, Susan Bordo argues, help us to 'guard against the feeling of comfortable oneness with culture and to foster a healthy scepticism about the pleasures and powers it offers' (1993: 30–1). To listen to one another's stories and to make the space for the telling of stories that interrupt dominant tropes is one way in which we can discover how people are variously comforted and discomforted in unexpected ways by their encounters with everyday practices in an institution. In this way, we can gain insights into how domination and exclusion are reproduced and how we ourselves collude in this process.

If continuities in institutional culture are in part reproduced by the unshakeability of a certain common story stock and by our complicity in leaving that story stock unchallenged – or, more than this, ourselves unthinkingly narrating the stories in the dominant anthology – it follows that the contrary is true: the reshaping of institutional culture involves a process by which we find ways to alter our existing story stock. Linde argues that stories will only be told if there are appropriate occasions for their telling:

> The existence of relatively formal or institutionalized occasions for telling particular stories is extremely important for the life of the story in the institution. If there is no time, event, place,

object, or practice that provides the occasion for the telling of a particular story within an institution, that story has little chance of entering into the stock of stories known and told by most members of the institution. A few people may find individual reasons and occasions on which to tell it, but it will not become part of the institution's representation of it[self] (2009: 45).

To provide occasions for the telling of stories that contest the dominant narratives of an institution's story stock involves acts of leadership and sometimes of courage, to speak against the tide. New stories do not simply arise as an inevitable outcome of institutional change, which is why institutional culture is resistant to change. The implication is that if we want to shift something about institutional culture, we need to shift something about the stories we tell, the opportunities we have to tell them, how we make those opportunities and who has the chance to tell their stories: we need, in short, to find ways of altering our story stock. And we need acts of leadership that consciously make available spaces for the telling of alternative stories and create a climate in which those stories can really be heard.

However, to avoid the telling of stories becoming reduced to the merely anecdotal and the possibility of the damaging elevation of isolated experiences and incidents to an interpretation of the whole of an institution's culture, I want to advocate an approach that draws on debates in feminist methodology in the social sciences and on participatory action research, which, I think, can provide us with the outlines of a project that is politically and socially significant, rather than located at the level of solitary individuals and isolated anecdotes. Discussing participatory action research, Wilfred Carr and Stephen Kemmis suggest that 'a group process' is required to enable 'the development of a learning community to generate a critique of the context in which the group operates' (cited in Pease 2000: 143). The aim is to transform the learning community 'into a critical community that subjects its own values and practices to scrutiny' (Pease 2000: 143). William Torbert (1991: 232) has described this as 'a practical community of inquiry' where people are 'committed to discovering propositions about the world, life, their particular organisations and themselves that they will test in their own actions with others'. The process is therefore one that involves 'dialogue, discussion, argumentation, critical reflection and theorising from experience' (Pease 2000: 143).

This idea brings to mind what some might regard as the rather dated and passé feminist project of 'consciousness raising'. It was Catherine MacKinnon (1982) who referred to consciousness-raising as the 'quintessential expression' of feminism. But consciousness-raising is not only part of a (Western) feminist tradition, it also has a long history in black identity politics, not least as embodied in the work of Frantz Fanon. Amina Mama (1995: 6) comments that the assertion of black identity can be understood to be 'about changing into a different kind of human being – about changing one's consciousness of one's position in the world, about constructing new subjectivities and rejecting the disempowering legacies of centuries'. It speaks to the idea of becoming aware, at a conscious level, of things that might be experienced, but not consciously known, thought about or understood. The development of critical analysis and understanding are seen to be the first step towards social change. Consciousness-raising 'enables participants to explore material about themselves in ways that are searching and insightful and while such a method focuses on the personal, it does not separate the exploration of subjectivity from the wider historical and political issues' (Pease 2000: 144).

Consciousness-raising is a process through which participants come to a greater understanding of how social relations play themselves out in our own lives, a way, as Chris Weedon (1987: 85) puts it, 'of changing our subjectivity through positioning ourselves in alternative discourses which we produce together'. Thus, rather than being seen as part of an attempt to shore up notions of a unified self that is more rationally self-aware, consciousness-raising can play a role in destabilising unified notions of identity, challenging previously held conceptions of the self and creating the possibility for senses of the self to be reconstructed. In 2003 I turned one of my academic classes into an experiment along these lines. Jessica, one of the participants, provides an account of what the process meant to her:

I realised that all that I think I know is actually about power and 'normalisation' processes instilled in me from when I was a child. I have never considered myself a racist. I went to a Catholic convent during my primary school years, at the time of apartheid, which actually allowed black children to attend the school and treated them in an equal manner. I remember playing with black children from a young age, they came to my birthday parties, etc. In other words, I was socialised to consider black people as my equal. It was after reading Bennet and Friedman's article and rereading the transcripts from my interview with Privani on race that I reconsidered my views. During the interview I went on about how I felt discriminated against, that now I was at a disadvantage. Is this not hiding something? Am I not reacting in horror at suddenly finding 'my foot on someone else's neck' and not being able to accept that my foot is causing pain, but apart from that it is *my* foot. It is the inability to accept this fact that perhaps is the power that is exerted upon me. Society tells me to ignore the fact that people are suffering, that I should just remain 'a white girl', born after apartheid and therefore not connected to the struggle and therefore not linked to it at all, and that I should just enjoy my privileged white background and in my neo-liberal mindset just make myself happy at any cost.

The process of consciousness-raising in a group context is one in which, through collective storytelling, people become newly aware of the highly differentiated nature of the ways in which a common context is experienced and of the fact that even within a very narrow social stratum of people who find themselves in an elite academic institution, there are relations of power present. Public telling of stories allows for the possibility of reply, negotiation and placing of stories alongside one another with mediating and interpretive outcomes. But it requires, along with the shared group setting, the use of the resources of wide-ranging social theory to enable participants to begin to find more sophisticated interpretations and to recognise patterns of experience that help to locate the individual in history and in social structures. While the goal of consciousness-raising may seem, as Bordo (1993: 30) comments, 'to belong to another era', in a cultural context that peddles individual choice and freedom as its major accomplishment, becoming more conscious of how our choices and attitudes are fashioned and constrained by social and historical circumstances is itself a 'tremendous achievement'.

One of the main drawbacks of storytelling/consciousness-raising is that it is a process that is located very much in the individual, implying a psychological journey of sorts in which individuals come to certain realisations within themselves and for themselves. Thinking about how to overcome this limitation, I have been greatly influenced by the work of Frigga Haug (1987, 1992), which I first came across in Bob Pease's book on masculinity politics (2000). In Haug's attempt to understand what action women can take to bring about their own emancipation, she asks: 'How can women learn to intervene in their own socialisation?' Her aim is to 'construct a practical theory which seeks to understand women's experience from the point of view of changing it' (1992: 16). Haug developed her method of 'collective memory work' in part as an outcome of her reservations about the politics of consciousness-raising. She describes a project that I believe has implications for the transformation of institutional cultures. In the early days of the women's movement, she reminds us, animated by the slogan 'the personal is political', women gathered together in small groups to discuss their day-to-day problems, which had the effect of leading them 'out of their isolation into the sense of a collective experience'. However, Haug points out, 'the mere exchange of personal experiences does not necessarily lead to greater understanding'. While such exchanges may initially provide comfort, these groups quickly ran out of steam and did not necessarily lead to action. Following Bertolt Brecht, Haug warns that 'experience does not necessarily lead to understanding, even though it is perfectly true that there is no understanding without experience'. This is the problem of remaining at the level of merely endlessly exchanging experiences. At the same time, however, those experiences are needed in order to animate our theories and root them in our day-to-day realities. This challenge of 'theory poor in experience and experience bereft of theory' leads Haug to propose a collective empirical project, which she calls 'collective memory work':

> To prevent a simple duplication of the everyday with all its prejudices and lack of theoretical insight, our task would be to analyse these stories collectively. In order to uncover the social construction, the mechanisms, the interconnections and significance of our actions and feelings, we must proceed historically. Our proposal, therefore, is to retain the strengths of the consciousness-raising groups, to make connections between the everyday and the larger context, while avoiding the vices of ignoring the totality and losing ourselves in untheorized details. Our project is one of collective memory work, with the emphasis on collective, and memory and work. Its product would be a great and essential empirical undertaking that would be both new and enjoyable (1992: 16–17).

Haug's is an avowedly political project. Structures, she avers, 'only survive as long as they are continually reproduced by those who live within them'. This implies in its turn that these structures can be altered by those who reproduce them. For Haug (1992: 8), people are not simply puppets at the behest of social structures: 'The process of socialization is itself an activity which requires acquiescence at every stage.'

Memory work moves away from the totalising logic of trying to get everyone to see the world in the same ('correct', 'true') way. Its aim is to identify how subjectivities are constituted discursively as well as recognising the possibility of contradictions within discourses. Subject positions are recognised as partial, overlapping, fluid and changing. Agency is seen to arise out of the possibility for alternative subjective positionings. While we cannot 'escape' as a group or as individuals from our material position in the social structure, our ideological and discursive position relates not only to our structural location, but also to the discursive construction of our subjectivity, which we *can* change.

We can, for example, learn to see the world from the perspective of lives and experiences that are not our own and to generate knowledge from the perspective of these other lives and experiences. If this were not possible, social science would not be possible, nor would any form of morality based on the desirability of weighing our own interests against the interests of others. In the following section, I try to model what such a project of storytelling might be like; I provide examples of how stories reveal the subterranean workings of institutional culture and show how analytical work based in social theory can have a profound impact on our relationship to the structures that powerfully call to our subjectivities.

The materiality of institutional culture

> Neither discursive practices nor material phenomena are ontologically or epistemologically prior. Neither can be explained in terms of the other. Neither is reducible to the other. Neither has privileged status in determining the other. Neither is articulable in the absence of the other; matter and meaning are mutually articulated (Barad 2007: 152).

While the current period is frequently designated 'postcolonial', as a wide literature on the geographies of apartheid shows (for example, see Coetzer 2013; Noble 2011), the continued influences of the legacies of apartheid and colonialism are perhaps most concretely felt in built environments, architecture, urban planning, monuments and other physical artefacts, design and physical planning choices. Transformation of institutional 'culture' therefore cannot avoid an engagement with concrete material manifestations of cultural practices, identities and subjectivities. However, when people talk about institutional culture they often allude to the built environment – architecture, spaces, chairs, artworks, curtains – at the level of symbolism. These material artefacts are often seen as repugnant symbols of the past and what is needed, it is argued, is a new set of symbols. But there has been little by way of a sustained attempt to theorise and conceptualise in a more detailed way the materiality of institutional culture and why it is significant in a way that goes beyond the merely symbolic or representational.

In the humanist tradition, agency has always been thought of as something attached to humans – a person has agency to the extent that what they do is willed and chosen, not predetermined. In referring to a 'new' way of thinking about materialism, I have in mind Barad's (2007: 3) argument that 'matter and meaning are not separate elements'. As she explains: 'We must understand in an integral way the roles of human and nonhuman, material and discursive, and natural and cultural factors in scientific and other practices.' The insight of new materialism is that we experience material things as also having agency over us. New materialists challenge the distinction between active/ intentional humans and passive/background matter to suggest that floors, tables, paintings, as well as the bodies we occupy and the stuff they are made of – the skin, the hair and so on – can be understood as powerfully acting upon us and implicated in the performative production of power (see Lenz Taguchi 2010: 4).

Bringing the two ideas of the present chapter together, narratives can be understood not only as a discursive tool, but also as one way in which we can come to a fuller understanding of the agency of the material in institutional cultures. In paying attention to the stories that people tell, we are able to gain an insight into the ways in which the materiality of the institutional culture is experienced, lived and negotiated. Hillevi Lenz Taguchi, who writes about pedagogy, illustrates this point about the agency of the material in particular institutional settings in a story she tells about her first day at preschool:

> On my first day of preschool the teacher took all of us into the large and light playroom. She told us to sit down on an assigned dot glued to the floor. The dots formed a large circle and by the main wall there was a soft red pillow where the teacher seated herself crossing her legs in front of her, telling us to do the same. I could feel the icy chilliness from the cool linoleum floor through my tights, my dot was in-between two other boys that I had never met before. They talked lively to each other and sat somewhat too close to me, so that our crossed legs would touch. I therefore stretched out my legs instead, which caused the boys to immediately fill out the

vacant space with their legs, so I could feel them against the side of my thighs. I felt sandwiched in-between them, almost not being able to breathe. 'You're not sitting on your dot,' I told the boy to my right. 'Can you move onto your dot, please?' The boy mocked me as the teacher told me to be quiet. I felt as if the dot on the floor was burning under my buttocks, screaming out to me 'Sit Still!' 'Don't move!' 'Be quiet!' I couldn't understand why the dots under those boys didn't do their job, not keeping them in place at all. The boy on my left suddenly swirled around and his feet hit my arm and the side of my stomach. I straightened and nailed my body even more firmly to the dot without saying anything. I was doing it right, but I was not in a position to do the reprimanding. The teacher simply laughed lightly at what had happened. Then she said something about how difficult it was to learn how to sit still – especially for boys this age – but, she explained, that this was exactly what preschool was all about: learning how to sit still on your dot (2010: 2–3).

Lenz Taguchi explains how this way of seeing helps us to interpret her story:

> ... material objects – can be understood to actively work on my body and make it sit in specific ways, depending on the meaning I make in a specific space as girl or boy, or as a female or male, young or old, ethnic minority or ethnic majority, etc. Sitting in a specific space can thus be understood as a material-discursive phenomenon that emerges in the intra-action that takes place in-between a subject, who is inscribed in discursive meanings, the body, the dot on the cool floor ... In this way [material objects] can ... keep us in place and force or enable us to sit in specific ways, depending on whether we are at a lesson, assembly, seminar, lecture or staff meeting. In this sitting, our sense of being emerges in the material-discursive intra-actions taking place – being empowered, or being subjected to disciplining, etc.... All spaces, and certainly

pedagogical spaces, call upon us and demand specific ways of sitting or moving, talking or socialising with different affective force and intensities, depending on the material-discursive interconnections and intra-actions at work in this space (2010: 5).

This story illustrates the intertwining of the discursive and the material layers of culture – the ways in which a person's subjectivity, their material environment and the physicality of her/his body interact to define the contours of lived experience. The material and the discursive are an intertwined relation. Note that not all the subjects are perfectly disciplined by the dots – they engage with the dots differently depending on their own embodied identities, prior experiences and capabilities. The discourses of gender and education that the teacher speaks – what boys are like and what they find difficult and what they must learn – are intertwined with the materiality of the dots of the floor and the subjectivity of the pupils happens (rather than 'is') in this intra-action between the ideas that inform the institution, between the representative who speaks and embodies those ideas and the room that exercises agency in its materiality.

Earlier I argued that a narrative understanding of the workings of institutional culture provides us with a way of 'getting at' institutional culture. The narrative understanding of institutional culture points us in the direction of collecting narratives and taking narrative seriously as a mechanism both for understanding and interrupting the reproduction of dominance, injustice and inequality. Similarly, to offer a theory of the agential in the material is to point us in the direction of what to be alert to in our observations about institutional culture. To get at the specificities of how institutional cultures are operating would be to pay attention to how the material life of the institution is exercising agency on us and to whose interests are and are not being served at particular moments of the exercising of agency by all the multifarious material components that make up any particular institution. It is also to recognise how different embodied existences in interaction with one another within the institutional space constitute a significant component of its materiality.

When acting as the dean of my faculty for a short time, I had to occupy a chair on a raised platform in order to chair a faculty meeting. And this chair had a high back, which made me look as if I was half the height I am – ironically, a literal diminishing of my stature by a material object whose purpose was to achieve the opposite: to elevate the dean above the ordinary faculty members. Understanding the agential in the material occasions us to ask what performative work I experienced the chair doing and how my subjectivity was being formed and enacted in this moment in between the intra-action of my body with the chair and the gaze of the other humans present in the room and their subjectivity in intra-action with their chairs and with other bodies and selves that were in the not-elevated part of the room. How does the chair's effect on my body and my stature (both literal and figurative) get read at the level of discourse and how is this entangled with the chair's materiality and the materiality of my body as well as the discourses that circulate about bodies such as mine – white, woman, academic, mother, corpulent?

Nirmal Puwar (2004: 1) uses the term 'space invaders' to evoke the idea of the dissonance that ensues when people who have been historically and conceptually excluded from a space – as she puts it, people who differ from the 'somatic norm' – arrive in that space – particularly in its elite positions. She suggests that these are dynamic moments, moments of disturbance, disruption, rupture and paradox, to be sure, but also moments of potential illumination. She uses the example of the fracas that ensued when plans were announced to install a bronze statue of Nelson Mandela in Trafalgar Square in London:

> The pending arrival of a black figure of leadership in this privileged domain, reserved for very specific types of heroes, raised a revealing dispute. The coupling of particular bodies with specific spaces is at the heart of this conflict, even though the issues are declared to be of a purely aesthetic nature (Puwar 2004: 4).

The Westminster Councils' Public Arts Committee objected to the statue being placed prominently at the north terrace of the square and suggested that it would be more appropriate to place it closer to South Africa House. The committee also did not like the size and shape of the statue's hands. Puwar comments: 'The unease generated by the position and posture of a black figure in a privileged public space invokes the constitutive boundaries of the [imaginative] nation. The consistency of the play of national symbols, stories and monuments is jarred by the impending arrival of this figure' (2004: 5). What Puwar is suggesting is that the arrival of jarring (somatic) difference in spaces hitherto experienced as exhibiting consistency – between space, artefacts (statuary, ornamentation, architecture and so on), symbols and the stories we tell about them – necessitates a troubling reimagining of those spaces: what they are, what they mean, who they are for and for what purpose. She proposes therefore that there is

> a connection between bodies and space, which is built, repeated and contested over time. While all can, in theory, enter, it is certain types of bodies that are tacitly designated as being the 'natural' occupants of specific positions. Some bodies are deemed as having the right to belong, while others are marked out as trespassers, who are, in accordance with how both spaces and bodies are imagined (politically, historically and conceptually), circumscribed as being 'out of place'. Not being the somatic norm, they are space invaders (Puwar 2004: 8).

Another story: I was the external examiner for a PhD at a foreign university. The viva for the PhD had to be conducted by video conference. I entered the video conference room alone in bright sunshine at 2.30 in the afternoon. The viva was a long and gruelling one, which I participated in alone, while my colleagues and the candidate were in their respective building abroad. When I was ready to leave the meeting room, it had grown dark. I discovered that I was locked in. In the pitch darkness, I was unable to find the red bands on the doors, which allow one to open them from inside. In a panic, I called someone from security on my cell phone and he told me how to get out. I was very afraid in the empty, dark building. I fumbled for the red release bar and ran through the back door into a car park that was unlit and empty and I was alone and terrified. I ran up the ramp and towards the main street where the lighting was much less bright than I needed it to be at that moment. There were few people around because it was the vacation. Here the materiality of poor street lighting and the institutional materiality that locks a person into a building that will be in total darkness and surrounded by locked doors and dark, silent, empty car parks when she emerges from her meeting combined to diminish me into a fearful, cringing, desperate subject, which my academic credentials and professional standing had no power to resist. Reflecting on this experience and how to recreate the possibility of fighting back in ways that I was powerless to do in the moment, I make the argument here that the possibility for resistance may lie, not only for me, but also for countless others, in telling these stories, however personal, small or mundane. I am also aware how my own identity and position in the academy makes it possible for me to speak in ways that might be denied to others. I am arguing therefore also that one of the things that people in positions of power, who want to contribute to transformation, might do is to create the conditions under which counternarratives might emerge, be told and be listened to.

The public telling of our stories provides the opportunity not only for our subjective experience to be 'seen', rather than remaining hidden, but also for that experience to be placed alongside other similar and different experiences and for its relationship to the determining influences of social structures and the possibilities for exercising agency to be analysed and theorised. Often our experience of discomfort when the materiality of the institution exercises its agency on and between and in us is dimly perceived, or perhaps that is not the right way to put it. It is sharply felt, not dim at all, but what is dim is the apprehension of its cause and the process of power that brings it into existence. It is easy in these moments to confuse the workings of power for some lack in ourselves – in fact, that is how power works when it works best: when we turn its disciplinary gaze upon ourselves. We are often ashamed to tell our stories and our shame helps to perpetuate our humiliation. It is only through courageous acts of leadership in our institutions that we shall genuinely be able to make the space available for the telling of counternarratives to become legitimised. Oppression is happening in small and hidden ways and it continues to happen because it is trivialised and because we are ashamed of our own inability to be unaffected by it.

Conclusion

What I have tried to do with this theoretical engagement with the materiality and the discursive is to offer some insight into the kinds of questions we should be asking in order to make sense of institutional culture. But I have also pointed to the kinds of practices and processes informed both by theory and by experience that we might engage in to change our institutional cultures. We can achieve this, I have further suggested, by making room for the telling of new stories. But I have argued also that these new tellings will not emerge organically. The courage of leadership is required to legitimise, to welcome and to create occasions for not only the telling of these small stories in public and group settings, but also their interpretation and analysis, using the powerful tools of social theory. In this way, we can come to understand and take seriously the idea that social reproduction happens not so much in grand gestures, but in the everydayness of pain and shame and humiliation.

In seeking more inclusive institutional cultures I want to add a caveat, however: to make the distinction between 'shared' and 'common'. I would venture to argue that the objective of collective memory work should never be the erasure of difference. We ought, in my view, to be suspicious of processes aimed at commonality or even 'unity'. Rather our project ought to be one of living with difference, the instigation of multiple possibilities. Confronted with the astonishment of encountering the other, our natural inclination is to reduce the dissonance by declaring the other 'just like me'. But strangeness, I have argued here, is a resource, rather than an obstacle to be overcome, particularly when we encounter it in ourselves.

References

Barad, K. 2007. *Meeting the Universe Halfway: Quantum Physics and the Entanglement of Matter and Meaning*. Durham: Duke University Press.

Barthes, R. 1977. 'Introduction to the Structural Analysis of Narratives'. In *Image-Music-Text*, 79–124. London: Fontana.

Barthes, R. and L. Duisit. 1975. 'An Introduction to the Structural Analysis of Narrative'. *New Literary History* 6 (2): 237–72.

Bordo, S. 1993. *Unbearable Weight: Feminism, Western Culture and the Body*. Berkeley: University of California Press.

Botman, R. 2008. '"The Doors of Learning and Culture Shall Be Opened": Perspectives on Changing Institutional Culture'. Speech by Professor H. Russel Botman, rector and vice chancellor, Stellenbosch University on the occasion of the conference on changing institutional culture held on 30 May 2008 at Stellenbosch University. http://scholar.sun.ac.za/handle/10019.1/21157.

Coetzer, N. 2013. *Building Apartheid: On Architecture and Order in Imperial Cape Town*. Farnham: Ashgate.

Deleuze, G. and F. Guattari. 2000. *Anti-Oedipus: Capitalism and Schizophrenia*. Minneapolis: University of Minnesota Press.

Dyer, R. 1997. *White: Essays on Race and Culture*. New York: Routledge.

Elliot, A. 2002. *Psychoanalytic Theory: An Introduction*. Durham: Duke University Press.

Ensor, P. 2002. 'Curriculum'. In *Transformation in Higher Education: Global Pressures and Local Realities in South Africa*, ed. N. Cloete, R. Fehnel, P. Maassen, T. Moja, H. Perold and T. Gibbon, 270–95. Lansdowne: Juta.

Goga, S. 2008. 'The Silencing of Race at Rhodes: Ritual and Anti-Politics on a Post-Apartheid Campus'. MA thesis, Grahamstown, Rhodes University.

Haug, F. 1987. *Female Sexualisation: A Collective Work of Memory*. London: Verso.

———. 1992. *Beyond Female Masochism: Memory Work and Politics*. London: Verso.

Higgins, J. 2007. 'Institutional Culture as Keyword'. *Review of Higher Education in South Africa*, 97–122. Pretoria: Council on Higher Education.

Jansen, J. 2004. 'How Far Have We Come?' *Mail & Guardian*, 13–19 August, Getting Ahead Supplement: 1.

Lenz Taguchi, H. 2010. *Going Beyond the Theory/Practice Divide in Early Childhood Education: Introducing an Intra-Active Pedagogy*. New York: Routledge.

Linde, C. 2009. *Working the Past: Narrative and Institutional Memory*. New York: Oxford University Press.

MacKinnon, C. 1982. 'Feminism, Marxism, Method and the State: An Agenda For Theory'. *Signs* 8 (Summer): 635–58.

Makhanya, M. 2011. 'Launch of the UNISA Charter on Transformation'. http://www.unisa.ac.za/contents/about/principle/docs/PROF_MAKHANYA_CharterLaunchAddress.pdf.

Mama, A. 1995. *Beyond the Masks: Race, Gender and Subjectivity*. London: Routledge.

Noble, J. 2011. *African Identity in Post-Apartheid Public Architecture*. Farnham: Ashgate.

Pease, B. 2000. *Recreating Men: Postmodern Masculinity Politics*. London: Sage.

Polkinghorne, D. 1995. 'Narrative Configuration in Qualitative Analysis'. In *Life History and Narrative*, ed. J. Hatch and R. Wisniewski, 5–24. Abingdon: RoutledgeFalmer.

Puwar, N. 2004. *Space Invaders: Race, Gender and Bodies out of Place*. Oxford: Berg.

Rhodes University. 2004. 'Rhodes University Equity Policy'. https://www.ru.ac.za/media/rhodesuniversity/content/documents/humanresources/Equity%20Policy.pdf.

Sikes, P. and K. Gale. 2006. 'Narrative Approaches to Education Research'. Faculty of Education, University of Plymouth. http://www.edu.plymouth.ac.uk/resined/narrative/narrativehome.htm.

Steyn, M. and M. van Zyl. 2001. '"Like That Statue at Jammie Stairs": Some Student Perceptions and Experiences of Institutional Culture at the University of Cape Town in 1999'. Research Report, Institute for Intercultural and Diversity Studies at the University of Cape Town. http://opencontent.uct.ac.za/Humanities/Like-that-statue-at-Jammie-stairs-Some-student-perceptions-and-experiences-of-institutional-culture-at-the-University.

Torbert, W. 1991. *The Power of Balance: Transforming Self, Society and Scientific Inquiry*. California: Sage.

University of Cape Town. 2013. 'UCT Policy on Internationalisation'. https://www.uct.ac.za/downloads/uct.ac.za/about/iapo/internat_pol.doc.

University of the Witwatersrand. 2013. 'Institutional Culture Programme'. http://www.wits.ac.za/aboutwits/governance/transformationoffice/18464/institutional_culture_programme.html.

Weedon, C. 1987. *Feminist Practice and Poststructural Theory*. Cambridge: Blackwell.

Waghid, Y. 2008. 'Changing Institutional Culture: A Pedagogical Prerequisite'. Paper presented at the Conference on Institutional Culture, Stellenbosch University, 30 May 2008.

2

'Feeling at Home'
Institutional Culture and the Idea of a University

SAMANTHA VICE

The notion of institutional culture is increasingly appealed to in discussions of the failure of South African higher education institutions to transform.[1] It is because of the culture of our higher education institutions, it is claimed, that so many South Africans who were disadvantaged under apartheid are still unlikely to leave our universities with qualifications or to remain and thrive within them. While this view must, of course, be incomplete as an explanation for the failures to transform, I acknowledge that institutional culture is a useful notion and explore a particular dimension of it in this chapter.

One phrase we often hear informally in this discussion is of making an institution a 'home' for those who work and live in it. In this chapter I focus on this experience of being at home, its ethical significance and the challenges it raises for transformation. Informing my exploration is my own experience of feeling at home at a particular university and more generally in the space of tertiary education in South Africa and abroad. While many reportedly feel alienated in our tertiary institutions, I am fortunate not to have experienced this; the university space and culture have generally accommodated me well. Certainly, over the last years, the fact of 'fitting in' and 'feeling at home' has become problematic, as I have reflected on the assumptions underlying it, and as the fraught world beyond the institution has increasingly impinged. While this has rendered my experience more complex and reflective, and has at times threatened my sense of being at home, the university has in general remained a space in which I am comfortable. It might therefore be helpful to examine this positive experience in order better to understand what is lacking and so troubling in the contrasting experience of alienation.[2]

My first aim is therefore to explore the phenomenology and ethical significance of being at home and, in contrast, of being alienated or uncomfortable. My second aim is to discuss the implications of the interpretation I offer for debates surrounding institutional culture and transformation. Influenced by debates in political philosophy, I suggest that transforming an institution into a place in which everyone feels at home will not be easy in a complex, plural society such as South Africa and in a complex institution such as a university.[3] My – tentative – conclusions on these matters may strike some readers as overly pessimistic, but it is important that a commitment to transforming institutional culture be informed by a real sense of the difficulties involved.

Some preliminary remarks are in order. Firstly, I assume throughout a standard sense of institutional culture as the 'way things are done'. As Melissa Steyn and Mikki van Zyl (2001) write of university institutional culture, it is the ' "sum total" effects of the values, attitudes, styles of interaction, collective memories – the "way of life" of the university, known by those who work and study in the university environment, through their lived experience'. I will, however, use the term in a narrower sense than some writers. For instance, I do not include the material aspects of an institution – the architecture, the furnishings, design and art.[4] These can be symbolic of the institution's values and can influence institutional culture in both obvious and subtle ways, but including them in the core of the notion itself, rather than as a contributing cause, in my opinion renders it unhelpfully broad. Furthermore, I do not define culture as itself an experience.[5] My interest in this chapter is in our experience of an institutional culture as homely or alienating. Given that different people can experience the culture in different ways, it seems best to keep the culture and the various experiences of it distinct. The problem is precisely that a culture can be experienced so differently by people from different backgrounds and with different commitments; some experience it as a home, others not at all.

My second concern is with the way an institutional culture is experienced and the ethical dimension of that experience, rather than with the causes or conditions of the experience. However, in the final section of this chapter, I suggest some factors that might influence the creation of a virtuous culture.[6] Third, John Higgins (2007: 106) notes that the 'current, dominant sense of the term in South Africa understands the institutional culture of higher education institutions through the lens of "whiteness critique"'. I do not assume this racialisation of critique. The influence of whiteness is, of course, central in South Africa, but norms in relation to gender, race, class, religion and able-bodiedness (and their intersections) also influence the culture of an institution, as do different views about the very purpose of a university.[7] Finally, I do not assume that understanding institutional culture is the only key to the successful transformation of higher education.[8] The transformation of higher education requires changes that are external to and independent of higher education itself and thus is not adequately captured in terms of the culture of an institution.[9] Institutional culture is only one complex dimension of a complex problem.

Institutional culture: 'Feeling at home' and 'being in one's element'

What would a transformed institutional culture look like? There is a quick answer to this question, which while incomplete, is not wrong: a transformed culture – a 'transformed' way of doing things and the set of values and norms that inform it – is one that is unprejudiced, welcoming of diversity in all morally legitimate forms, intent on acknowledging and transforming a damaging legacy, responsive to its history and context. It is welcoming to all the people who constitute it or have dealings with it and is conducive to their flourishing. A transformed institutional culture is, therefore, in miniature, a reflection of a socially and politically transformed society. The mission statements of most South African universities illustrate this and Rhodes University's provides a representative example. In pursuit of its mission, Rhodes University undertakes

- to develop shared values that embrace basic human and civil rights;

- to acknowledge and be sensitive to the problems created by the legacy of apartheid, to reject all forms of unfair discrimination and to ensure that appropriate corrective measures are employed to redress past imbalances;
- to create a research-based teaching and learning environment that will encourage students to reach their full potential, that is supportive of students from disadvantaged backgrounds, and that will produce critical, capable and skilled graduates who can adapt to changing environments;
- to promote excellence and innovation in teaching and learning by providing staff and students with access to relevant academic development programmes . . .;
- to provide a safe and nurturing student support system as well as a diverse array of residential, sporting, cultural and leadership opportunities that will foster the all-round development of our students, the university and the region as a whole . . .;
- where appropriate, to assist in the development of the Eastern Cape Province by making available the university's expertise, resources and facilities;
- to play a leading role in establishing a culture of environmental concern by actively pursuing a policy of environmental best practice (Rhodes University 2014).[10]

I quote from this document in some detail to show the familiar liberal range of values and goals taken to be relevant to a transformed university in South Africa. They are, when not concerned with strictly academic matters, simply those of a post-oppressive, liberal, democratic, environmentally aware society.[11]

While laudable, nothing about these broader values is peculiar to an institution or a university. A university is a place of work and study, in which a diverse array of people – perhaps more diverse than in many other organisations – spend their days together, in common or solitary pursuits that ultimately have something to do with the creation or transmission of knowledge and understanding. What does it mean for this kind of educational institutional culture to be transformed?

I want to look more deeply at institutional culture and its transformation by taking seriously one commonly heard expression, which reveals what a valuable (and hence a 'transformed') culture is thought to be. We say that institutions should strive to provide a 'home for all' their members, especially in the light of a past in which many were marginalised or denied access. The expression is familiar to us as an institutional and national ideal and worth taking seriously for at least that reason; exploring it will help us to get to the heart of what we value about a place of work and study.[12] Admittedly, I offer a particularly substantive interpretation of a good institutional culture as a 'home' and I do not claim that all those who discuss institutional culture will agree with my interpretation. However, I hope to further defend my method by putting the expression to work and seeing if it yields any interesting results.

The notion of 'home' is perhaps more familiar in relation to institutions than to organisations, according to one way of drawing that distinction. Institutions have a social, religious or educational purpose with a tradition and longevity that survives beyond a particular time and group of people; their purpose (for instance, education) may never come to an end. An organisation, in contrast, is any 'organized body of people with a particular purpose' (*Oxford English Dictionary*), which could be purely commercial or practical. It ends when the purpose is fulfilled or set aside or when the people leave, rather than surviving those changes. As I discuss later, this difference is relevant when considering the ethos of an institution and the challenges it faces. So what does it mean to say that the culture of our tertiary institutions should be such as to provide a 'home for all'? What is it to feel at home in an institution?[13]

The experience of feeling at home in a place is not easy to articulate. Like many good things, if it is there, it is often more or less invisible – a framework in which we live and of which we are usually not aware. Like happiness, its attainment is not entirely up to us; we can hope to feel at home and we can do what is in our power to feel that way, but ultimately it is an experience that arises from a complex confluence of factors, some of which are out of our control. Of course, 'feeling at home' is a metaphor when applied to anything but one's actual home and it is an extremely complex one. Home, writes Theano Terkenli (1995: 327), is 'a multidimensional and profoundly symbolic term that cannot be mapped as an exclusively spatial concept'; it is, rather, 'one aspect of human emotional territory'.[14]

This use of 'home' is obviously normative. All things being equal, 'home' is a positive space and being at home is a valuable experience. However, this is not uncontroversial and things are often not equal. Iris Marion Young (1997: 134) claims that 'house and home are deeply ambivalent values'. 'Home' can be a space that is beneficial to some at the expense of others, restrictive of personal growth and autonomy, suspicious of change and difference, complacent and conservative. And these dangers can arise precisely from its positive aspects — security, comfort, familiarity. So an immediate criticism of the attempt to understand transformation in this way is to note that the fact that many people are at home in institutions struggling to transform is precisely the problem — people's very comfort impedes change and so they need to be dislodged from their homes in order for transformation to happen. Furthermore, being jolted out of comfort every now and again can be a valuable experience in itself; my own experience of discomfort in the face of new realisations and a deepening understanding of the university and its place in society has been good for me. Sometimes, therefore, the orienting and sustaining framework needs to become visible if change is to happen, both personally and institutionally; sometimes we need to be made uncomfortable for our own and others' good. And sometimes we come to a greater appreciation and knowledge of home itself by leaving it or interrogating it, accepting the good of it, while recognising the potential or actual threats within it.[15]

I accept these concerns and return to them later in this chapter. However, like Young (1997: 134), I am 'not ready to toss the idea of home out' completely.[16] It is important not to neglect what is valuable when admitting the force of these criticisms. 'Home' can exist in both properly virtuous and distortedly vicious forms. Throughout this chapter, I explore the tension between the danger of being inappropriately 'at home' and the real value of that phenomenon. I hope to rescue the value while admitting the dangers. In order to do so, my strategy, perhaps unusually, is to explore the complex expression and experience of 'feeling at home' in conjunction with another equally complex figural expression – 'being in one's element': being in a situation or environment that naturally fits one's fundamental 'type' or character. One reason for this strategy is to save and examine the positive aspects of 'feeling at home', so that they are not lost in the debate over the negative aspects. My suggestion is that the positive aspects of feeling at home are best captured in terms of 'being in one's element', an expression that also escapes the problems of the former expression.

There is no necessity of understanding a homely institutional culture in terms of the expression of 'being in one's element'. However, there are a number of further reasons that make this strategy fruitful: there are intuitive and conceptual links between the expressions that are mutually enriching and 'being in one's element' is a less domestic and private notion than that of 'being at home' and so is perhaps more appropriate to an institutional context. Most importantly for my purpose, 'being in one's element' is helpful in explaining what is valuable about a good institutional culture and allows us to appreciate what is thought to be valuable in the experience of feeling at home. Finally, it draws out features that are significant for the analysis of transforming institutional culture.

The *Oxford English Dictionary* defines the relevant sense of 'element' as follows:

> That one of the 'four elements' which is the natural abode of any particular class of living beings; said chiefly of air and water. Hence *trans.* and *fig.* (a person's) ordinary range of activity, the surroundings in which one feels at home; the appropriate sphere of operation of any agency.

To be in one's element is therefore to be in one's natural abode, appropriate to one's character, nature and activities, and in which one feels secure, enabled and productive. My suggestion is that if one 'feels at home' in an institutional culture, this is how the institution is experienced in one's day-to-day involvement – as enabling and comfortable. To transform an institutional culture in any way more specific than the values given to us in universities' mission statements is to strive to produce an institution that provides such an experience for as many people as possible.

The expression 'being in one's element' has its limits, but it is useful for bringing out a number of features of the experience of feeling at home in an institution that are relevant here. Firstly, there is a 'feeling' and 'experience' of being at home. However, these need not be articulated or present as a discrete feeling. Often the sense of being at home is made apparent by its absence; we are retrospectively aware of it only when it is missing (see Terkenli 1995: 328, 331). For this reason, the expression of being in one's element is useful because when we are in our element, we are probably precisely *not* conscious of being so. Agency and experience are unimpeded and 'natural', just as they should be, so not worthy of comment or present in our reflective awareness. Fish are probably not aware of their watery element, nor birds aware of the air that supports their familiar flight. This means, too, that 'feeling at home', while having deep emotional resonance, should not itself be thought of as necessarily an occurrent emotional experience. We are most at home, this expression suggests, when not aware of it and most aware of it when it is absent.

A second and related point is that feeling at home is enabling and productive: we are in the 'appropriate sphere of operation' of our agency. This points to a central professional value of the experience: when we feel at home in an institution, we can perform our appropriate professional tasks unimpeded and with more success, with less friction and frustration. Constitutive of this are the habits that develop in concert with others in the institution, which facilitate activity and ease everyday interactions (see Terkenli 1995: 326; Wise 2000: 302ff.). Out of our element, habits break down or meet resistance; friction and gravity impede. Because not feeling at home has effects on productivity and professional success, it is something that an institution should care about, even if only for the most instrumental reasons.

Third, the experience of being in one's element is *relational*: there is a fit between a person and the institutional 'way of doing things'.

Both sides of the relation need to be in a particular way to fit each other. It is already clear that attempts to foster the experience when it is not there will be complicated, as at least two parties need to be a certain and complementary way. I return to this below. Finally, feeling at home is a constituent of fulfilment and flourishing. We are not only productive, but are personally fulfilled in our natural element. Fish out of water die; birds with no chance to fly are frustrated in their characteristic activities and purpose. This, too, has the consequence that achieving transformation in an institution will be a complex task.

Thinking in these terms brings out the value of being at home in an institution, especially for academics. Professionally we are enabled and productive and, if we also take our work seriously as an expression of our identity and our deep value commitments, then both professionally and personally we flourish. An institution such as a university, in which academics, at least, often feel that work is also personally enriching and fundamental to their identity, is therefore ideally a place in which professional activity and personal growth meet. Being in one's element means one can both *do* what one has to do and *be* who one authentically is. For many academics, therefore, the personal is the professional. One can then also see why not feeling at home could be so debilitating for them and why it is not only a problem of professional productivity. Alienation or discomfort is more than not knowing the ways and the habits that ease everyday professional relations, not knowing how things are done. All this is discomforting enough, with obvious effects on productivity and satisfaction. But furthermore, if we are 'out of our element' in our professional space, our personal flourishing, our sense of belonging and our sense of deeply 'fitting' with and endorsing the guiding values and goals of the place in which we spend so much of our lives, will also be undermined. We are unmoored, out of the milieu in which we belong, neither fitting the space nor having it fit us in return. We will not find ourselves and our deepest commitments mirrored in the institution's narratives.[17] The intermingling of professional and personal life is therefore both a blessing and a curse of academic life, as it may be in other professions too.

The value of the experience and the impact of its absence are important to recognise and think about, especially in the light of the familiar criticisms of 'feeling at home'. Being in one's element is *good* for one, both professionally and personally; it is something we wish for others and regret, for their sakes, when it is absent. A lack of 'fit' between one's character and one's space of agency is a symptom of a life not how it ought to be and it can be a criticism of an institution if its members are not in their element. The transformation of institutional culture is important precisely so that more than the historically advantaged can be in this valuable state. It is therefore a value that should be claimed for everyone, rather than rejected because it has historically been unavailable to many.[18]

Of course, any normative account must leave room for inappropriate instances. We do not praise those who flourish in an unfair, intolerant or unjust setting; something is then wrong with both the institution and the person who thrives within it. As I acknowledged earlier, home can be a restrictive and overly secure space, in which one is protected from any strangeness or discomfort that might challenge one.[19] However, employing the expression 'being in one's element' is helpful here and allows us room for evaluation. 'Being in one's element' need not entail the uncritical comfort that many are suspicious of when thinking about the notion of home and it brings with it a way of evaluating inappropriate thriving. The experience is not essentially about *feelings*, about feeling complacent and unchallenged. Rather, it refers to successful agency and to the complementary fit between one's character and one's environment. This is compatible with – indeed it could require – growth, challenge and episodes of intense discomfort as one develops in a developing environment. Even within one's element, one has to face change, challenges and threats; one needs to be flexible. Surviving even in one's natural sphere of agency requires the ability to recognise and respond appropriately to change. One's element is not hermetically sealed.

In a transitional or transforming society, the need to adapt and respond appropriately to change is particularly pertinent and those who struggle to do so will find it difficult to flourish. This therefore suggests one reason for preferring the expression 'being in one's element' to 'feeling at home'; the former includes the ability to respond appropriately to changing circumstances.

Exploring the expression 'being in one's element' rescues, I hope, what is significant in the experience of feeling at home while admitting the dangers. This interpretation, however, raises difficulties for the transformation of institutional cultures and in the next section I look at these difficulties in more detail.

Challenges for transformation

I have offered a substantive interpretation of feeling at home in an institution, one richer than simply knowing how things work and knowing one's way around. If we understand 'feeling at home' in an institution as also 'being in one's element', a transformed institutional culture is one that is conducive to both professional success and personal flourishing. However, this interpretation brings with it consequences for this debate that we might not be happy with and that leave us with a choice: we can reject the substantive understanding of 'home' explored here, through the analysis of 'being in one's element', and opt for a thinner notion or we can accept the aptness of the expressions and commit ourselves to tackling the issues, both theoretical and practical, they raise. Some of these issues arise particularly for a university and might not apply, or not in the same way, to other institutions. I do think that both expressions are useful enough to retain, so I want to conclude this chapter by suggesting a way of approaching the challenges, although I cannot resolve any of them.

To begin with, how we experience an institution is a function of the different spaces within it, perhaps each with its own culture. My own happiness within the university is, I suspect, crucially a matter of the ethos of my department – the support and respect of colleagues I respect in turn, an ethos of equality, fairness and vigorous debate. Someone else might not feel at home – feel out of her element – not necessarily because of the larger institution per se, but because of politics or animosities or indifference within the department, school or faculty of which she is a part. An institution, therefore, is a nested collection of spaces, some of which may be experienced as more homely than others, and an analysis of institutional culture must recognise the added complexity this brings. The transformation of an institution requires the transformation of discrete spaces, as much as of the official, public ethos and presentation. In a university, in which departments, schools and faculties have a measure of autonomy from the central administration and from each other, this again brings challenges for transformation.

There are deeper difficulties raised by my substantive interpretation of feeling at home. The first relates to the assumptions about work and flourishing that this interpretation contains. I noted that, for many academics, feeling at home in the university contributes to both personal and professional flourishing. However, those for whom the personal and the professional are more distinct and whose identity is not essentially bound up with their professions – those for whom a job is simply a job or studying simply a means to some later life plan – might not have such a substantive experience of fulfilment in the institution. One question to ask is whether in attempting to make an institution a home for everyone, there is an assumption that the personal and the professional ought to be, at least in that institution, blurred. In contrast, that is, one might be productive and efficient and enjoy one's work or study and then leave it behind at five o'clock and return to one's far more important life outside. Or, one might work in a purely professional capacity and have no personal stake in the core functions of the university – the situation, perhaps, of many support and administrative staff. If 'feeling at home' is to be anything more than this (undoubtedly valuable) experience of being content and productive in one's place of work or study, then defining it in terms of *element* is useful. As mentioned earlier, being in one's element brings with it both productive activity and flourishing in a sense deeper than being content. However, if we remain with this interpretation, we might wonder whether it is possible for an institution to make everyone, in all kinds of positions, feel at home in this richer sense and whether, more strongly, its leaders have a duty to ensure it.

Of course, this concern depends upon our taking two figurative expressions seriously. Perhaps an institution's aim to make everyone feel at home is meant less substantively, or meant more substantively only for academics, or meant to apply only to a setting in which administrative and management tasks are also carried out by academics – the collegial system, which is vanishing in large institutions and under pressure even in smaller ones.[20] However, differentiating academic from other positions does not seem right either, especially if we are trying to rid the institutions of potentially divisive distinctions.[21] Transforming the culture of an institution is supposed to remove distinction, hierarchy and alienation and supposed to make everyone, whether pursuing academic, support or management tasks, feel equally welcome and valued in pursuit of a project that everyone can see the importance of in some way.

A second worry is related and arises from the assumption that one institution ought to provide a space for the substantive flourishing of people with diverse capacities and talents, diverse conceptions of the good and diverse needs. Is this a reasonable expectation and can university leadership be held to it? How can a university enable flourishing for academics, administrative and management personnel, students, support staff and the extra-institutional community, if it is a stakeholder too?[22] Universities face the particular challenge that many of their members live, as well as work and study, in it. They are, for many people, not places that can be left behind at the end of the day and so are literally homes for these people. In addition, people are at home in different spaces and, as mentioned previously, being in one's element requires a fit between two parties. An institution will need to attract the kind of people that it believes will fit the (transformed) institutional ethos and not only academics who might share a conception of a university, but also administrators and managers, students and support staff. Is it possible to ensure such a fit? Given reports of increasing antagonism between academics and what is often perceived as intrusive and unsympathetic management; given divergent views on academic freedom and on the uses and value of research, even among academics; given a support staff who have little reasonable hope of participating in or fully benefiting from the core functions of the institution they serve; given the pressures on management to transform and be financially viable in a climate of scarce resources; given students who increasingly – we are told – think of themselves as consumers with rights to success — given all these tensions, is it even a coherent goal? If not, we need to ask *who* can legitimately be uncomfortable and in what ways. To whom is an institution's duty of accommodation?

These questions are not as crass as they might initially sound. In the transformation of universities, some will be made uncomfortable. The discomfort of those who work according to an ethos that is no longer acceptable can perhaps be justified by the imperative to transform and by unreasonable recalcitrance. However, those newly on the losing side cannot always be accused of ill will or prejudice. In some cases, conflict is caused by the practical or in principle impossibility of accommodating what might be equally reasonable demands.

A third problem is that to have a character at all is to exclude some things and make others essential or marked; character is after all constituted by definite and differentiating characteristics. How does an institution both have character, stand out as something particular and valuable, and at the same time accommodate the many needs and values of its members? Is it possible for an institution to have any character, depth and tradition without leaving some people feeling alienated or, less grandly but perhaps no less unfortunately, uncomfortable or dissatisfied? Borrowing from the debates in political philosophy that have been guiding my thoughts, we can ask whether it is possible for an institution to have a distinctive culture at all and still be 'neutral', tolerant and welcoming with respect to the ways of doing things and the different values of its very different members.

I do not want to exaggerate the difficulties posed by these three, related problems. One obvious response is that precisely because universities are nested collections of spaces, we can create different spaces for different people, all nested within the larger university culture.[23] It is a mistake to think that transformation is of *one* institutional culture, rather than the transformation or creation of different spaces. This strategy certainly alleviates some problems. Service and administrative staff, as much as academics and students, should have spaces in which they can (reasonably) create their own 'ways of doing things', their own narratives and traditions, and which ought to be respected by others. Furthermore, there should ideally be points of access into new spaces for those able to function within them. However, the deeper problem remains, with which the political debate about multiculturalism and the politics of recognition is concerned: when there are tensions or clashes between different ways of doing things, what standard (whose standard) do we use to adjudicate? In times of economic privation, whose needs and values do we prioritise? The way these tensions are managed will have a lasting effect on who feels at home and who does not and will reveal, as Lionel Thaver (2006: 23) reminds us, the fundamental reality, beyond the various subcultures, of the 'institutional order that arises out of the common practices and procedures' of central administration and the 'institutional "home base"'.

Another response to my worries reminds us that all institutions and organisations contain people with varying needs and values. If it were impossible for different people to be content and productive, no workplace would ever function, and if there is even minimally a professional code of conduct, people can work together productively and amicably. Furthermore, it is not difficult for an organisation to set out a regulating framework of (for liberals at least) uncontroversial values, such as non-discrimination on the grounds of religion, race, gender or class. Any institution can and ought to do at least this much and most South African universities have publically committed themselves to a notably similar set of policies and values. However, what such a framework comes down to in practice might be contentious, and well-intentioned policies do not always translate into real change in behaviour and attitudes. This is what many in the debate on institutional transformation are concerned about: while universities might have noble-sounding policies and statements, people's habits and comfort – their very 'feeling at home' – can impede the transformation of the institution into a place in which other, traditionally marginalised people also feel at home.

These three difficulties arise partly from a growing responsiveness to the needs of non-academics in the university and to an increasing sense that universities need to be more socially aware and responsive to their history and context. However, we should not ignore the fact that universities are essentially places oriented around a commitment to learning and teaching and thus, arguably, academics are their defining employees. South African universities need to find ways of retaining their essential function while responding to a complex socio-economic reality, not an easy task in our highly politicised context. A fourth and final issue I wish to consider therefore focuses on academics and the very nature and function of the university.

Part of the difficulty is the fact, already noted, of the relation between the professional and personal lives of the employees of universities. For many academics, the relation is blurred; they have a deep stake in the institution's espousing certain values and ways of doing things because those are also their own values. However receptive we think a university ought to be to external economic, social and political pressures, it is certainly (importantly) true that academics are core to the university's purpose and functioning. If they are unhappy, alienated or unproductive, a university cannot function or retain any sense of purpose. This is not to ignore or belittle other employees or to say that they are the ones who ought to be made uncomfortable if we have to choose. Not at all. Academics can be frustratingly complacent and suspicious of change. It is, rather, to say that if there is a problem keeping academics in their element, it is a problem affecting the core of a university itself. It is to say that the university might as well be another kind of institution. How academics experience the university is central to its purpose and character. I return to this point in the final section.

A further aspect of this issue, which is closely related in the minds of many academics, is even more fundamental to universities – the divergent views of the very function, the very 'idea', of a university. Different ideas about what a university essentially is will affect one's experience of working and studying within it. For those taken by the idea of the research university, or the idea of a university as offering a liberal, universal and theoretical education, for instance, the increasing pressure for universities to be more socially oriented, relevant or receptive to market forces will impact on their integrity and flourishing as a researcher and on their sense of identity as a member of a university they respect.[24] This raises the question of whether there is a core value or function of a university, to which other functions and values ought to be subordinated, and which acts, in Gordon Graham's (2008: 162) words, as a 'regulative ideal' to guide and articulate policy and ethos. If we can find one, then perhaps *it* should constitute the essence of an institution's culture.[25] In a cohesive and collegial university, administrators and managers should be as committed to this guiding ideal as the academics are and there should not be fundamental disagreement surrounding policies and long-term direction.

In South Africa, however, this is contentious. The historically advantaged universities have tried to further research and teaching, along with professional and vocational education. With issues of social justice so pressing, they are now also forced to consider the vexed issue of social relevance in a way that affects the traditional views of a university as in some ways importantly independent of practical pressures. I am not sure whether we can expect consensus on how this should work in our fluid and troubled context, where so much is at stake. My point is that without a guiding idea of its very purpose, a university will be hard pressed to develop a coherent ethos, in terms of which internal conflict could be managed and which could provide a framework within which all its members are at home. The 'idea of a university' is therefore crucial in the debate about institutional culture and is as relevant and pressing, even if for a wider array of reasons, than it was when Cardinal Newman first discussed it.[26]

Traditions, articulation and stability

In the absence of consensus on a guiding ideal, what should institutions do to make themselves, as far as it is feasible, a 'home for all', in a way that still expresses a distinctive culture? It is always a simpler matter to provide a negative critique than to offer solutions, but in this final section I review, at a very abstract level, a way of engaging with institutional transformation.

The 'idea of the university' is 'not the sort of thing that can be fully realized and permanently secured,' writes Graham (2008: 162). 'Rather, it is a regulative ideal that gives us our bearings and against which trends and tendencies are to be judged.' In light of the discussion so far, and guided by the thought that academics are core to a university's identity and culture, my suggestion is that engagement in good faith with the idea of the university should be of central concern in the institution and guide attempts to transform it. I want to conclude by exploring this, still focusing on academics, and drawing on ideas of *tradition* (MacIntyre 1981), *articulation* (Taylor 1989, 1991) and *stability* (Rawls 1973).

A university is the bearer and expression of traditions, which partly constitute its culture. While critics have rightly charged tradition with being, often, conservative and unwelcoming to many, tradition is at the same time essential to maintaining an institution at all and to giving it a distinctive character. An institution continues beyond the lifespan of particular people and tradition is one way it is able to do so. The problem, therefore, is not that universities have traditions; the problem lies in the particular content and inspiration of those traditions. Tradition, and the distinctive institutional character it forms, is probably not something that can be completely imposed and managed, which adds to the difficulties attending transformation. It grows organically, influenced by many factors beyond anyone's control. We may find ourselves with traditions, whose complete genealogy even the official institutional narratives may not be able to tell us. Yet it is important for the health, character and continuity of a university that it understands and articulates its traditions, even in the attempt to transform itself into something new and better. How else can it outlive the particular people who live and work in it at any particular time? Furthermore, many come to work and study in a university precisely because of its traditions – they hope to join a long tradition of systematic study on what it means to be human, whose institutional origin *in this form* happens to be European.[27] It is essential to the humanities, at any rate, that we retain our connection with that past; achievements within philosophy and the arts are not superseded in the way those in the sciences are.[28] They are part of the very long story we tell in the effort to understand ourselves.

Charles Taylor's 'presumption' in favour of the value of cultures is relevant here. It seems reasonable, he says, to think that cultures

> that have provided the horizon of meaning for large numbers of human beings, of diverse characters and temperaments, over

a long period of time – that have, in other words, articulated their sense of the good, the holy, the admirable – are almost certain to have something that deserves our admiration and respect, even if it is accompanied by much that we have to abhor and reject (1994: 72–3).

Echoing this point, Alasdair MacIntyre (1981: 207) writes: 'Living traditions, just because they continue a not-yet-completed narrative, confront a future whose determinate and determinable character, so far as it possesses any, derives from the past.' No institution that has lasted will have a tradition and culture so debased as to contain nothing valuable and no seeds for progress within it. It will contain possibilities for a future that is hopefully better than what we have, but with which we can identify because its form is already embedded in the tradition, however inchoately. In our struggle to reimagine universities in South Africa and to disentangle ourselves from our dependence on European and American models, it is important not to reject entirely our institutional history.

Traditions connect us to our past and to a future our past makes meaningful for us, but they need not be conservative or reactionary. 'A living tradition,' MacIntyre (1981: 207) writes, 'is an historically extended, socially embodied argument, and an argument precisely in part about the goods which constitute that tradition.'

> So when an institution – a university, say, or a farm, or a hospital – is the bearer of a tradition of practice or practices, its common life will be partly, but in a centrally important way, constituted by a continuous argument as to what a university is and ought to be or what good farming is or what good medicine is. Traditions, when vital, embody continuities of conflict. Indeed, when a tradition becomes Burkean [that is, stable and conservative], it is always dying or dead (MacIntyre 1981: 206).

The conception of a tradition as an extended argument is important. It reminds us that institutions can maintain a coherent tradition that nonetheless contains ongoing argument and dissent, which, rather than being destructive, can partly constitute their distinctive character. It is how this argument is managed, the spirit in which it is undertaken, the attitudes we take towards each other as interlocutors and the end that is envisioned that are crucial to an institution's ethos. We argue, but ideally about the same thing, often with passion because we agree that it matters and to many of us both professionally and personally. According to MacIntyre (1981: 207), traditions are sustained and strengthened by the exercise of certain virtues and undermined by their absence. If we are mindful of the virtues that sustain traditions and the vices that undermine them – 'lack of justice, lack of truthfulness, lack of courage, lack of the relevant intellectual virtues' – even our ongoing arguments can be creative and good-spirited. This ongoing argument needs to be contained and managed, of course (and here is a role for university leadership), but it needs to be there or universities will stultify into complacency, acquiescence or, at worst, into the mouthpiece of fashion and power. They will lose the critical, open-minded and open-hearted spirit that is essential to their purpose and that characterises them at their best.

While not explicit about this, Graham's understanding of a guiding ideal incorporates this idea. He writes:

> Intellectual ideals need constant renewal. Otherwise they disappear and die. But their renewal depends crucially on their intellectual articulation. This means setting out what makes them ideal and why they are worth adhering to and pursuing, despite the fact that the vicissitudes of real life will forever prevent their full realization (2008: 162–3).

As Taylor (1991: 22) understands it, the articulation of our values has a 'moral point', in 'making the force of an ideal that people are already living by more palpable, more vivid for them' and in revealing where our guiding ideas exist in 'debased and deviant forms' (21). Articulation is, for Taylor, a moral task. This role of articulation is especially pertinent to South African universities, as we struggle to articulate our both valuable and problematic dependence on European traditions, and as we try to imagine alternatives that are responsive to our context, yet still continuous with our intellectual history.

Articulation and argument are important for keeping the necessary traditions supple and responsive, for helping us to excavate the often inchoate ideals that we pay allegiance to and for reimagining them into better, less debased and more context-sensitive forms. Furthermore, and this is my final point, they can lead to what John Rawls, in relation to justice, has called 'stability'. The conception of justice in a well-ordered society is stable, he says, because those taking part in just social arrangements 'acquire the corresponding sense of justice and desire to do their part in maintaining them' (1973: 454). Stable conceptions of justice ensure that citizens' potentially 'disruptive inclinations' are overridden for the sake of the justice they affirm. The broader point here is that a stable institution generates its own support, by fostering in its participants the very ethos and motivations that define its culture and enable its survival. And, as Taylor (1989: 96, 1991: 22) writes, in articulating the ideals and commitments that we are often moved by in a non-specific way, we can be empowered to live up to them more fully.

One idea of the university, according to Graham (2008: 165), is 'as a place in which the pursuit of truth and understanding are given special protection, not to the exclusion of useful or socially relevant subjects, but not principally in their service either'. Perhaps this idea, minimally, can unite us. Although the condition Graham states – that truth and understanding should not principally be in the service of social relevance – might be controversial in our context, it is, I think, necessary if universities are to remain a distinctive kind of institution, with a core purpose that is not diluted by social, economic and political pressures. The task, then, for each university, is to figure out, in community, how to express this ongoing project in a particular and character-full way in its institutional culture and, in doing so, generate support for it. If we are all trying to make a home together in which the pursuit of truth and understanding is definitive of its purpose, in full appreciation of the difficulties and inevitable conflicts, the very effort can be productive and unifying.

Thinking of traditions as sustained arguments, and stressing the need for ongoing articulation, might seem to be in tension with the other notions informing this discussion, those of home, element and stability.[29] We think of feeling at home as being in harmony with our surroundings; we saw how being in one's element facilitates agency, productivity and flourishing and we saw how stability can override disruptive impulses and generate support for a guiding ideal. In contrast, engaging in an ongoing argument and continuous articulation is potentially antagonistic and disruptive. However, MacInytre's point is that extended arguments can be creative, rather than destructive, and constitutive of continuity and character. With careful guidance and commitment to rigorous and respectful engagement, arguments about its own constitution and ideals can sustain and vivify an institution. I hope, too, to have reinterpreted the notion of home, through the analysis of 'being in one's element', so that it is compatible with disagreement and perhaps animated by it. Home, therefore, need not be a conservative or reactionary space. Just like healthy families, a healthy institution should be able to accommodate the disagreement that is inevitable, as long as it is disagreement about issues recognised by all as important and engaged with in a respectful and tolerant spirit.

This strategy has the advantage of offering even recalcitrant members of an institution – those whose feeling at home is perhaps an impediment to transformation – a way to engage on their own terms. As the notion of stability has suggested, for those to whom it matters that they work in a university, and for whom the ideals of teaching and learning, the pursuit of truth and understanding have both personal and professional resonance, the ongoing debate must matter and they have a stake in participating in it. They are playing a game, the fairness of which they value, by rules they have agreed to obey. If the goal is to create an institutional culture that distinctively embodies and expresses a commitment to the pursuit of truth and understanding, all other disagreements and proposed changes can be assessed and structured according to this shared goal.

Finally, this strategy reorients a question I raised earlier. In the light of the difficulties I have discussed, does a university leadership have a duty to create a space for the substantive flourishing of all its members? The discussion now suggests that if there is a duty, it is the duty of all members of an institution, especially those for whom its purpose and values matter personally as much as professionally.[30] We all need to create a distinctive, fair and generous culture together and have a duty to do so in the various ways our different talents and interests make possible. This will include the creation of individual spaces to fit individual needs, whether academic or not. If the university is not a home for some of its members, it is the responsibility of all of us, not only those in leadership roles and not only those who are not at home, to change this and work towards *making* a home for all.

Nonetheless, the discussion throughout this chapter has centred on academics. As they are central to the existence and purpose of a university, this is perhaps unavoidable and not in itself problematic. I have suggested that an ongoing discussion on the idea of a university, undertaken in an appropriate manner, and the attempt to give a distinctive character to this idea in each institution, can create a uniting ethos for a university, in which its members may feel at home. This ongoing argument is most naturally thought to be the domain of academic and management members of the university and the suggestions in this final section are probably not as relevant to those who do not participate directly in the academic pursuits of the university. The point made earlier, that a university is a collection of nested spaces, ameliorates this problem somewhat, if the creation of different kinds of spaces for different kinds of people is facilitated and, importantly, if there exists the possibility and support for people to move from non-academic into academic spaces. While this offers some potential solutions, it does not remove the deeper issues. However, if we cannot provide a home for all in a rich sense, in which professional and the personal lives are connected and reinforcing, we must at least strive to forge an institution in which a home for some does not mean alienation for everyone else.

Notes

1. My thanks to Bruce Janz, Sally Matthews, Pedro Tabensky and the anonymous reviewers for helpful advice and comments, to audiences at the Institutional Culture Roundtable at Rhodes University and at the Rhodes Centre for Higher Education, Research, Teaching and Learning (CHERTL) doctoral students' gathering and to the South African National Research Foundation (NRF) for financial support, which aided my research.

2. This chapter can be seen as a companion to my (2010) paper, 'How Do I Live in This Strange Place?', in which I explore the experience of not being entirely at home in a place.
3. My thoughts are influenced by debates on liberalism and the challenges it faces from the politics of recognition and multiculturalism. The 'politics of recognition' is Taylor's influential term from his essay of the same name (1994). See Kymlicka (1995) for a liberal response to multiculturalism, which addresses similar issues in a political context to those I raise here.
4. As Louise Vincent does in Chapter 1 of this volume.
5. The University of the Witwatersrand Institutional Culture Programme defines institutional culture as 'the lived experience of the university by all those who inhabit it'. http://www.wits.ac.za/aboutwits/governance/transformationoffice/18464/institutional_culture_programme.html.
6. I am using 'virtuous' in a standard philosophical sense, to capture what is appropriate and excellent for a particular kind of thing. In persons, this will refer to excellences of character, which issues in appropriate conduct, thought and feeling; in institutions, it will refer to appropriate policies and activities, relations between people and institutional culture.
7. Sally Matthews's helpful contribution in Chapter 3 of this volume explores this issue.
8. Higgins (2007: 97) notes that some recent analyses argue that 'it is simply the massive fact and bulk of institutional culture that may be the main obstacle in the way of the successful transformation of South Africa's higher education system'.
9. Higher education cannot be transformed without transforming the schooling system that feeds tertiary institutions, without addressing poverty and exclusion in society, without extending the status that is currently attached to universities alone to other institutions that educate for valuable skills and are equally important for society. And so on. Universities themselves do not have direct, or even great, control over these factors, yet are dependent upon them for their own functioning, transformation and integrity.
10. I have excluded statements that are purely concerned with academic matters. See http:// www.ru.ac.za/static/policies/vision_mission.html.
11. While other universities' mission statements are less comprehensive than that of Rhodes, all have some socio-political and environmental element, though some are more narrowly focused on academic concerns than others. For example, the University of KwaZulu-Natal's mission is to be a 'truly South African university that is academically excellent, innovative in research, critically engaged with society and demographically representative, redressing the disadvantages, inequities and imbalances of the past' (http://www.ukzn.ac.za/about-ukzn/vision-and-mission). The University of Stellenbosch

aims to 'create an academic community in which social justice and equal opportunities will lead to systemic sustainability' (http://www.sun.ac.za/english/management/rector/Documents/Institutional%20Intent%20and%20Strategy%202013-2018.pdf). The University of Cape Town's mission is more focused on research, teaching and other academic concerns than Rhodes and KwaZulu-Natal, but in the final section states that it 'promotes a more equitable and non-racial society', 'supports redress in regard to past injustices' and 'is affirming and inclusive of all staff and students and promotes diversity in demographics, skills and backgrounds' (http://www.uct.ac.za/about/intro/). The mission statement of the University of the Witwatersrand concentrates on academic concerns (http://www.wits.ac.za/aboutwits/3160/introducingwits.html). The University of Fort Hare's extensive and substantive 'charter' is, perhaps surprisingly given its history, less inclined to political language than other universities' statements. The values most discussed are humane and scholarly, though the familiar socio-political values do appear (http://www.ufh.ac.za/mission). It would be an interesting exercise, but one that is beyond the scope of this chapter, to compare South African universities' mission statements with those in other countries.

12. With respect to institutions, the management of Rhodes University, including the vice chancellor, have used the phrase frequently. Thaver (2006) offers an overview of the uses of what he calls the concept of 'home-at home' for the analysis of institutional culture. See Matthews (2010) on the short-lived 'home for all' campaign in South Africa, which called on white South Africans to acknowledge the injustices of apartheid and attempt reparations.

13. In this chapter I use the expressions 'feeling at home', 'being at home' and 'homely', interchangeably, though a more careful analysis would reveal significant differences in tone and value.

14. Compare Porteous (1976), in which he explores 'home' as a 'psychic space'.

15. See Terkenli (1995: 328). I have also been influenced by Monahan (2013). Many feminist philosophers have long been suspicious of the notion of home: see Weir's (2008) overview of the debates and, for instance, Honig's (1994) critique of the use of this notion in political and moral philosophy.

16. Young's (1997) essay is a valuable exploration, within the context of feminist debates, of both the positive and negative aspects of 'home'. See Weir (2008) for a helpful discussion of Young's essay and bell hooks (1990: 43) for a reminder of the value of home and its potential to be a 'site of resistance and liberation struggle'.

17. On narrative and institutional culture, see Louise Vincent's contribution to this volume, Chapter 1. For an influential exploration of narrative, tradition and institutions, and identity, see MacIntyre (1981: Chapter 15). I return to MacIntyre later in this chapter.

18. Young (1997: 161) makes this point with regard to 'home'.
19. See Minesh Dass's Chapter 4 in this volume.
20. A collegial institution is one run or managed by academics, in which there is an equal 'community of scholars' (Graham 2008: Section 5).
21. According to Hashatse (2013), various official documents state that Rhodes University aims to become the 'employer of choice' for all kinds of people.
22. Furthermore, as Castells (2001) reminds us, universities are complex institutions, with many functions that are often contradictory, which can only further complicate their attempts to transform.
23. Thanks to Sally Matthews for this point.
24. See Graham (2008) for a helpful survey of different historically influential ideas of the university and the classic texts collected in Mooney and Nowacki (2011).
25. The University of Fort Hare's mission statement provides the best expression of a 'guiding' ideal I have found. See http://www.ufh.ac.za/mission.
26. See John Henry Newman's classic study, *The Idea of a University*. Sections are reprinted in Mooney and Nowacki (2011).
27. My point, obviously, is not that non-Europeans never examined human life or had no intellectual activity, tradition and institutions. But the university as we know it is European in form.
28. On this difference between the arts and the sciences, see Jones (2012).
29. Thanks to Pedro Tabensky for pressing me on this point.
30. Murali Ramachandran originally suggested this idea, in conversation.

References

Castells, M. 2001. 'Universities As Dynamic Systems of Contradictory Functions'. In *Challenges of Globalization: South African Debates with Manuel Castells*, ed. J. Muller, N. Cloete and S. Badat, 206–23. Cape Town: Maskew Miller Longman.

Graham, G. 2008. *Universities: The Recovery of an Idea*. Exeter: Imprint Academic.

Hashatse, T. 2013. 'Rhodes University 2006–2011: Review of Transformation Related Strategy, Plans and Initiatives'. Grahamstown: Equity and Institutional Culture Office, Rhodes University.

Higgins, J. 2007. 'Institutional Culture as Keyword'. *Review of Higher Education in South Africa*, 97–122. Pretoria: Council on Higher Education.

Honig, B. 1994. 'Difference, Dilemmas, and the Politics of Home'. *Social Research* 61 (3): 563–9.

hooks, b. 1990. 'Homeplace'. In *Yearning: Race, Gender, and Cultural Politics*, 41–9. Boston: South End Press.

Jones, W.E. 2012. 'Higher Education, Academic Communities, and Intellectual Virtues'. *Educational Theory* 62 (6): 695–711.

Kymlicka, W. 1995. *Multicultural Citizenship*. Oxford: Clarendon Press.
MacIntyre, A. 1981. *After Virtue: A Study in Moral Theory*. London: Duckworth.
Matthews, S. 2010. 'Differing Interpretations of Reconciliation in South Africa: A Discussion of the Home for All Campaign'. *Transformation* 74: 1–22.
Monahan, M. 2013. 'The Strangeness of This Place: A Response to Samantha Vice'. Unpublished paper.
Mooney, T.B. and M. Nowacki. 2011. *Understanding Teaching and Learning: Classic Texts on Education by Augustine, Aquinas, Newman and Mill*. Exeter: Imprint Academic.
Porteous, J.D. 1976. 'Home: The Territorial Core'. *Geographical Review* 66 (4): 383–90.
Rawls, John. 1973. *A Theory of Justice*. Oxford: Oxford University Press.
Rhodes University. 2014. 'Vision & Mission Statement'. http://www.ru.ac.za/static/policies/vision_mission.html.
Steyn, M. and M. van Zyl. 2001. ' "Like That Statue at Jammie Stairs": Some Student Perceptions and Experiences of Institutional Culture at the University of Cape Town in 1999'. Research Report, Institute for Intercultural and Diversity Studies at the University of Cape Town. http://opencontent.uct.ac.za/Humanities/Like-that-statue-at-Jammie-stairs-Some-student-perceptions-and-experiences-of-institutional-culture-at-the-University.
Taylor, C. 1989. *The Sources of the Self: The Making of Modern Identity*. Cambridge: Cambridge University Press.
———. 1991. *The Ethics of Authenticity*. Cambridge: Harvard University Press.
———. 1994. 'The Politics of Recognition'. In *Multiculturalism: Examining the Politics of Recognition*, ed. A. Gutmann, 25–73. Princeton: Princeton University Press.
Terkenli, T.S. 1995. 'Home as a Region'. *Geographical Review* 85 (3): 324–34.
Thaver, L. 2006. ' "At Home", Institutional Culture and Higher Education: Some Methodological Considerations'. *Perspectives in Education* 24 (1): 15–26.
Vice, S. 2010. 'How Do I Live in This Strange Place?' *Journal of Social Philosophy* 41 (3): 323–42.
Weir, A. 2008. 'Home and Identity: In Memory of Iris Marion Young'. *Hypatia* 23 (3): 4–21.
Wise, J.M. 2000. 'Home: Territory and Identity'. *Cultural Studies* 14 (2): 295–310.
Young, I.M. 1997. 'House and Home: Feminist Variations on a Theme'. In *Intersecting Voices: Dilemmas of Gender, Political Philosophy, and Policy*, 134–64. Princeton: Princeton University Press.

3

White Privilege and Institutional Culture at South African Higher Education Institutions

SALLY MATTHEWS

If there is one thing that almost all commentators on higher education in South Africa agree on, it is that higher education institutions need to be transformed, at least in some ways and at least to some extent.[1] Most commentators also acknowledge that transformation remains incomplete and many (see, for example, Badat 2009; Mabokela 2003; Potgieter 2002; Thaver 2010) relate this incompleteness to a failure to transform institutional culture. However, while the transformation of institutional cultures is widely recognised as necessary, there is much uncertainty about both what is meant by the term 'institutional culture' and how it can be transformed.

In this chapter I discuss some of these difficulties, drawing on literature on white privilege to tentatively suggest some ways in which some of these difficulties, particularly those relating to race, may best be overcome. Literature on white privilege is helpful in showing how racism and racial inequality persist, even once openly racist laws and practices have been eradicated. Although this chapter focuses particularly on institutional transformation related to race, I would like to stress at this point that I do not mean to suggest that institutional transformation ought to focus only or even predominantly on race. Issues of class, gender, sexuality and disability are some of the other areas that need attention. Also, while this chapter focuses particularly on the question of institutional transformation at historically white higher education institutions, this is not to say that historically black institutions do not also face challenges relating to the transformation of their institutional cultures. Furthermore, as is true in many other chapters in this volume, I should note at the outset that my focus is particularly on academics, rather than on students or support staff and that several, although not all, of the illustrations and examples I use are drawn from the context of Rhodes University.

Race and the South African higher education context

While the apartheid-era higher education sector included universities designed to cater for black students, the largest and most well-resourced universities catered principally for white students.[2] Until the 1990s, the student and staff bodies of such universities were overwhelmingly white. Considerable progress has been made in increasing the numbers of black students at such universities, to the extent that many of these formerly white universities now have majority black student populations, even though white students are still overrepresented, if one bears in mind that whites make up less than 10 per cent of the South African population.[3] However, the academic staff component at such institutions remains overwhelmingly white: in most historically white universities more than 70 per cent of current academic staff is white.[4]

Thus, despite the existence of employment equity programmes designed to promote the employment of black staff, little progress seems to have been made in respect of reaching a point where the academic staff profile of universities, particularly historically white universities, comes anywhere near being representative of the population as a whole. While universities have complied with regulatory frameworks that have been put in place with the aim of ensuring the appointment of more black staff, this compliance has not yielded significant results (Soudien 2010: 882; DOE 2008). Thus, it is not that there are no policies in place to encourage, even to compel universities to employ more black staff, nor that universities fail to comply with such policies; rather, it seems that the existence of and compliance with policies are not enough to ensure transformation. The report of the Soudien Committee, which investigated issues concerning transformation at South African higher education institutions, concluded: 'All institutions have complied with the broad transformation requirements placed before them', but nevertheless commented that 'discrimination, in particular with regard to racism and sexism, is pervasive in our institutions' and that 'a disjunction [exists] between institutional culture and transformation policies' (DOE 2008: 13–14).[5] Responding to this report, the organisation Higher Education South Africa (HESA), which brings together vice chancellors of 23 South African universities, concluded that there is an 'urgent need to move beyond policy formulation . . . to create an observable shift in the cultures of institutions which in many instances, albeit in difficult to define and sometimes barely perceptible ways, continue to legitimise the subordination of the disabled, of women and of black people' (HESA 2011: 4).

It may be argued that more policies or more stringent ones are needed, but, as will become clearer later on in this discussion, the transformation of institutional cultures is not something that can be achieved straightforwardly through the introduction of new policies and practices. Also, it must be acknowledged that there are a number of different factors that come together to result in the failure to appoint or retain black academics. This chapter focuses on one such factor – institutional culture – but I do not mean to suggest that if we transformed institutional cultures, the problem would immediately be solved and black academic staff would quickly increase in number to form the majority at such institutions and the whole approach to learning and research would, as a consequence be transformed. Clearly, a whole range of factors, both historical and contemporary, have led to a situation where, particularly in some fields and particularly at very senior levels, there are relatively few black academics. While I would certainly argue that this dearth of black academics has to do with untransformed institutional cultures, this is not to say that this is the single determining factor, but simply that it is sufficiently significant to make it worth further consideration.

Race and white privilege in post-apartheid higher education institutions

In his discussion of the use of the term 'institutional culture' in the South African higher education context, John Higgins (2007) argues that the term is used as a kind of 'buzzword', which brings to mind a rather intangible set of issues that stand in the way of transformation. Other commentators on institutional culture stress that it is a 'slippery notion' and a 'hard to define phenomenon' (Ensor cited in Higgins 2007: 97; Jansen 2004: 1). It is a term that has all kinds of connotations, making it difficult to provide a simple definition. At best, it could be said that the term refers to the values, attitudes, perceptions, practices and ways of doing things that become embedded in an institution, even while they are not necessarily explicitly part of university policy or procedure.

As Higgins notes, in South Africa the term is most often used to refer to concerns relating to race and transformation – it 'figures as a kind of shorthand term for the powerful currents of racial feeling still active in South African society' (2007: 97). But while discussions on institutional culture in South Africa clearly have to do with race, there is little clarity about exactly what it is that needs to change so as to make institutional cultures more welcoming to black South Africans.

In attempting to pin down what institutional culture is and how it operates, several South African universities have tried to find a way to measure institutional culture, often through so-called 'institutional climate surveys', but while these are very useful in identifying some of the perceived problems people experience within particular institutions' cultures, they are less helpful in getting us to see exactly how such cultures operate and can be changed. One thing such surveys make clear is that institutional cultures are experienced very differently by people of different backgrounds. For example, the University of Cape Town's 'Institutional Climate Survey Report' reveals that 75 per cent of black African academic staff think racial discrimination is a problem on campus, while only 54 per cent of white academic staff agree (UCT 2007: 111). Similarly, Kezia Lewins's (2007) research at both the University of the Witwatersrand and the University of Cape Town reveals sharp disjunctures between perceptions of racism on the part of white and black staff members.

One reason why there may be such different perceptions regarding the extent of racial discrimination is that the form of racial discrimination that dominates today in universities as well as broader South African society is less explicit and obvious than it was in the past.

During the apartheid era, black people were openly prevented from attending particular higher education institutions or from occupying particular positions in these institutions. Unlike in the contemporary context, racial discrimination was explicit and undeniable. Today, while explicit incidents of racism do occur, discussions of the operation of racism at South African universities highlight the subtle and complex nature of much contemporary racism.

When asked to explain why and how they felt discriminated against, it becomes clear that many black academics have a sense that they are experiencing racism, but this racism operates in ways that make it difficult to pinpoint. Consider the following comments made by black academics working at formerly white universities:

> Racism has become subtle. The victims can smell it a mile away. The problem is how to articulate it (cited in DOE 2008: 41).

> Racism is ubiquitous, it can't be seen and then you feel you must be 'mad' . . . You feel it, but can't pinpoint it (cited in DOE 2008: 41).

> I am not certain if my experiences can be classified as discrimination or [if] they are just a figment of my imagination (cited in DOE 2008: 42).

> The racism is so sophisticated, it is almost difficult to say it is happening . . . this has led some of us who are black to think we are being paranoid or seeing racism when it is not so (cited in Potgieter 2002: 9).

> It's almost stuff that you can't quite put your finger on, and I think that's the more dangerous stuff, because if it's overt, it's out there, you know we can confront something, we can do something about it. But as I said, part of the difficulty is you're almost always trying to make sense of why am I feeling uncomfortable in my skin, what's going on. And having to

constantly go and say no, actually it's not me, something's going on (cited in Portnoi 2009: 380).

These quotes, as well as some of the narratives discussed later in this book (see, in particular, Chapter 5 by Thando Njovane) reveal that while many black academics experience racism, their experiences often relate to incidents where race was not obviously and explicitly at issue. As the HESA report puts it, there are 'myriad small ways in which slights, insults and prejudices can act to mould experience with discriminatory results' (2011: 5). In the contemporary setting, these slights and insults are not typically put in explicitly racist terms, but black academics often sense a racialised aspect to their experiences.

It is important to acknowledge at this point that it is possible that someone may *wrongly* feel as if there is a racialised aspect to their experience. However, because contemporary forms of racism often do not involve an explicitly racist subject who knowingly acts in a racist way, it is complicated to determine whether or not a particular incident is racist. Thus, while we have to be cognisant of the possibility of someone being wrongly accused of racism, a claim of racism cannot simply be dismissed because there is no hard evidence for it.[6] Rather than being taken seriously, some black academics discuss the dismissive or negative experiences they have had when they point to the implicitly racist nature of some or other negative experience they have had at formerly white universities. For example, Samuel Raditlhalo (2007) relates two incidents where black academics were themselves accused of racism after they suggested that racism underlay the problematic behaviour of students under their instruction. It seems that raising the possibility that racism is operating in subtle but important ways places black academics at risk of themselves being accused of racial prejudice, being oversensitive or overpoliticising things. Discussing the situation of being 'other' in the academic environment, M. Neelika Jayawardane (2007: 48) argues:

> Many academic 'Others' have heard the refrain: 'Why are you taking this so personally? Why do you always read things politically?' Some colleagues of mine, who usually find me an

easy-going, and Gracious Native, are quick to reposition me as 'Political' when I've responded to some awful encounter by describing, labelling, and interrogating the unjust situation.

In her discussion of racism at the University of the Witwatersrand, Lewins (2007: 92) raises a similar issue, noting that some black academics feel that to label incidents as racist and to draw attention to them is not advisable: calling something racist 'puts people's backs up and they come out fighting' – hence it is better to brush off such incidents, rather than to try to highlight them.

These comments relate to another point picked up on by Lewins (2007: 92–6), which is that some white academics seem to think that not being racist entails not mentioning racial categories or being colour-blind. Lewins discusses white academics who seemed awkward about making any reference to race or asked her during interviews for permission to use terms such as 'race' or 'black'. The black academics interviewed for Lewins's research used such terms freely and expressed frustration at the pretence of colour-blindness on the part of some white colleagues. It seems that some white academics think that not being racist means not noticing or talking about race, thus explaining the discomfort that emerges when black academics point out the racist nature of some of their experiences. They may think that the best way to avoid being racist, or being perceived as racist, is to not use racialised language at all and so they end up avoiding the topic of race altogether.

Responding to claims of racism by refusing to talk about race or being critical and suspicious of the person who raises such claims is problematic. However, the use of the disciplinary procedures universities have put in place to deal with incidents of racism is difficult where there is no concrete evidence that racism is the problem. Policies and procedures are of little help when we have to respond to subtle and ambiguous situations where race seems relevant, but is not explicitly and openly at issue. This is not to say that policies and procedures may not at times be of use when dealing with subtle forms of racism, but it seems that policies and procedures are insufficient in dealing with many contemporary incidents of racism.

The operation of racism in post-segregationist settings

When thinking about how to respond to these more subtle forms of racism, broader discussions on how white domination persists in post-segregationist settings are helpful. Literature on contemporary forms of white supremacy and white privilege show that the end of state-sanctioned, explicit racial segregation does not automatically result in the attainment of racial equality and justice. As Lucius Outlaw (2004: 166) puts it, with reference to the United States, white supremacy may no longer be the 'reigning public philosophy', but the 'inertial racism of white predominance' continues. The repeal of racist laws is certainly important for achieving racial justice, but changes in the law do not straightforwardly result in changes in beliefs and practices, which are the consequence of centuries of white supremacism (MacMullan 2005: 277).[7] However, contemporary forms of racism are often or even typically distinct from earlier, cruder forms of racism and must thus be addressed in a different way. To explore these differences, Shannon Sullivan (2006) makes a distinction between white supremacy and white privilege. She uses the term 'white supremacy' to refer to conscious, deliberate forms of white domination and 'white privilege' to refer to 'a constellation of psychical and somatic habits formed through transaction with a racist world', which are often unconscious, but have the effect of maintaining white domination (63).[8] Sullivan, whose particular focus is the United States, but whose work has relevance for countries such as South Africa, notes that in post-segregationist societies both white privilege and white supremacy continue to operate, but, she argues, the less conscious and explicit forms of racial domination – those she calls 'white privilege' – predominate. As she puts it: 'While big-booted forms of conscious oppression still exist, in the early twenty-first century white domination tends to prefer silent tiptoeing to loud stomping' (5).

In making these distinctions, Sullivan is not suggesting that contemporary forms of white domination are any less pernicious than earlier forms. Indeed, she says that white privilege is 'just as, if not more destructive than white supremacy, even if (or, perhaps, precisely because) it is not as spectacular' (2006: 55). Her aim in making a distinction between white supremacy and white privilege is to emphasise that contemporary forms of white domination are different from earlier forms and thus need to be approached differently. White privilege cannot be addressed in the same manner as more explicit forms of white domination since one of the difficulties that white privilege presents is that it is not an explicit, conscious form of domination. Rather, it functions through the 'whitely habits' that white people are likely to continue to have, even though they may reject explicitly racist beliefs. In explaining what she means by the term 'whitely habits', Sullivan says that she is not claiming that contemporary forms of racism are simply a 'bad habit' – something annoying, such as biting one's fingernails, but not really fundamentally important (2). Rather, by 'habit' she refers to 'an organism's subconscious predisposition to transact with its physical, social, political, and natural worlds in particular ways' (23). Such whitely habits may include, for example, a blindness to the way in which white domination and racism benefit all whites, a tendency to view the white experience as 'normal', an easy assumption of authority and a tendency to assume the appropriateness of one's position of dominance.[9]

Sullivan's discussion shows how racism is not only, or even primarily, a set of conscious beliefs about the superiority of white people. Rather, it is a way of being in the world that privileges white people and disadvantages and dehumanises black people, even when this is not the obvious or conscious intent of the white people concerned. Furthermore, as the idea of the *habits* of white privilege makes clear, racism is not only about beliefs and ideas, but also about bodily reactions, such as a white woman unthinkingly holding her bag more tightly when passing a black man in the street or the unconscious change in tone perceptible in some white people's voices when talking to a black person.

Sullivan's argument is thus that white privilege operates in largely unconscious ways. She stresses that she does not mean that whitely habits are simply habits we have not reflected upon and that could easily become conscious once our attention has been drawn to them. Neither, on the other hand, does she mean that they are completely inaccessible to intelligent inquiry.[10] What she means is that white privilege is not only perpetuated through intentional acts, but also through ways of being in the world that reinforce white domination, even without the conscious intention of white people, and that are very difficult to bring to the conscious attention of the people concerned.

Talking of whiteness as habit also helps to explain why even white people who are openly opposed to racism and consciously committed to eradicating it may sometimes continue to act in ways that perpetuate white domination. As bell hooks (1989: 113) points out, whites can 'embody white supremacist values and beliefs even though they may not embrace racism as prejudice ... [in so far as] their actions support and affirm the very structure of racist domination and oppressions that they profess to wish to see eradicated'. To say this is not to say that such whites are necessarily dishonest or disingenuous in professing a commitment to ending racism; it is to say that the habits of white privilege are difficult to see and to root out and that a conscious commitment to ending racism is not sufficient to uproot the various underlying attitudes and ways of being which, as Terrance MacMullan puts it, function 'below the radar' (2009: 145). It also means that it is possible to accept that many white people may be innocent of consciously perpetuating white supremacism, while still needing to be held accountable for the perpetuation of white domination through habits of whiteness (183).

The recognition that white privilege often operates in ways that are difficult to discern, especially for white people, has led some writers on the topic to spend quite some time reflecting on how to make it visible and particularly on how to make it visible to white people, who often fail to see that they remain privileged in post-segregationist societies, regardless of the dismantling of explicit racist laws and practices. For example, Alison Bailey (1998) and Peggy McIntosh (1988) both talk about the frustration they experience when teaching white students about white privilege. In their experience, even when white students accept that black people experience oppression and exclusion, they are often unwilling to accept the corollary: that they themselves experience privilege. Reflecting on her students' reactions, McIntosh notes that she and her students had been taught 'to recognize racism only in individual acts of meanness by members of [their] group, never in the invisible systems conferring unsought racial dominance on [their] group from birth' (1988: 6). When one regards racism as only having to do with individual acts of meanness, white people who do not actively work to put black people at a disadvantage come to believe that they do not contribute to racial injustice. Racial injustice, as they see it, is a consequence of the actions of individual (bad) whites against blacks, with other (good) whites standing by innocent and unaffected.

If we think of racism only as being the kind of explicit, conscious thoughts and acts that characterised apartheid and other forms of state-sanctioned segregation, we might come to think that not being racist means not noticing or not talking about race. However, as some contemporary writers point out, apparently race-neutral approaches often function to perpetuate racism and racial inequality. For example, Ruth Frankenberg (1993) and Sullivan (2006) show how so-called colour-blindness can actually function to obscure and perpetuate racial inequalities and racist oppression. Sullivan argues that in the United States the civil rights movements of the 1960s made it increasingly socially unacceptable for white people to openly espouse racist beliefs. As a result, a kind of colour-blindness emerged as the acceptable way in which white people were supposed to treat black people. The 'good' white person was the person who did not notice race at all (Sullivan 2006: 5). However, as Frankenberg (1993: 7) points out, the colour-blind strategy allows white people to distance themselves from racism, presenting it as something other (bad) white people do. Thus, racism is presented as something that relates to bad white racists and poor black victims, but has nothing to do with the white person who does not hold or express any explicitly racist views.

In contrast to this picture, authors writing on white privilege show how many post-segregationist societies continue to privilege white people in all kinds of ways and argue that those who thoughtlessly accept these privileges are complicit with injustice. Rather than being colour-blind, Frankenberg argues that white people need to be 'race-cognisant' (1993: 157–76). By this she means that white people ought to recognise that race plays an important role in shaping the experiences of both black and white people. 'Race-cognisant' white people are willing to critically interrogate their own (often unwitting) complicity in the creation and perpetuation of racial injustices. Through this kind of awareness, race-cognisant white people can play a role in making racial injustices visible and can 'use their critique of the racial order and their own positions within it as the basis for participation in changing . . . the material relations of racism' (241).

The literature on whiteness and white privilege in post-segregationist settings reviewed above raises two issues that are helpful when thinking about how to transform institutional cultures. Firstly, this literature suggests that white privilege persists in post-segregationist settings, but that it is difficult, especially for white people, to see how it functions and thus that in order to overcome racism in post-segregationist settings, considerable work is needed in making privilege visible. Second, this literature, particularly the literature on white privilege as habit, suggests that because white domination in post-segregationist settings occurs largely through unconscious habit rather than conscious, explicit intent, it may be best tackled indirectly. Thus, direct attempts to shift people's views and behaviour may be insufficient and may need to be accompanied by mechanisms that are likely to foster the unlearning of 'whitely' habits and the learning of new, less problematic ones. The rest of this chapter expands on these two claims.

Revealing privilege in higher education institutions

Taking into account some of the difficulties described above, some writers use metaphorical language and illustrations to assist white people living in post-segregationist settings to recognise that they are privileged and to begin to understand how white privilege operates. A much-quoted and very helpful metaphor on white privilege is provided by McIntosh (1988: 2) in her essay on white privilege as an 'invisible knapsack'.[11] In this essay she describes white privilege as being 'like an invisible weightless knapsack of special provisions, maps, passports, codebooks, visas, clothes, tools and blank checks', which help white people to navigate their way more easily through the social landscape. McIntosh goes on to draw up a list of items in this invisible knapsack in an attempt to help white people to recognise their privilege. This list includes a wide variety of privileges, some seemingly insignificant on their own, which assist white people to move more easily through their lives. Here are a few examples of the items on her list:

- Whether I use checks, credit cards or cash, I can count on my skin colour not to work against the appearance of my financial reliability;
- I can do well in a challenging situation without being called a credit to my race;
- I can easily buy posters, postcards, picture books, greeting cards, dolls, toys and children's magazines featuring people of my race;
- I can take a job with an affirmative action employer without having co-workers on the job suspect that I got it because of my race;
- I can be sure that if I need legal or medical help, my race will not work against me;
- I can choose blemish cover or bandages in 'flesh' colour and have them more or less match my skin;
- I can be late for a meeting without having the lateness reflect on my race (McIntosh 1988: 5–9).

McIntosh drew up this list in order to try to push white people to recognise ways in which they remain privileged in post-segregationist settings. When confronted with a list like this, it is harder for white people to deny that their race privileges them even in a post-segregationist setting.

In trying to reveal white privilege in the South African higher education context, similar techniques may prove helpful. As Melissa Steyn (2007: 3) points out, institutional cultures are not visible to everyone – the dominant culture of an institution 'was shaped around, and arose out of, a specific cultural base [and] needs to be made visible to those who function within it'. Similarly, Louise Vincent (in Chapter 1 of this volume) argues that research into institutional culture needs to make the 'normal strange' and surface the workings of the dominant culture(s), making the dominant recognise that they are indeed dominant. If white academics cannot see that the university context privileges them, they will be unlikely to be sympathetic to black academics' concerns about subtle forms of racial discrimination and probably not motivated to play a role in opposing such discrimination. My earlier overview of various discussions of black academics' experiences of racism in post-apartheid higher education institutions shows that black academics detect racism in contexts where it may seem absent to many white academics and that some black academics have found some white academics unsympathetic to their claims of continuing racism. Thus, there is a need to push white academics to see how they remain privileged in formerly white higher education institutions and to acknowledge that black academics may experience such institutions more negatively than they do.

The use of metaphors and illustrations such as McIntosh's knapsack may help white academics to better recognise their own privilege. In a presentation on transformation at Rhodes University, I drew up a list modelled on McIntosh's in which I identified some of the 'special provisions, maps, passports, codebooks, visas, clothes, tools and blank checks' that white academics at Rhodes University may have in their 'invisible knapsacks' of privilege (1988: 2).[12] While I drew up the list with Rhodes University in mind, I suspect many items will be applicable to other universities in South Africa and beyond. Here are a few items on the list:

- My students are not surprised to find someone like me lecturing them and tend to accept me as an authority on my subject;
- On campus I am generally assumed to be an academic staff member, rather than a student, outsider or non-academic member of staff;
- The texts I prescribe for my students are mostly written by people who look pretty similar to me. It's clear to my students that people like me are experts on my subject;
- No one complains about my 'funny' accent;

- When I attend a faculty meeting, there are lots of other people there who look like me and who come from a similar background to me;
- Meetings proceed in a manner familiar to me;
- I'm accustomed to people cleaning up after me and the people cleaning my office are accustomed to cleaning up after people like me;
- I understand the jokes made during staff meetings and I find them funny;
- Students are wary of complaining about me to the head of department. They assume the head of department will side with me;
- I feel comfortable at the local pub where some staff and students hang out after departmental seminars;
- If I make a mistake, I don't worry that my mistake is going to confirm a stereotype others have about people of my race;
- I'm not worried that people think I was appointed just because of my race;
- My mother tongue is spoken all day at my workplace;
- No one struggles to pronounce my name.

This list, like the original one by McIntosh, aims to assist white people to recognise their privilege. I used it in the original workshop with the aim of helping white academics at Rhodes University to see what black academics might mean when they claim to continue to feel disadvantaged at the university. I reproduce the list here in the hope that it might help to illustrate more concretely what I mean when I say that whites continue to experience privilege in post-segregationist higher education settings.

In recognising their privilege, white academics may also be pushed to recognise that confronting racial inequalities and racial discrimination at higher education institutions is not only about preventing and condemning explicitly racist incidents. Rather, addressing racial injustice must also be about recognising that white academics may experience South African universities in far more empowering ways than black academics do and that this makes it harder for black academics to flourish in these settings.

Tackling white privilege indirectly

Revealing white privilege may help white people to recognise ways in which institutional cultures nurture and protect some people, while making others feel unwelcome or vulnerable and unsure. This recognition will, hopefully, result in greater sympathy and concern on the part of white academics with regard to the experiences of black academics who feel alienated or out of place at formerly white universities. However, making privilege visible to the privileged is insufficient to combat the subtle forms of racism that are the principle manifestation of white domination in post-segregationist societies. As mentioned earlier, some commentators on race argue that contemporary forms of white dominance are often perpetuated through the operation of unconscious 'whitely habits' of privilege.

If racism operates in this way, it is unlikely to be overcome through rational argument alone. In explaining this point and its implications, Sullivan (2006) discusses the shift in the thinking of W.E.B. Du Bois, who initially believed that the best way to combat racism was to teach white people more about black people in order to fill the gaps in their knowledge. However, Sullivan reminds us that Du Bois later came to believe that what he had initially thought was an 'innocent lack of knowledge on white people's part' was actually 'more complex and sinister' (2006: 20). Rather than being simply a product of ignorance, white people's racism, Du Bois came to see, was 'carefully (though not necessarily consciously) constructed, maintained, and protected'. Sullivan does not stress this point principally to push home the maliciousness of racism, but rather to emphasise that racism is not eliminated simply by presenting new information that discredits the conscious arguments people might present in its defence. Rather, she argues, white dominance is maintained not only through white people's conscious beliefs about the racial superiority of white people, but also – and increasingly – through unconscious habits of whiteness.

This does not mean that it is not worth pushing white people to recognise their privilege – it is important to think and talk about race and to encourage more people to acknowledge the ongoing salience of race in post-segregationist societies. However, while conscious reflection on race and racism is necessary, it will not be sufficient to uproot white privilege because habits of white privilege can most likely not all be 'surfaced' in a way that would allow them to be tackled at a conscious level. As Sullivan points out, even if logical arguments against racism do succeed in getting white people to consciously reject racist beliefs and ideologies, these arguments do not necessarily have much impact on white people's unconscious habits. It seems, then, that rather than only trying to confront racism directly, it may be that 'the hidden, subversive operations of unconscious habits require indirect, roundabout strategies for transformation' (Sullivan 2006: 9). And, Sullivan continues, because these habits are formed through white people's interaction with a racist world, it may be that the best way to force changes in these habits of whiteness will be to change the environments that feed them. As she puts it, because of 'the constitutive role that the world plays in the formation of habit, the particular type of indirect assault needed is one that transforms the social, political, institutional, economic, aesthetic, physical, psychological, and other conditions for the composition of white privileged habits' (2). White people have come to develop habits of whiteness because they have been immersed in contexts that validate whiteness, but if they are exposed to environments which do not, these habits will slowly begin to change. Thus Sullivan suggests that if white people relocate out of the environments (be they geographical, literary, political, social and so on) that have led to the development of these habits of white privilege, they will begin to unlearn them.

When thinking about the transformation of institutional cultures, the arguments outlined above suggest that policies against racism and attempts to make white privilege more visible to white people will not on their own succeed in transforming institutional cultures. Policies that declare racism to be unacceptable or that outline the appropriate disciplinary procedure to follow when racist incidents occur are important, but on their own such policies are unlikely to succeed in eradicating racism since contemporary racism operates in such unseen and complex ways that it is difficult to identify and punish it.

Furthermore, while making privilege visible through strategies such as those described earlier can help white academics recognise their own privilege and become somewhat more sensitive to the concerns of black academics, Sullivan's discussion of the habits of privilege suggests that the operation of white privilege is unlikely to ever become fully accessible to conscious reflection and thus unlikely to be overcome through rational reflection and argumentation alone.

Rather, it may be that white privilege will be eroded if and when white academics are pushed out of the environments that have led to the development of whitely habits. If, for example, white academics are increasingly placed in situations where being white is not 'normal', are exposed to academic literature that comes out of contexts other than the West, are placed in situations where their dominance is questioned or undermined, they are likely to slowly unlearn habits of white privilege. Unfortunately, this means that while we cannot undo white dominance at historically white institutions until we tackle white privilege, white privilege is most likely to be unlearnt when whites no longer dominate.

While to some extent I think it is true that white privilege can only be unlearnt when whites cease to dominate a particular space and that whites are likely to continue to dominate it unless they unlearn white privilege, I do think there are some possible ways around this rather self-perpetuating and depressing situation. Firstly, white people can at least become somewhat aware of their privilege and at least partly committed to undoing it and, if they do develop this awareness, white people may be more willing to push themselves into environments in which they may unlearn the habits of white privilege. Thus, while Sullivan is right to emphasise that white privilege cannot simply be unlearnt through rational reflection and argument, the recognition of white privilege and reflection upon it can push white people to embrace environments in which they are likely to unlearn whitely habits. Thus, the project of revealing white privilege and encouraging white people to play a role in undoing it is of value, even if we acknowledge that white privilege operates in ways that resist conscious reflection. Second, in the South African context, whites are a numerical minority and as black South Africans become more insistent on fighting against their exclusion from particular spaces, contexts that feed white privilege will surely diminish. Whites can, and do, flee from spaces where they do not dominate, but in the South African case (unlike in societies where white people are a numerical majority and black people are marginalised politically) the avenues for such flight will surely become fewer and narrower.[13] Also, while current white academics were mainly socialised during the apartheid era and thus unavoidably grew up in an environment that nurtured the development of whitely habits, younger white academics have grown up in an environment that has been less likely to nurture this development to the same degree. Although there are some reasons to be pessimistic, surely it is likely that, slowly, whitely habits are being and will continue to be eroded.[14]

Attempts have already been made at engaging university communities on issues relating to race in ways that are a little more creative and roundabout than straightforward argument. For example, the University of the Witwatersrand and Rhodes University have both used drama to stimulate reflections among students and staff about racial and other forms of discrimination and stereotyping (see Nebe 2008; Sutherland 2011). Drama allows for a more personal, visceral engagement with the issue of racism and thus may be more effective at shifting unconscious attitudes than more abstract, intellectual discussions would be. These alternative ways of trying to shift attitudes and practices are worth further exploration.

Conclusion

When one considers the possibility that the continuing 'whiteness' of many South African higher education institutions may not be easily changed through the introduction of policies against racism and procedures to be followed, those who are committed to transformation may be left feeling rather defeated. However, the foregoing does not suggest that transformation is impossible, only that it may require more roundabout strategies. In so far as contemporary white domination is perpetuated less by explicit intent and action than by implicit attitudes and 'whitely' habits, we have to recognise that confronting racism is about both revealing white privilege and trying to create environments that encourage the dismantling of privilege through changing the environments that feed whitely habits.

I would like to make two final comments. Firstly, it is important to acknowledge that the above suggests that changing institutional culture will not be a quick and easy process. As Sullivan (2006: 33) points out, it is somewhat suspicious when a white person argues that the elimination of racial domination will take a long time; however, as she stresses, if we want to undo racism as effectively as possible, we need to take into account how it operates so that it can be better fought. Given that racism in post-segregationist societies often operates in complex, ambiguous and subtle ways, it needs to be confronted thoughtfully and often indirectly in order to be confronted effectively and we need to be cautious about too quickly considering the work of transformation to be complete.

Second, because this chapter has drawn principally on literature on white privilege, and particularly on literature by white theorists who are trying to think about ways in which white people can play an appropriate role in ending racism, it has disproportionately focused attention on what white people ought to do in response to continuing racism at South African higher education institutions. However, what the final section makes clear is that confronting white privilege requires changing the environments that feed such privilege and, given the pernicious and changing nature of white privilege, the changing of such environments is not something best entrusted to white people. Importantly, what this means is that the project of transforming South African higher education institutions has to be a predominantly black-led project because, as I argue at greater length elsewhere, white people can best unlearn white privilege through engagement with and confrontation by black people.[15] Such engagement and confrontation need not be explicitly about race or explicitly aimed at ending white privilege, but it seems safe to say that as long as white people are not made aware of their privilege, or made uncomfortable by it and are not made to slowly question and unlearn the deep-seated assumptions that continue to inform their actions in all kinds of ways, white domination of South African higher education institutions will continue.

Notes

1. This chapter developed out of a workshop presentation, which formed part of Rhodes University's 2011 *Imbizo*. I am grateful to Tshidi Hashatse for inviting me to participate in this workshop and for suggesting the relevance of white privilege literature to discussions on higher education.
2. For a history of higher education in South Africa, see Bunting (2002) or Reddy (2004).
3. For a more detailed discussion on race and student enrolment in South Africa, see Soudien (2010) and Steyn (2007).
4. For statistics and a discussion of the situation at the University of the Witwatersrand and the University of Cape Town, see Lewins (2007). Some universities provide updated statistics on their equity profile on their websites – for example, Rhodes University (http://www.ru.ac.za/humanresources/policiesandinfo/employmentequity/eestats/), the University of Pretoria (http://www.up.ac.za/services/equity/index.html) and the University of Johannesburg (http://www.uj.ac.za/EN/ABOUTUJ/TRANSFORMATIONOFFICE/EMPLOYMENTEQUITYFORUM/Pages/home.aspx).
5. This committee's full title was the Ministerial Committee on Transformation and Social Cohesion and the Elimination of Discrimination in South Africa's Public Higher Education Institutions. It was chaired by Professor Crain Soudien and is thus sometimes referred to as the 'Soudien Committee'.
6. For further discussion of this issue, see Raditlhalo (2007: 18).
7. On this topic, see also MacMullan's more recent work (2009:144–6).
8. Other authors use 'white supremacy' to refer to both conscious, deliberate and unconscious, more subtle forms of white domination – see, for example Mills (1997). I think both usages are appropriate, but the distinction Sullivan makes between white supremacy and white privilege is useful for my purposes here.
9. For an overview of the idea of 'whitely' habits, see Matthews (2012). For a longer discussion of 'whiteliness' and 'whitely' habits, see Frye (1992), Sullivan (2006), Taylor (2004) and Jones (2004).
10. Sullivan summarises her position in the introduction (2006: 5–7), but for a longer and more detailed defence of the idea that white privilege can operate in an unconscious way, see her Chapter 2.
11. Another helpful metaphor is provided by Kimmel (2010: 1), who describes white privilege as being like 'this breeze at my back'.
12. The presentation discussed here was part of Rhodes University's *Imbizo* held in July 2011. The *Imbizo* was an event in which various members of the Rhodes University academic community reflected on the past five years at Rhodes University and thought about a future path. One of the panels was on institutional culture. The word '*imbizo*' is an isiZulu word meaning

'meeting' or 'gathering' and is often used in the South African context to refer to planning meetings. The presentation I made is available at http://www.ru.ac.za/media/rhodesuniversity/content/institutionalplanning/documents/Institutional%20Culture%20-%20Sally%20Matthews%2022June2011.pdf.

13. Indeed, one of the places they flee is to higher education institutions such as Rhodes University and the University of Stellenbosch since such institutions remain sufficiently white as to make it easier for white people to avoid having their views and ways of being challenged.
14. Jansen (2009) argues, for example, that many young, white South Africans hold rather similar views to those of their parents. It is not obvious and should not simply be assumed that younger white South Africans are significantly less racist than their predecessors.
15. See Matthews (2012).

References

Badat, S. 2009. 'Theorising Institutional Change: Post-1994 South African Higher Education'. *Studies in Higher Education* 34 (4): 455–67.

Bailey, A. 1998. 'Privilege: Expanding on Marilyn Frye's "Oppression"'. *Journal of Social Philosophy* 29 (3): 104–19.

Bunting, I. 2002. 'The Higher Education Landscape under Apartheid'. In *Transformation in Higher Education: Global Pressures and Local Realities in South Africa*, ed. N. Cloete, R. Fehnel, P. Maassen, T. Moja, H. Perold and T. Gibbon, 35–52. Lansdowne: Juta.

DOE (Department of Education). 2008. 'Report of the Ministerial Committee on Transformation and Social Cohesion and the Elimination of Discrimination in Public Higher Education Institutions', 30 November. https://www.cput.ac.za/storage/services/transformation/ministerial_report_transformation_social_cohesion.pdf.

Frankenberg, R. 1993. *White Women, Race Matters: The Social Construction of Whiteness*. Minneapolis: University of Minnesota Press.

Frye, M. 1992. *Willful Virgin: Essays in Feminism*. Berkeley: Crossing Press.

HESA (Higher Education South Africa). 2011. 'Sector Position Paper on the Report of the Ministerial Committee on Transformation and Social Cohesion and the Elimination of Discrimination in South Africa's Public Higher Education Institutions', March. http://www.hesa.org.za/report/sector-position-paper-report-misterial-committee-transformation-and-social-cohesion-and-elimi.

Higgins, J. 2007. 'Institutional Culture as Keyword'. *Review of Higher Education in South Africa*, 97–122. Pretoria: Council on Higher Education.

hooks, b. 1989. *Talking Back: Thinking Feminist, Thinking Black*. Cambridge: South End Press.

Jansen, J. 2004. 'How Far Have We Come?' *Mail and Guardian*, 13–19 August, Getting Ahead Supplement: 1.

———. 2009. *Knowledge in the Blood: Confronting Race and the Apartheid Past*. Cape Town: University of Cape Town Press.

Jayawardane, M.N. 2007. 'Taking Things Personally, and Publicising the Private: Encountering Erasure on the Frontlines of Academia'. *Social Dynamics* 33 (1): 31–51.

Jones, J. 2004. 'The Impairment of Empathy in Goodwill Whites for African Americans'. In *What White Looks Like: African-American Philosophers on the Whiteness Question*, ed. G. Yancy, 65–86. New York: Routledge.

Kimmel, M. 2010. 'Introduction: Toward a Pedagogy of the Oppressor'. In *Privilege: A Reader*, ed. M.S. Kimmel and A.L. Ferber, 1–12. Boulder: Westview Press.

Lewins, K. 2007. 'How Open Are Our Doors? A Comparison of Academic Staff Transformation at the University of Cape Town and the University of the Witwatersrand', PhD diss., University of the Witwatersrand, Johannesburg. http://wiredspace.wits.ac.za/handle/10539/2150.

Mabokela, R.O. 2003. '"Donkeys of the University": Organizational Culture and Its Impact on South African Women Administrators'. *Higher Education* 46 (2): 129–45.

MacMullan, T. 2005. 'Beyond the Pale: A Pragmatist Approach to Whiteness Studies'. *Philosophy & Social Criticism* 31 (3): 267–92.

———. 2009. *Habits of Whiteness: A Pragmatist Reconstruction*. Bloomington: Indiana University Press.

Matthews, S. 2012. 'White Anti-Racism in Post-Apartheid South Africa'. *Politikon* 39 (2): 171–88.

McIntosh, P. 1988. 'White Privilege and Male Privilege: A Personal Account of Coming to See Correspondences through Work in Women's Studies'. Working Paper No. 189. Wellesley College. http://www.iub.edu/~tchsotl/part2/McIntosh%20White%20Privilege.pdf.

Mills, C. 1997. *The Racial Contract*. Ithaca: Cornell University Press.

Nebe, W. 2008. 'Identity Transformation through Theatre: The Case Study of the Wits Transformation Office Identity Pending Project'. Symposium on Knowledge and Transformation: Social and Human Sciences in Africa, Stellenbosch, November. http://152.112.253.5/Event_Page-24.phtml.

Outlaw, L. 2004. 'Rehabilitate Racial Whiteness?' In *What White Looks Like: African-American Philosophers on the Whiteness Question*, ed. G. Yancy, 159–72. New York: Routledge.

Portnoi, L. 2009. 'Transformative Change? Institutional Formalities and Institutional Realities'. *South African Journal of Higher Education* 23 (2): 373–85.

Potgieter, C. 2002. *Black Academics on the Move*. Cape Town: Centre for Higher Education Transformation.

Raditlhalo, S. 2007. 'Talent, the Staying Power of Racism, and Transformation: Transatlantic Observations'. *Social Dynamics* 33 (1): 3–30.

Reddy, T. 2004. 'Higher Education and Social Transformation: South African Case Study'. Report of the Council of Higher Education (CHE). http://www.che.ac.za/sites/default/files/publications/HEandSocialTransformationReport_25Feb2004.pdf.

Soudien, C. 2010. 'Grasping the Nettle? South African Higher Education and Its Transformative Imperatives'. *South African Journal of Higher Education* 24 (5): 881–96.

Steyn, M. 2007. 'The Diversity Imperative: Excellence, Institutional Culture, and Limiting Assumptions at Some Historically White Universities'. *Communitas* 12: 1–17.

Sullivan, S. 2006. *Revealing Whiteness: The Unconscious Habits of Racial Privilege.* Bloomington: Indiana University Press.

Sutherland, A. 2011. 'The Role of Theatre and Embodied Knowledge in Addressing Race in South African Higher Education'. *Studies in Higher Education* 38 (5): 728–40.

Taylor, P. 2004. 'Silence and Sympathy: Dewey's Whiteness'. In *What White Looks Like: African-American Philosophers on the Whiteness Question,* ed. G. Yancy, 227–42. New York: Routledge.

Thaver, B. 2010. 'The Transition to Equity in South African Higher Education: Governance, Fairness, and Trust in Everyday Academic Practice'. *International Journal of Politics, Culture and Society* 23: 43–56.

UCT (University of Cape Town). 2007. 'Institutional Climate Survey Report'. http://www.uct.ac.za/downloads/uct.ac.za/about/introducing/transformation/reports/institclimatesurvey07.pdf.

PART II

RHODES UNIVERSITY: A CASE STUDY

4

Making Room for the Unexpected
The University and the Ethical Imperative of Unconditional Hospitality

MINESH DASS

Teatime at Rhodes University: A personal experience of discomfort

One of the more difficult institutional practices I had to negotiate when I first came to Rhodes University (hereafter referred to also as Rhodes) from the University of Johannesburg was something called teatime. Apparently at 10.15 each morning, just as I was starting to get into my day's duties, I was obliged to stop working, go and have a warm beverage, perhaps a cigarette, and make conversation with my colleagues. Here, it seemed to me, was Rhodes at its antiquated best, continuing a ritual handed down from a colonial past, of which it seemed both embarrassed and strangely proud. Let me not focus too much on this colonial heritage, though it is a spectre that haunts the institution.

In any event, my rejection of teatime was not based primarily on its historical origins. And it was not that I did not enjoy the university-sanctioned break, or the conversation, or the delicious cakes that were sometimes put out. It was simply so very different to what I was accustomed to. I did not come from an institutional culture that gathered each day for tea. For this reason, I could not fathom the value placed on it by others in the department.

In those first few weeks as a new staff member, and mostly because I was nervously preparing to lecture the first-year students, I assumed that I could miss the daily pastime without raising any concerns. Then I attended the new staff orientation workshop, at which other new academics also expressed wonder at this fairly unique daily routine. Those running the workshop informed us that while, of course, teatime was not compulsory, it was nevertheless very important. They assured us that during those fifteen to twenty minutes each day, we would get to know the department, the staff and the postgraduate students and that much of the business of the week would be discussed, perhaps even decided, at that time. It occurs to me now – though this thought never crossed my mind at the time – that orientation, by its very nature, is a dangerously one-sided process. Its purpose and design is conservative in that it takes those who are new, and therefore different, and positions them in relation to that which already exists. When you take into account how scared or anxious most new academics are, and that the orientation programme speaks with the authority of the institution, there is little surprise that what new appointees (such as myself) come away with is a sense that this is how the university does things, this is how it has always been done and this is how I should do it from now on.

So, shocked and distressed by my own arrogance in assuming that teatime did not matter, I dutifully began going (even though, I should add, I do not drink either tea or coffee and I do not smoke). Sure enough, a great many departmental matters were discussed. I heard mention of the 'loss of DP' and of possible dates for something called a shredding meeting. DP losses, I thought, must have to do with Tony Leon's political failures. 'Shredding' was a term I knew vaguely from skateboarding and so I puzzled at the thought of middle-aged and, quite frankly, elderly men doing outlandish tricks on 'Sweet Boards' provided by the great Rhodes itself.[1]

You might well point out that I could simply have asked people to explain things I did not understand and I often did exactly that. Yet, strangely, the informal nature of the occasion made that more difficult, not less so. It was as if, since everyone was just gathered to chat to friends, my stalling conversation to ask obvious questions was simply unfair. I understood that teatime was a chance to relax, to be collegial – that, in a very real sense, it was a university-established practice designed to encourage hospitality.

Why was it then that I felt so ill at ease, so very unwelcomed, precisely during a period in the day created to make me feel at home? I do not deny that, in part, it had to do with my own misconceptions and prejudices, even my shy nature. To what extent should I therefore have felt responsible for my own uncertain beginning at this university? This is a question to which I will return shortly.

First though, I would like to suggest that for me teatime is difficult because of the inherent limitations of the hospitality it is able to provide. It is premised, quite obviously, on the notion that one likes tea, coffee or cigarettes. When I stood among my colleagues without these physical objects, I felt less like I belonged there. For quite some time, I could not grasp why this should be so, even though the answer is quite simple. Drinking tea, having a smoke – these are routines that characterise the Rhodes academic culture. The humble cup of tea therefore has a symbolic and normative function. In its way, it contributes to the communal feeling of the department and the university as a whole. So naturally, there was much at stake in my refusal of it.

Furthermore, I think that, in a sense, I did not really speak the language of the institution. DPs, shredding meetings, the difference between exercises and essays, CHERTL (Centre for Higher Education, Research, Teaching and Learning), Barratt (the largest lecture venue on campus) and numerous other terms were as foreign to me as a dialect of German spoken only in certain parts of Switzerland. The informality of the gathering only strengthened my sense that here was a community at ease with itself. And I quickly realised that it was my job to become more like them. I needed to learn the lingo, read the signs (and drink them, too, it seemed). Even if I did not really get the joke, I would have to learn to laugh anyway. Every admission, however subtle, of a lack of common ground would implicitly ensure that 'they' remained the department and I remained someone on the outside, looking in. If I asked for an explanation or clarification, I would also, unwittingly, declare my strangeness. And if I suggested a way of doing things that did not correspond with established practices, it would also make me seem alien and other.

The principle and the paradox of unconditional hospitality

I would like to be clear: I am in no way suggesting that my colleagues were intentionally ungenerous, unkind or unsupportive. Rather, what I am attempting to think through are the unintentional, systemic conditions that mediate the relationship between those who belong (to Rhodes, or to any other community for that matter) and those who do not. These conditions of hospitality ensure that it is always, in some sense, an exclusionary gesture and that our attempts to welcome others are always premised on something quite unwelcoming.

Principally, this paradox is explained by the very nature of community. In spite of the many ways in which a group may attempt to open its borders and invite others in, it cannot do so indefinitely. Always, and precisely so as to be a community in the first place, it must deny someone the right of access. The irony of this concept is beautifully captured by E.M. Forster in his finest novel, *A Passage to India*. Two Christian missionaries discuss with a group of Hindus the house of the Lord, which the Bible assures us has many mansions. The Hindus wonder if perhaps the Lord, in his infinite grace, would allow the monkeys their 'collateral share of bliss' (Forster 1979: 58). The younger missionary, a Mr Sorley, being more advanced, concedes that perhaps God would indeed allow monkeys into heaven (though his partner Mr Graysford disagrees). Emboldened, others ask if he would also allow access to the wasps, the oranges, even the bacteria that live inside people. At this preposterous suggestion, the young cleric becomes upset and declares: 'We must exclude someone from our gathering, or we shall be left with nothing.'

The question, though, is what is the worth of such a hospitality that limits, excludes and prescribes? For instance, the English Department at Rhodes University had to impose its language and its ways of doing things on me in order for me to do my job properly.[2] I had to change my practices so that they were more in line with the department's. That is patently obvious. And yet, what is it to welcome another in, but only on the condition that they speak and look and behave as you do?

The effect on me of this form of welcome was a profound sense of displacement and loss. I felt hopelessly caught between two opposing poles of classification: either I would be the foreigner, and be treated accordingly, or I would become like my host and therefore less like myself. As you may well imagine, neither of these options seemed fitting and I resisted on both fronts. On the one hand, I wanted not to be seen as unusual, as lacking in understanding or common ground. On the other hand, I actively refused to consider myself a member of the department. In truth, the irreconcilable nature of this double bind left me terribly isolated, unsure and confused. In a town as geographically remote and small as Grahamstown, these feelings were naturally exacerbated. Moreover, I must reiterate, this was not because members of the department were not collegial. In fact, it is precisely the kind of collegiality they generously advanced that I would like to critique or problematise.

This troubled beginning to my life at Rhodes is not provided to elicit sympathy or pity. Rather, I have given the example of my own lived experiences so that you may see how issues of hospitality play out in the everyday moments of people in a university. Indeed, I hope to show that they will impact, in the most profound sense, on the future of Rhodes and tertiary education in South Africa more generally. For there is no doubt that the challenges that face higher learning in this country are about access. The questions of who will be given this education and who will be employed by the various universities (and who will not) are fundamental to how we will construct the higher education landscape and how it might (or might not) contribute to the development of social justice.

In order to broach this issue of institutional reform, I must briefly (all too briefly, in fact) draw on some aspects of French philosopher Jacques Derrida's notion of unconditional hospitality, which I believe is crucial to what this institution is and would like to be. According to Derrida (2000: 25): 'The absolute or unconditional hospitality I would like to offer . . . presupposes a break with hospitality in the ordinary sense, with conditional hospitality, with the right to or pact of hospitality'. He then elaborates, arguing: 'We are taking account of an irreducible pervertibility. The law of hospitality, the express law that governs the general concept of hospitality, appears as a paradoxical law, pervertible or perverting. It seems to dictate that absolute hospitality should break with the law as right or duty.' To put it otherwise, contends Derrida:

> Absolute hospitality requires that I open up my home and that I give not only to the foreigner ... but to the absolute, unknown, anonymous other, and that I *give place* to them, that I let them come, that I let them arrive, and take place in the place I offer them, without asking of them either reciprocity ([the] entering into a pact) or even their names (2000: 25).

Absolute or unconditional hospitality does not, in any way, assume knowledge of the guest who might then enter. It asks, instead, that s/he is allowed to be utterly anonymous (hence, even her/his name is not demanded) and radically other to the one who acts as host. It does not require that the guest resemble her/his host in any way. For the host must allow the guest to take place without any prior knowledge of her/him, without any demand for commonality and without imposing one language and culture. To meet the extraordinary ethical imperative of absolute hospitality, one may not even consider the guest as a foreigner in the usual sense of the word, since that term designates merely a negation of all that is familiar, comfortable and homely. In other words, the absolute alterity of the guest is dissipated by considering her/him foreign.

If such an infinite form of hospitality seems absurd or impossible at the very least, it is, nevertheless, for Derrida, an ethical imperative. For hospitality is a deeply conventional practice (hence, a gesture of hospitality in one culture can be seen as rude or meaningless in another). Such conventionality always assumes prior knowledge of the guest. We are inclined to welcome in those we know, or think we know, at any rate. Such hospitality is also premised on fixed notions of private property and on ideas of safety and security. As such, conditional, conventional hospitality bespeaks a desire to maintain power over one's home and one's sense of self. It is, in the most literal sense of the word, conservative.

Despite appearances to the contrary, the principal work of limited hospitality is to preserve the world of the host; it is not *for the guest* and, as such, it is not properly hospitable as it is premised on exclusion (here Derrida and Forster are in perfect agreement). The many forms of conditional hospitality thus designate a kind of violence because they all work by prescribing, determining and knowing the guest only in terms of the host. What is established in the process is a diminished form of the guest, a limiting of the other, which allows for disregard, abuse and harm.

Accordingly, Derrida insists on the necessity of unconditional hospitality, which he contends is the only one worthy of the name, because its radical lack of convention or limit means that it is utterly inclusive and hence it meets the criteria that surely haunt the very concept of a welcome. It does so precisely by demanding the impossible, which is that we respect the infinite unknowability of the other, at the cost of any sense of our home as comfortable, safe or inviolable.

Furthermore, according to Derrida, there is for this reason a 'pervertibility' that mediates these two forms of hospitality. On the one hand, unconditional hospitality is impossible – any form it might take in the world would have to be finite, limited and conditional. On the other hand, those finite forms are not ever enough and therefore they are premised on the unlimited form, which is their condition of possibility. Any act or gesture of hospitality that does not attempt to be absolutely, infinitely respectful of the otherness of the other, fails to be hospitable. But, by the same token, that failure is inevitable and is written into the nature of hospitality as a law.

Rhodes University and its challenges

Universities struggle with this irreconcilable tension in all their interactions, both internally and with the world beyond. It is worth mentioning that Derrida has himself considered the difficulties of establishing, once and for all, the borders of what is called the university. According to Derrida, it is 'not certain that the university itself, from within, from its idea, is equal to this task [of university responsibility] or this debt: and this is the problem, that of the breach in the university's system, in the internal coherence of its concept' (2004: 92). Indeed, my interest in Derrida's work lies precisely in considering whether higher learning is capable of responsible or ethical action when its very conception might be problematic, when, in other words, its limits are always in danger of a breach from that which, historically and theoretically, has always been envisioned as 'outside' of the parameters of the university. Paradoxically, what I would like to suggest is that such a 'breach' might be a condition of possibility for ethical and responsible conduct; that, in fact, the 'outside' (which has come 'inside') is precisely where the university is obliged to orientate its ethics.

In order to elucidate these ideas of responsibility, I would like to consider some of the more obvious limits that plague the South African university and Rhodes in particular. As the demand for higher learning grows ever larger in this country, each institution must establish physical, intellectual and administrative limits on its student numbers and the make-up of its student body. Rhodes, for instance, has always prided itself on being a small university in comparison with, say, the University of Johannesburg or the University of the Witwatersrand, with slightly more than 7 000 students currently enrolled. Furthermore, it is the determined hope of those who conceive of the shape and size of this particular institution that the percentage of the student body studying at postgraduate level should increase. The reasons for positioning the university in this way are numerous and in some cases very persuasive. They take into account the physical location of Grahamstown, the size of the town, its capacity, as well as the state of higher education in this country. In other words, the reasoning is both pragmatic and, in a sense, guided by what Rhodes believes to be its moral duty in providing a particular kind of learning space in South Africa. Yet this logic is always susceptible to criticism. When one takes into account the geographical isolation, the small student numbers, the relatively high fees and so on, collectively these factors bespeak a desire for a certain kind of student and a particular kind of tertiary education that should be provided. In other words, by its very nature, and despite the reasoned, often moral logic the institution uses to justify its size, shape and nature, it will always run the risk of being seen as elitist, marginal and unwelcoming of others.

Even the difficulties that have, on occasion, arisen between the university and members of the town point to the complexities of monitoring the borders that define this academic space. I do not wish to simplify or misrepresent the divergent interests of the town or the university and I am also wary of implying that the relationship between the two is only hostile, for it is far more complex than that. So I will point out one recent example, a small but telling matter of a disagreement between some Grahamstown residents and Rhodes University. On 14 August 2013, Dr Saleem Badat, the vice chancellor, wrote an open letter to the Makana municipality, describing his, the university's and the town's distress at the water crisis, which had arisen yet again. At the time of the letter going to press, parts of the town had been without water for nine days, though it would be six more before water services were properly restored. To his great credit, Dr Badat begins this letter, which he also sent to government, with the following words: 'Rhodes University views itself as an integral part of the Makana region and the Eastern Cape. We are willing to shoulder responsibility in the search for collective solutions to problems that confront our community' (Badat 2013). He describes the dire situation at some residences on campus and admits the possibility of closing the university. In the letter, he asks if the municipality is fully aware of the damage such an extreme decision would cause. He writes: 'Can you at all imagine the chaos that will occur if the university has to close its doors? Or the economic impact that this will have on the town, which is highly reliant for its economic well-being on the university operating?' Again, one can see that there is a concerted effort on the part of the vice chancellor to position the institution as a part of Grahamstown, in effect, as a member of a larger community. That said, we should perhaps pause here to consider the importance that Dr Badat assigns to Rhodes within this community. While this is simply a reality, the tone (which is in danger of being patronising) and nature of such remarks might account for the anger felt by some townspeople in the wake of this letter. The letter ends with the following plea:

> Rhodes University also calls for intervention at the highest level of government. We request an urgent investigation at the provincial and national government levels into water supply and water quality in Makana. We call upon the ministers of

Higher Education and Training, Public Works, Water Affairs and Provincial and Local Government and the Eastern Cape MEC for Local Government to ensure that water security in Makana is secured for current and future generations (Badat 2013).

It seems that this call has been heard and heeded. After an investigation by government, the *Sunday Times* reported: 'Cacadu district municipality has pledged R3-million of the R6-million needed to refurbish pumps at the Grahamstown reservoirs' (Skiti 2013). So, it could be said that Rhodes stood by its community; that its interests and those of the town were totally convergent and its intervention led to a positive outcome. Yet some residents of the town were not at all happy about the situation. The *Sunday Times* article notes, for example, the outrage of Thandeka Ndlovu, who lives in the Ethembeni informal settlement: 'We've been here since 1993 and our taps were installed in 2003, but there is hardly any water in them. Is it because they are better than us that Rhodes gets listened to?' she asks the reporter. I think that it would be very dangerous indeed to ignore the complaints of those such as Thandeka Ndlovu who think that the university gets preferential treatment. Also, implied by her statement is a critique of the money and privilege that benefits Rhodes, though it does not necessarily lead to the socio-economic advancement of the poor of Grahamstown.

The university does have a community engagement programme. In fact, Rhodes identifies three main areas of activity for academic staff: teaching and research, quite obviously, while community engagement is the third. In the English Department, for instance, two projects are currently underway. The first is the Cycle of Knowledge poetry group, which includes local poets, students from the institution and academic staff. The second involves Ntsika Secondary School students in a reading group. In both cases, the hope is that the particular expertise of the department might be of benefit to the broader community and that the community should also enrich the institution in turn. It is undoubtedly difficult to quantify the good that such projects have done for Rhodes and for Grahamstown, but what should be clear is that the university is not unaware of its responsibility for engendering social justice beyond its borders.

The question then arises: realistically, honestly, what more can we do? How much more can Rhodes give? At what point is it simply unfeasible to intervene any more or in any other way? These are valid questions, which I can only imagine have caused many sleepless nights for Dr Badat (the previous vice chancellor), Dr Mabizela (the newly appointed vice chancellor) and the administrators of this tertiary centre. They gesture at the interminable, relentless, overwhelming responsibility that universities have for their own and for others. Incidents such as the one I have just described remind us of the never-ending obligation we have to push beyond borders that we are, nevertheless, always, out of necessity, creating and maintaining. Derrida would call this the ethical imperative of infinite hospitality.

The open-ended pursuit of knowledge

It is in the very nature of the word 'university' to orientate itself in accordance with such an ethical ideal. To be, in the most profound sense, universal, universities must open their borders in the most radical manner. That this is simply not possible does not negate the necessity of the ethical imperative. What this points to, again, is the aporia of conditional and unconditional hospitality. It may be that it is impossible to be infinitely hospitable, and welcome everything in, but it is equally impossible to be hospitable if one imposes limits to others' access to one's home. The imposition of limits is not welcoming, ethical or generous. It is self-centred, wilfully disrespectful of alterity – in a sense, violent.

Similarly, I would argue that by virtue of what a university is and what it is for, it is also obliged to strive for unconditional hospitality. In order to set out this argument, I turn to Stefan Collini's excellent book, *What Are Universities For?* Collini is a long-time advocate of universities and he writes extremely persuasively in reaction to those he feels are placing them under unfair scrutiny, outright attack or who simply misunderstand their true value and purpose. In particular, he argues cogently that the debate over the 'usefulness' or 'utility' of university study and academic work more generally is misplaced.

The difference between a vocational college or company think tank, for example, and a university is, at the core, the kind of questions and research that can be carried out in universities. According to the critics, vocational colleges train people to work in the so-called real world and make changes there, while a university engages in irrelevant, unnecessary, insular work.[3] This criticism, contends Collini, is premised on a false understanding of what it is that universities actually do. His point is that academic work is simply open-ended, that it places no a priori restrictions on what aspect of given subject matter might be studied or in what forms such study might be conducted. For this reason, the nature of university research is that it is 'undertaken under the sign of limitlessness – that is to say, not just, as with the development of all knowledge, subject to the testing of hypotheses or the revision of errors, but where the open-ended quest for understanding has primacy over any application or intermediate outcome' (2012: 55). Instead of endlessly asking about the utility of such study, Collini alerts us to the fact that its very reason for being is to question knowledge and reveal the contingency of current understanding. As such, he observes that 'there is no way to prescribe in advance what will and will not be fruitful ways to do that' (56). What we think of as 'useful' belongs to a here and now that academic study is obliged to consider contingent. Its work is endlessly to subject this contingent knowledge to critique, speculation and evaluation. Therefore, the call for utility is futile precisely because it tethers the academy to a limited understanding of things, which is its duty and nature to problematise.

Clearly then, open-endedness and limitlessness are innate to the academic project. It is our work, we who call ourselves academics, to go beyond the knowledge that has thus far been passed on to us. It is demanded of us that we extend the boundaries of enquiry, that we shift the horizons of knowledge. And that we never think of any body of ideas as finite, complete or absolute. Accordingly, we are called on to open ourselves to that which we do not yet know, that which we do not anticipate, that which is radically, infinitely other to all we know or have thus far experienced. This is perhaps not the primary message of Collini's book, but it is an unavoidable corollary of it.

Collini's reasoning seems to me the most meaningful and thoughtful response I have yet read to the scourge of utilitarianism that seeks to turn universities into companies and students into clients (a move Dr Badat, for instance, has often rejected publically; he did so at the new staff orientation programme I mentioned previously). Most academics would agree with Collini: research that gears itself toward relevancy curtails in advance the nature of the work it will produce. The open-ended pursuit of knowledge is therefore important if the academy is to produce new forms of thought, which may, ultimately, change the world in ways that can, perhaps, be measured and quantified. Nonetheless, such utility or relevancy must be a by-product, not an exhaustive goal of the work.

Yet, in practice, universities are inclined to produce certain kinds of research. The reasons for this can, I think, be linked to issues of hospitality. For instance, all institutions tend to hire staff who meet certain criteria. Any academic who has been involved in drawing up a 'list of requirements' for an advertisement of a new post knows this all too well. My concern is that, in prescribing the kind of staff member required, the institution also prescribes the type of thinking that this new appointee will almost certainly produce. Those who claim to love the limitless scope for research offered by universities might find that their practices do not match their ideals; that, in practice, they welcome in only certain kinds of people and, by association, certain kinds of knowledge-production. I have tried to show that not only is this type of practice perfectly reasonable, but also that it is, in many instances, so implicit and invisible as to appear natural. Nonetheless, open-ended research requires open borders. To the extent that any institution establishes borders, it must be aware that these boundaries might well defeat the noblest aims of higher learning. The more forcefully it polices these limits and refuses some access, the more determinedly it might create knowledge that is utilitarian, that is, knowledge that serves at the behest of an already established authority – which almost certainly has as its major purpose its own conservation.

None of this is to say that higher learning is or will become an inhospitable intellectual terrain. I would argue that everything will depend on how we as a community (for that is surely what we are) respond to the ethical demand for unconditional hospitality. Not to impose one's culture, language or ways of knowing on the other is to allow for the unexpected. It is only on the condition that we respect the other's alterity that we might actually experience something we could not predict in advance, something outside our frame of reference and, thus, revolutionary. If unlimited hospitality burdens us beyond measure, it also holds out the promise of a future that need not be defined in terms of the violent, destructive realities that have come to define the present moment. In other words, in the impossible task of overcoming our own limitations and boundaries, lie possibilities we cannot yet fathom.

To return to the personal, slightly silly example with which I began this discussion, I do not think it was wrong or mistaken of the English Department to ask that I assimilate myself into its culture. The institutional, departmental, academic and pragmatic reasons for its doing so are easily understood. Yet, to what extent did the department attempt to exceed these limitations, which were necessary in the sense that they helped to establish the borders that defined the world I was entering? Was there an effort made to do the impossible, by which I mean, not to do what was necessary, in order that I might have the space to do something unexpected? And, equally, did I do enough to avoid prescribing, delimiting and assuming knowledge of the academic space that I had entered? Did my misconceptions and prejudices not also limit the possibility of an unforeseen encounter?

The answers to these questions are undoubtedly complex. For one thing, the department is not a monolithic entity and my interactions in it reflect a varied, multifaceted reality. As for my own limitations, there are those I am able to identify and those I am not. I have certainly failed at times to be within the department on its own terms, rather than on mine. Similarly, my feeling is that, on occasion, the department did not respect what I might offer beyond simply acquiescing to its needs and cultural constraints.

My personal example matters little in the grand scheme of things. Any member of any community struggles in her/his relations with that of which s/he is nevertheless a part. What does matter though is what will happen tomorrow. It is within our power to turn every tomorrow into a rehashing of today. Our reasoning for doing so will appear faultless. There were conditions we had to place on the future in order to survive today. That is surely what we will say. And we will acknowledge that something has been lost in the process, but, we will argue, at the least we have preserved ourselves. We will be what we have always been. The irony, of course, is that what we have always been are universities. And thus, as Collini has suggested, we have always been, by definition, limitless, open-ended, orientated towards the unknown, unknowable other. If there is a conservatism that I would ascribe to, it is not the one I have too often encountered from some academics; the one that says, let us not change things and let us not question prevailing wisdom because then we will be forced to produce a certain kind of knowledge, which would be utlitiarian in nature. I would counter by saying that a better, more ethical conservatism would conserve our right and our need always to question, critique and change. This is the core value that needs preserving, protection and ever-vigilant attention. If tomorrow there is no teatime, or the syllabus is altered to reflect a changing student body, well, let us not cry havoc and let slip those petulant, ruinous dogs of war.

We cannot, in my estimation, afford to walk that dead road to a dead world. We must orientate ourselves towards that which we do not know and are unable to anticipate in advance. Only then will we create hospitable universities worthy of the name.

Notes
1. For those who might be unfamiliar with such concepts, as I was, allow me to provide a brief explanation. DP stands for 'Duly Performed' and indicates that a student has met the set of predetermined requirements to continue in any given course. In the English Department, for example, a learner may lose her/his DP if s/he does not attend a certain number of lectures and/or tutorials, or if s/he does not hand in assignments. DP also stands for the Democratic Party, of which Tony Leon was, at the time, the leader. Shredding meetings are held to read through proposed exam questions. Staff then debate the merits of the questions, any wording issues and the general nature of the papers. The name is derived from the fact that once the exams are finalised, the draft papers are shredded for security reasons. I would also add that in my case, I was lucky enough to be appointed an excellent mentor by the department. She explained several foreign concepts to me when I first arrived. That said, in some cases, and

shredding meetings are a good example, one really has to see it and participate in it to understand it fully.
2. In fact, I think that it makes a great deal of sense that Rhodes (or any tertiary institution) should expect new staff members to fall in line with its pedagogical practices. It is for this reason that I have chosen not to focus on pedagogy, but rather on the more invisible effects of culture. My sense is that the either overt or covert demand that others adopt and adapt to the culture of the institution is a dangerous one, which no institution has the right to make of those who enter its space, while the need for new staff to understand and repeat the technical procedures and teaching ethos is far more reasonable and is surely to be expected. That notwithstanding, in asking a new staff member to accept the pedagogical practices germane to the institution, I suspect that what might be lost in the process is the possibility of teaching strategies or ideas that are new and perhaps excellent. This naturally goes against the very spirit of taking on staff who have been trained or who have studied elsewhere. For surely the hope is precisely that they will bring something new to the party? Ideally, of course, a staff member would adapt to the culture of a new institution, while also being allowed to suggest new practices. That said, it is a distinct possibility that the power associated with the institution's culture might make speaking up quite difficult for the new appointee. There is, no doubt, a privilege that the university's culture enjoys, which can, though it need not, be somewhat debilitating to new staff. In a different context, Amanda Hlengwa discusses a similar concern in Chapter 7 of this collection. Her insightful analysis of the accelerated development programme at Rhodes and the appointment of what she calls 'safe bets' relates to the inherent limitations of 'safe' forms of transformation, which may, at the end of the day, allow little that is new to enter.
3. Collini is speaking specifically of British universities and is quite willing to admit that in other countries the situation is probably quite different. I am therefore aware that his argument is not entirely relevant to South Africa where many colleges have been shut down. Nevertheless, his core critique of the useful versus useless debate is certainly applicable here and wherever else there are universities.

References
Badat, S. 2013. 'An Open Letter to Makana from Rhodes University'. http://activateonline.co.za/an-open-letter-to-the-mayor-the-municipal-manager-and-the-makana-municipality-councillors-from-rhodes-university/.
Collini, S. 2012. *What Are Universities For?* London: Penguin Books.
Derrida, J. 2000. *Of Hospitality: Anne Dufourmantelle Invites Jacques Derrida to Respond.* Translated by Rachel Bowlby. Stanford: Stanford University Press.

———. 2004. 'Mochlos, Or the Conflict of the Faculties'. In *The Eyes of the University: Right to Philosophy 2*, translated by Jan Plug et al., 83–112. Stanford: Stanford University Press.

Forster, E.M. [1924] 1979. *A Passage to India*. London: Penguin Books.

Skiti, S. 2013. 'Town up in Arms over Water Crisis'. http://www.timeslive.co.za/sundaytimes/2013/08/25/town-up-in-arms-over-water-crisis.

5

The Violence beneath the Veil of Politeness
Reflections on Race and Power in the Academy

THANDO NJOVANE

> Soon we will be strangers. No, we can never be that. Hurting someone is an act of reluctant intimacy. We will be dangerous acquaintances with a history (Kureishi 2013: 2).

Deliberations on institutional culture in the South African higher education system are necessarily always connected to the country's legacy of dual systems of oppression, namely, colonialism and apartheid. Where higher education institutions in this country are concerned, issues of race and power, both inherited from this horrific history, significantly influence pedagogical practices and social relations in the learning and teaching environment. Mamphela Ramphele, for example, observes:

> It is to be expected that institutions founded by white males for white males would have very strong male cultures. Academic institutions world-wide reflect an ethos flowing from the dominant roles that men have played as students, teachers and researchers. In South Africa's case, our socio-political history has left a deep imprint on the higher-education landscape. Racism, sexism and authoritarianism are deeply embedded in the cultures of many institutions (2008: 210).

Similarly, in her article on the limitations of the 'inter-racial contact' in South Africa, Louise Vincent argues that while people of different races have experienced more exposure and contact with each other since the demise of apartheid, 'this increased "contact" does not amount to greater racial integration' (2008: 1426). She goes on to claim that in this setting, 'contact occurs within a context of unequal power relations in which "whiteness" continues to be privileged over "blackness"'. The issues Vincent raises here, and elsewhere in her work, gesture towards the difficulties encountered by teachers and students of various races within this socio-political space. These difficulties, I aim to show, may also be traced back to the fact of entanglement and the pathology of politeness prevalent in post-apartheid South Africa. According to Sarah Nuttall, entanglement is 'a condition of being twisted together or intertwined, involved with; [a condition which] speaks of an intimacy gained, even if it was resisted, or ignored or uninvited' (2009: 1). In addition to the remnants of South Africa's violent past, as well as the socio-economic and educational disadvantage from which most black students at Rhodes University emerge, teachers are bound by an unwritten contractual obligation that teaching in this environment carries, an obligation that requires not only scholarly rigour, but also an ethical engagement with students.

Using Ramphele and Nuttall as points of departure, I examine the dynamics of interpersonal relations in light of the race, power, entanglement and violence at Rhodes, focusing specifically on experiences of black females. I do so by providing a series of interrelated narratives based on both my experiences of being a student at this institution, as well as those of other black females, in order to reveal how policy does not necessarily translate into ethical action. As Vincent, citing Charlotte Linde (2009: 8), points out in Chapter 1 of this volume: 'Laws, policies and institutional frameworks may change, but "social and cultural structures, practices, habits of mind and heart, remain stable over time"'. The narratives that follow are discomforting precisely because they gesture towards that which remains concealed in this context. They represent a reality that has been concealed behind screens of silence and extreme politeness. Vincent also notes:

At any given moment in any given social milieu, there will be discourses that are dominant, hegemonic, powerful and influential and there will be those that are marginalised, subordinated and suppressed. One way of understanding institutional culture at this discursive level is to understand the culture of an institution through the stories we tell about it and ourselves and ourselves in relation to it – and indeed the stories that the institution itself, *qua* institution, tells, authorises, negates, suppresses, circulates and propagates. Institutional culture, in short, can be understood as something that is 'narrated'.

Official narratives and acceptable ways of viewing the world thus play a crucial role in determining who gets to speak, when and how, and who is simply not allowed to have an opinion. A black person writing and/or talking about race in a context that purports to be not only liberal, but also socially responsible, causes a certain hesitation because this writing or speech act is, more often than not, perceived as either 'pulling the race card' or being accusatory, which is to say, what is said or written is mostly received defensively. This defensiveness results in the black person feeling that s/he is not so much raising a concern as being a 'problem'. In short, one grows increasingly weary of relentlessly engaging in 'verbal toyi-toying', so most people just learn to cope in silence. Coping under such conditions, however, involves having to perform a role, rather than simply being one's honest self in order to function. This speaks to the role that tolerance – in the form of a performance of politeness – plays in perpetuating injustice. At the same time, 'black South Africans experience the absence of a willingness to engage passionately and sincerely with questions of prejudice, stereotypes and racism as deeply disrespectful and a mark of continuing white arrogance' (Vincent 2008: 1448). As such, as Vincent argues in Chapter 1 of this volume: 'To say, for instance, that one "never thinks of race", as many white people do, is not an indicator of enlightened thinking; it is rather an indicator of a profound and hurtful blindness to one of the most important privileges of whiteness – the privilege of "race" "not mattering" '. The unwillingness to engage with the issue of race is often disguised as 'colour-blindness', which constitutes a form of denialism rendered pathological by the very fact that it dismisses critical analysis of the lived experiences of black people. Therefore, genuine politeness, in the sense of being mindful, thoughtful and considerate of others, is appropriated in order to legitimise unethical interactions between subjects. In this regard, Slavoj Žižek's (2008: 41) reflections on the function of tolerance in liberalism are relevant: 'Today's liberal tolerance towards others, the respect of otherness and openness towards it, is counterpointed by an obsessive fear of harassment. In short, the Other is just fine, but only insofar as his presence is not intrusive, insofar as this other is not really other.'

Tolerance is intimately related to denialism because it maintains hegemony by evading the question of difference. I am reminded of Amanda Hlengwa's Chapter 7 in this volume, where she discusses the notion of the 'safe bet', which implies that sameness is more desirable than difference. Likewise, in Chapter 4, Minesh Dass maintains that 'in spite of the many ways in which a group may attempt to open its borders and invite others in, it cannot do so indefinitely. Always, and precisely so as to be a community in the first place, it must deny someone the right of access.' In light of this, tolerance or the performance of politeness reveals itself to be volatile, since it already assumes that there is a hegemonic and epistemological structure that needs to be safeguarded.

I first arrived at Rhodes in 2005 with stars in my eyes and filled to the brim with notions of equality and non-racialism, primarily because I had never seen myself as a victim of racism before. I was astonished when, upon arriving at my residence, I discovered that the two double rooms were occupied by two black girls and two white girls respectively because one of the parents had complained that she did not want her daughter to share with a black girl. As an isolated incident, this did little to decrease my reverence for the rhetoric of the 'rainbow nation' I had grown up espousing. However, since then, the accumulation of seven years of hateful and hurtful violence has changed me in irrevocable ways. For example, while I continue to have good friends and mentors of all races, I tend to be somewhat suspicious of most white people until I have known them long enough to realise that they are not racist, or are at least struggling to break out of the racist order that formed their minds. Similarly, while naturally a cheerful person, I feel myself rotting on the inside as a result of racially motivated injustices against others. Above all, I am disillusioned. The world of my childlike vulnerability, trust and love for other human beings, irrespective of race, has been contaminated.

Given South Africa's traumatic history, the notion of colour-blindness is synonymous with the erasure or muting of black people's experiences. In essence, then, it is a call for a convenient amnesia to the benefit of those who stand to profit from it. Žižek (2008: 41) point outs: 'My duty to be tolerant towards the other effectively means that I should not get too close to him, intrude on his space. In other words, I should respect his intolerance of my over-proximity.'

The irony inherent in Žižek's claim here is that, in practice, tolerance perpetuates and even exacerbates intolerance and insidious violence. In other words, intolerance *feeds off* tolerance. The issue of tolerance is thus intimately bound up with issues of what voices and experiences are validated or excluded in discourses on institutional culture. For a happy black person, this issue is irrelevant. For an unhappy, weary one, however, the message is clear: find ways of coping or get out.

In light of this, success in the academic enterprise is premised on whether or not those who are entangled with each other in this context nurture or abuse those under their power. Clause 3.1.1.4 of the 'Rhodes University Equity Policy', for example, stipulates that the institution is 'committed to ensuring that all members of the university are treated with respect and courtesy' (Rhodes University 2004: 5) – where courtesy implies genuine politeness. Upon reflection, however, I cannot really say that I have ever felt that to be the case until I worked with someone who embodied such values when I was a Master's student. Because of this person's care and respectfulness, I was able to remain at Rhodes in spite of many occasions that made me ready to throw in the towel and go elsewhere, simply because I could no longer endure the pain of existing in this context. Prior to this, I was always acutely aware that I was at the fringes, that I could never relax or be comfortable because I did not belong and I was reminded of this at every turn.

Like Ramphele, Vincent (2008: 1447) notes the existence of 'powerful institutions whose history and residual character is colonial and "white" in deeply embedded ways', which black students tend to experience as 'deeply painful, dislocating, disruptive, unsettlement, angering, confusing and difficult'. During a seminar with several peers and a lecturer in my fourth year, for instance, there was discussion of the concept of the 'noble savage'. One of the students turned to me, the only black person in the class, and declared, 'Oh, Thando, you can be our noble savage!' This was followed by much laughter. I suppose this incident may be regarded merely as a joke that I took too seriously. I suppose one could, in one way or another, explain the fact that the lecturer in charge of the seminar did not intervene on my behalf by pointing out the impropriety of the situation. However, for me, this incident highlighted a fact I was already aware of: I did not belong and my educational endeavour was not something that was seen to come as naturally to me as it did to those who looked the part.

Furthermore, this incident reveals a prevalent view of black people who do not conform to racial essentialist stereotypes as 'exceptional'. These 'exceptional' black people have to contend with people saying profoundly offensive things, such as: 'You speak *so* well! Where did you learn to speak like that?' or making repulsive comments, such as: 'I fucking *hate* black people, but you're cool.' Frustration and anger arise because there is no decisive way of dealing with such verbal violence. It is insidious precisely because the people who say such things do not necessarily intend to be offensive; in fact, they assume that they are admitting me into an exclusive club and that their words should be read as compliments.

In that same year, I received an essay back from a senior staff member. This essay had no mark and no comments, apart from a capitalised 'B.S.' on the cover page and intermittently throughout. The staff member then told me he would not give me a mark and that he wanted me to rewrite the paper. I was stunned. My astonishment saw me looking for possible explanations for this unfathomable interchange. I did not want to believe that the B.S. did not stand for 'bad sentence' or 'bad structure'; after consulting some of my peers, it emerged that B.S. could only stand for one thing: bullshit. Yet, I still could not believe it. It couldn't. Regardless of whether or not this comment was racially motivated, no teacher would ever write that on a student's paper and, besides, he was *so* nice. Always so nice.

Of course, this incident might be written off by some as simply being an example of poor pedagogical practice, rather than an incident that relates in any way to race or to institutional culture. However, it is relevant that my reaction to the incident was a result of my subjective position as a black female in a predominantly white department in which my race was overemphasised. Consequently, poor pedagogical practice as a symptom of exclusion is of crucial importance.

A few years later, I would come to the realisation that niceness or politeness is learned and does not necessarily reflect the character of a man. The more I thought about it, the more I came to understand that this was the very man who would make offensive black jokes in my presence and when I questioned it, he defended himself by telling me it was okay because his 'black friend' told it to him. While I cannot be sure to what extent this incident had to do with race, my interactions with this staff member have left a bitter taste in my mouth. As a result, I have attempted to explain these incidents to myself to lessen the impact, to recover some of the dignity I lost in the interchange. I doubt he even remembers or considers the impact his words and deeds have had on me. T.S. Eliot (1974: 111) aptly describes my feelings:

> Half the harm that is done in this world is due to people who want to feel important. They don't mean to do harm; but the harm does not interest them. Or they do not see it, or they justify it because they are absorbed in the endless struggle to think well of themselves.

This professor's inability to acknowledge, let alone measure, the damage inflicted was reflected when, after I had graduated with my Master's degree, we crossed paths at a coffee shop and he introduced me to someone by referring me as 'one of ours'. Needless to say, I was enraged by this description, primarily because it suggested that I was suddenly being accepted into the fold I no longer wished to be a part of. I am thus entangled with him and the type of teacher he represents through violence, through bullshit. Our intimacy is premised on his power over me and by a humiliation, the residual effects of which, despite my achievements since then, I have yet to overcome. Ramphele (2008: 73) notes how the assumption of black inferiority is 'not simply something one shrugs off like a bad cold. It is branded deeply into one's psyche by doors that have been shut in one's face, resulting in repeated humiliation.' Likewise, the professor is unwittingly entangled with me, through his blindness or denial of the impropriety of his brutal engagement with his student.

The dynamic of entanglement, humiliation and denial further illustrates the relationship between power and authority in the academy. For academic staff, authority and power are unquestionable characteristics of their jobs. In the context of post-transitional South Africa, however, the unquestioned attribution of these powers proves somewhat problematic. Within the student-teacher relationship, to apply a rubric set up by Ramphele, power manifests itself in two ways: it can either constitute the capacity to act in order to influence or it can mean the limitless capacity to do as one wishes. On the one hand, while I cannot be sure if the senior staff member's actions were racially motivated, I can confidently infer that they reflect a displaced and inappropriate display of unrestricted power. On the other hand, it is almost impossible for me to dismiss the fact that his authority over me is the result of a colonial attitude, which despite his liberal pretensions and his one black friend who tells him racist jokes, means that he still regards black people as essentially inferior, even if he does not realise it. I say this because the bullshit comment is not only pedagogically out of place because it is a personal attack, it also negates my attempt to gain an education by *not* focusing on what is wrong with the essay and how this can be rectified and improved.

Instead, the comment implies that there is something fundamentally amiss with the person producing the work.

At a recent conference hosted by Rhodes University, three relevant issues came up. Firstly, the keynote speaker, Robert Young, spoke about the ambiguity inherent in writing about and speaking about subalterns by pointing out that the intelligentsia has always spoken on behalf of the subaltern, thereby unwittingly performing the role of the oppressor. Second, a senior staff member from Rhodes, in responding to a suggestion that certain curricula be revised so that the establishment is less colonial, claimed that some departments find it difficult to retain black students because the black students apparently think of certain subjects as 'white'. Third, a black female friend and peer jokingly proposed that she feels discomforted by the fact that her department has no black people and, despite the existence of numerous black academics in the field, all the invited speakers whose pictures are plastered all over said department are white. She then pleaded that those in power at least put up a picture of a black person, without having to go so far as to invite them to come and speak. No, that would be asking too much. A mere picture would do. All of this was, of course, seemingly said in jest and yet very serious issues were being raised.

In postcolonial theory, the subaltern can be loosely defined as a social category of person who is socially, politically and geographically outside the hegemonic power structure of the colony and of the colonial homeland. Grahamstown's local history and the colonial values, still prevalent in the segregation of people by class and race in the geographical make-up of the town, favour whiteness. Black female postgraduate students typically perceive Rhodes as 'incredibly white with a performative upper-middle-class attitude'. In other words, they perceive the space as privileging middle-class and elitist values. They also note that almost all the black people at the institution have 'white accents' and that those who do not are an anomaly and are marginalised. Coexistent with this attitude is the perceived pressure to be a 'good black', who has the right accent, is interested in things white people want to talk about, works hard to impress white people and who, above all, fits in. In other words, the acceptable kind of black person is one who does not disturb the status quo. Notably, the maintenance of the status quo in this context directly correlates to the extent to which the other does not disturb the comfort of the dominant structure into which one arrives as a 'guest'. In Chapter 4 of this volume, Dass, using Jacques Derrida as a point of departure, notes that this phenomenon amounts to 'limited hospitality': 'The principal work of limited hospitality is to preserve the world of the host; it is not *for the guest* and, as such, it is not properly hospitable as it is premised on exclusion.'

The incidents referred to above further conform to Žižek's conception of how objective violence operates: there are two interrelated forms of violence, subjective and objective. While subjective violence is the most visible since it is 'performed by a clearly identifiable agent' (2008: 1), objective violence manifests itself in two forms: systemic and symbolic. The latter, which is relevant to my discussion here, is primarily embodied in language. Postcolonial theorists have historically regarded language as the 'medium through which a hierarchical structure of power is perpetuated, and the medium through which conceptions of "truth", "order" and "reality" become established' (Ashcroft, Griffiths and Tiffin 1989: 7). The unspoken mandate to adhere to the status quo mentioned earlier may be read as an instantiation of symbolic violence precisely because it relies on the language used both to victimise and to exclude black students and staff. For instance, throughout my seven-odd years at Rhodes University, the first time I was taught by someone who was not white was for a month during my fourth year. This lecturer lasted only a year and, after a public and racially charged altercation with one of his colleagues, left the institution. More recently, a black female academic gave a presentation as part of her interview process in a predominantly white department. A white Master's student commented that she had thought the lecture was good, but that she had found the presenter's accent 'distracting'. Another renowned black researcher and teacher was reported to his department by white students who complained that they could not understand what he was saying, also because of his accent. Black students complain of having their pronunciation corrected by white peers, who tell them, 'that's not how you pronounce' this or that word.

These incidents serve to highlight the unfathomable link between accent and competence made in the minds of these people – and others like them. As Žižek (2008: 72) observes: 'White racist ideology exerts a performative efficiency. It is not merely an interpretation of what blacks are, but an interpretation that determines the very being and social existence of the interpreted subjects.' This prejudice is by no means new, nor does it point to anything other than racism. It speaks to an inherited colonial culture, which privileges whiteness while reinforcing black oppression, thereby delimiting the kinds of spaces that black people can comfortably inhabit. This is particularly alienating for black students who, as a result of being deprived of mentors and teachers who, for lack of a better phrase, 'look like them', come to regard academic pursuits as something reserved for white people. This sense of being an intruder in a space reserved for white people is echoed by my peer in her plea for a photograph of a black person. Upon my asking why only a photograph and not a person, she responded, 'They're not ready for that, for the body of a black person.' The senior staff member's seeming confusion about the high turnover of black students is thus misplaced, since it reflects the invisibility of black experience in this context, an experience that fails to conform to accepted and acceptable forms of being. His reasoning that the only thing preventing these students from pursuing higher degrees in 'white subjects' is their resistance to the label is flawed in so far as it dismisses the inhospitable social conditions within the departments in which these subjects are housed. In Chapter 1 Vincent notes that '. . . transformation is not only or even perhaps most importantly about getting different types of bodies (black, female, etc.) into the institution and into its structures of power, but it is about unsettling what counts as normal and by implication what is privileged and what is rendered illicit, strange, abnormal'. Read with reference to Dass's claim regarding the notion of limited hospitality, Vincent's contention suggests that the very use of the term 'white subjects' already assumes that anyone who is not white is an intruder.

In addition to the colonial attitude and repression of blackness in this space, some black students have to contend with the expectation that they are likely not to succeed in their studies. Although predominantly not articulated as clearly and explicitly as the bullshit comments mentioned earlier, this is nevertheless a feature of black experience at Rhodes University and, it is likely, at many other formerly white higher education institutions in South Africa. During my years at Rhodes, I have, for example, come across fellow teachers and tutors who constantly express their concern for the 'second-language speakers' – a polite code for black students – who seem to make it in spite of their apparent disability. Although this term can be used to describe individuals whose mother tongue is Afrikaans, in this case, it is always with reference to black students. The truth of the matter is that the majority of black students speak at least two or three languages. Studying in English is thus usually an exercise in translation. The intended polite tone of this phrase is undermined by the fact that it already designates non-first-language speakers of English as falling outside the category of the normal or natural. Concomitant with this rhetoric is the humiliation of having a lecturer literally pat me on the head while congratulating me for winning an award. His congratulations were also undercut by the qualifying statement, 'for a second-language speaker'. As such, because language is 'the first and greatest divider ... we and our neighbours (can) "live in different worlds" even when we live in the same street' (Žižek 2008: 66). The patronising treatment of those who, against all expectation, succeed in their studies extends to certain teachers treating their students as 'projects' – as the pat on the head illustrates.

In some classroom situations, black students are subjected to alienating and racist rhetoric. When they are not being called 'noble savages', white students and teachers often nonchalantly use offensive terms. For instance, a student related to me an incident in which she was in a tutorial session and the other students were 'throwing around words like "barbaric" to describe Xhosa initiation practices'. She admits to holding back her knee-jerk reaction in an attempt to respond 'academically', while also feeling that the criticisms were directed at her personally. Her unsettlement, she reports, not only stemmed from the fact that her family practises traditional Xhosa rituals, but also from the feeling that, because she did not hold the same views as her peers, she was somehow inferior. The interaction made her feel like an unrefined person who needed to be moulded into something else: 'I know I have my own voice, but it feels like they are trying to forge and then force another voice out of me.' This sense of alienation and of being appropriated is reminiscent of Jean-Paul Sartre's preface to Frantz Fanon's *The Wretched of the Earth* in which he describes the colonisation of the black mind: 'They picked out promising adolescents; they branded them, as with red-hot iron, with the principles of western culture; they stuffed their mouths full of high-sounding phrases, grand glutinous words that stuck to their teeth' (2004: l).

It is self-evident that the language used during tutorials privileges whiteness, which is equated with progress and civilisation, while blackness is associated with the obverse. The effect of this incident on the psyche of the student in question is noteworthy. Read alongside the quoted passage, it suggests that in order to get the 'right' kind of education, the student has to deconstruct her very identity. In other words, the success of her academic endeavour depends on whether or not she is willing to part with who she is in order to pander to what she is expected to be. Ironically, clause 3.1.3.3. of the 'Rhodes University Equity Policy' (Rhodes University 2004: 8) states: 'In its teaching and learning policies, including curriculum development, assessment and evaluation, the University recognises the need to accommodate learner diversity, in particular linguistic and cultural diversity.'

A glaring disparity exists between the formal commitments of the university and the reality of what occurs in teaching situations here. The fact that the university does not explicitly support the ethos demonstrated in the above anecdotes does not translate into perceptible action. The crucial question then becomes: how does covert racism thrive, despite national and institutional policies that forbid it? It may be argued that the gap between policy and practice is enabled both by power structures, which unwittingly suppress the voices/narratives of those in positions of dependence, and by the fact that this particular institution forms only a microcosm of a much bigger social reality. As recent media coverage of racist incidents at the University of Stellenbosch and the University of the Free State – to name but a few – reveal, Rhodes University is not exceptional in its struggles with issues on race, sex and gender, etc. The role of narrative then becomes all the more crucial in addressing such concerns at both an institutional and a national level.

My conclusion is no conclusion at all. Upon being requested to write this chapter, I was initially thrilled to transcribe my hurt and anger. At the same time, I felt it was my responsibility to speak for all those who have endured similar treatment, in the hope that those who come after us will have avenues for correcting injustices meted out against them. Moreover, it occurs to me that I have also interacted with some wonderful human beings who have never reduced me to a student number or a race. These people, such as my Master's supervisor, Sue Marais, continue to be very dear to me. Consequently, I have hope that someday transformation will not only be a policy on paper, but rather a way of being that reshapes minds deeply distorted by colonialism, apartheid and its living legacy.

References

Ashcroft, B., G. Griffiths and H. Tiffin. 1989. *The Empire Writes Back: Theory and Practice in Post-Colonial Literature*. New York: Routledge.
Eliot, T.S. 1974. *The Cocktail Party*. London: Faber and Faber.
Kureishi, H. 2013. *Intimacy*. London: Faber and Faber.
Linde, C. 2009. *Working the Past: Narrative and Institutional Memory*. New York: Oxford University Press.
Nuttall, S. 2009. *Entanglement: Literary and Cultural Reflections on Post-Apartheid South Africa*. Johannesburg: Wits University Press.
Ramphele, M. 2008. *Laying Ghosts to Rest: Dilemmas of the Transformation in South Africa*. Cape Town: Tafelberg.
Rhodes University. 2004. 'Rhodes University Equity Policy'. http://www.ru.ac.za/media/rhodesuniversity/content/documents/humanresources/Equity%20Policy.pdf.
Sartre, J. 2004. 'Preface'. In *The Wretched of the Earth* by Frantz Fanon, xliii–lxii. New York: Grove Press.
Vincent, L. 2008. 'The Limitations of "Inter-Racial Contact": Stories from Young South Africa'. *Ethnic and Racial Studies* 31 (8): 1426–51.
Žižek, S. 2008. *Violence: Six Sideways Reflections*. New York: Picador.

6

What about the Queers?
The Institutional Culture of Heteronormativity and Its Implications for Queer Staff and Students

NATALIE DONALDSON

Debates on transformation and equity in higher education, in South Africa and globally, have focused primarily on achieving equality in terms of race and, to some extent, gender. Very little attention has been paid to the issue of sexualities and how the culture of higher education institutions directly and indirectly promotes and performs heteronormativity. This chapter looks specifically at Rhodes University in order to exemplify the problem of heteronormativity, which is not unique to Rhodes University, but is rather a defining mark of institutional cultures both locally and internationally. Using examples of personal experiences as well as university policies, I show how Rhodes University promotes and performs a culture of heteronormativity. Since heteronormativity results in exclusionary practices for 'non-normative' genders and/or sexualities, I outline the implications of this for staff and students at Rhodes University.

Gender, sexuality and higher education
Writing about transformation in higher education with a specific focus on sexualities is difficult. With much of the focus on equity being about race and – to some extent – gender, South African universities have neglected to acknowledge that sexual diversity is a significant and necessary aspect of transformation. What we seem to have forgotten is that the end of apartheid and the implementation of the 1996 South African Constitution signalled the beginning of the end for not only racial inequality, but also inequalities based on

gender and sexuality. Like race, the gendered and sexual practices of South African citizens were policed and repressed through apartheid legislation, such as the Immorality Act of 1957 and the Sexual Offences Act of 1969 (Gevisser 1994). What most South Africans remember about these two acts is that they prohibited sexual practices between white and black citizens. However, a significant part of these two laws also placed strict regulations and limitations on sexual practices between same-sex South Africans (Posel 2005). The Constitution of 1996 was drawn up within a discourse of human rights and transformation, with a specific focus on addressing the social inequalities of apartheid. While social and cultural beliefs about same-sex sexualities remain embedded in prejudice, 'sexual orientation' was included in the new Constitution, making South Africa the first country in the world to offer same-sex sexualities constitutional protection against prejudice and discrimination (Francis and Msibi 2011).

There is an intimate link between the 1996 Constitution and higher education institutions, which were and still are regarded as having the potential to shape knowledge and identities and, as such, have become specific targets for implementing state transformation initiatives to achieve social change (Hames 2007). The 1997 'Education White Paper 3: A Programme for the Transformation of Higher Education' makes this connection quite clearly:

> All institutions of higher education should develop mechanisms which will: Create a safe and secure campus environment that discourages harassment or any other hostile behaviour directed towards persons or groups on any grounds whatsoever, but particularly on grounds of age, colour, creed, disability, gender, marital status, national origin, race, language, or sexual orientation (cited in Hames 2007: 57).

Rhodes University has implemented strategies and policies – mostly focused on recruitment and selection – in an attempt to achieve racial transformation. In the same way, gender transformation strategies and policies have focused on employing more female academics, as well as implementing policies to deal with issues of sexual harassment. Furthermore, relevant policies such as the 'Unfair Discrimination and Harassment' policy explicitly include 'sexual orientation', as do the university's various communiqués about prejudice and discrimination. The university also tends to use politically correct terms such as 'partner' and 'Ms'. However, because higher education institutions do not actively and regularly challenge normative conceptions of gender and sexuality, in South Africa (and globally) they remain largely patriarchal and heteronormative (Bennett and Reddy 2009; Francis and Msibi 2011; Hames 2007, 2012).

The use of the term 'heteronormativity' should not be confused with the term 'homophobia'. While homophobia refers to a fear of and/or prejudice against same-sex sexualities, heteronormativity refers to the ways in which gender ideologies are constructed to position heterosexuality as 'natural' and 'normal', while same-sex sexualities are rendered 'other' and therefore abnormal (Fox 2007; Francis and Msibi 2011; Macintosh 2007; Shlasko 2005). Heteronormativity is not always as overt and blatant as homophobia, sexism and racism, but the implication of heteronormativity is that all 'other' identities are measured against heteronormative standards and those that do not conform are deemed deviant and amoral; at worst, abnormal and in need of correction (Ferfolja 2007). Higher education institutions are not necessarily homophobic, but the institutional cultures of higher education in South Africa tend to promote and reproduce heteronormativity in terms of the discourses employed, rather than making a concerted effort to transform how we understand gender and sexuality. The ways in which we talk continue to reproduce heterosexist notions of gender and sexuality through discursive constructions of heterosexuality as unchallenged, assumed and normal (Francis and Msibi 2011; Hames 2007). In addition, conversations about sexuality have been limited to lesbian, gay, bisexual, transgendered, intersex, asexual and queer (LGBTIAQ) campus organisations and/or queer academics, which serves to reinforce the perception that sexuality is not a genuine concern for higher education institutions.[1] Very little is done by those who have actual decision-making power in higher education institutions to improve the social and academic lives of queer staff and students on campus and in the classroom (Hames 2012). Rhodes University is not unique in its reproduction of heteronormativity and it must be acknowledged that it is possibly one of the safer universities in South Africa for queer genders and sexualities. We have a visible LGBTIAQ organisation (OutRhodes) that aids in creating awareness and attempting to ensure that a safe space exists for queer students and, to some extent, staff. As in other chapters in this book, Rhodes University is simply being used as a case study to explore how the institutional cultures of higher education institutions do very little in terms of transforming our understanding of gender and sexuality.

According to the Rhodes University vision and mission statement, the university aims 'to develop shared values that embrace basic human and civil rights' and 'to acknowledge and be sensitive to the problems created by the legacy of apartheid, to reject all forms of unfair discrimination and to ensure that appropriate corrective measures are employed to redress past imbalances'.[2] While Rhodes University has made *some* strides in addressing the gendered (employing more women) and racial inequalities (employing more black staff and accepting more black students for study) of apartheid, it has done little to address and challenge heteronormativity and its implications for staff and students. The culture of Rhodes University (as in many universities in South Africa) is one where 'the unspoken ways, symbols, the various spoken, written and electronic evidence that makes up the prevailing culture ... the day-to-day experiences, social interactions and communication' (Hames 2012: 72) promote and reproduce a culture of heteronormativity, creating an exclusionary environment for staff and students who transgress conservative understandings of gender and sexuality.

Inclusion is not transformation

Rhodes University tends to promote discourses of inclusion and anti-homophobia when addressing issues related to queer genders and sexualities. The focus is on attempting to ensure that queer individuals feel comfortable, accepted and included or, at the very least, tolerated. However, there are a number of problems with these strategies of inclusivity. While inclusion strategies may be promoted with good intentions, they assume that the problem is one of ignorance and, as such, the solution becomes simply to help heterosexual individuals understand that it is acceptable for others to be queer (Fox 2007; Hames 2007; Macintosh 2007; Shlasko 2005). Homophobia, as a result, becomes personalised and prejudice against queer genders and sexualities is seen as a fear of the unknown, while 'pervasive systemic heterosexism and heteronormativity' is left unchallenged (Fox 2007: 501). Inclusion strategies also focus on incorporating queer genders and sexualities within existing normative frameworks. What is ignored is that these systems were and still are socially constructed to exclude queer genders and sexualities and, by merely focusing on assimilation and incorporation, these systems continue to privilege 'white, middle-class, male heterosexual values and desires' (502).

Looking at policy is a useful starting point for looking at the kinds of values enshrined in institutions since it gives staff and students an idea of what kind of culture the university is striving towards. University policies argue that the institution affords benefits and privileges to all staff and students. However, on closer inspection, the discourses used in policy work to construct certain kinds of benefits for certain kinds of people, thereby creating inclusionary and exclusionary criteria for who actually receives these benefits and privileges. The first policy I want to look at is the 'Parental Leave and Benefits' policy of Rhodes University.[3] I focus on this policy not because it is particularly reprehensible, but because it is a clear example of how heteronormativity functions and how it is embedded in institutional culture. I use my discussion of this policy as a means of demonstrating how inclusion strategies are not enough if we want to see real transformation.

Policies that implicate family planning and, by extension, gender and sexuality, are useful to analyse since parenting and 'the family' are institutions constructed within heteronormativity, where essentialist and biological discourses position the ideal family structure as one where one parent is the female mother and the other is the male father. These essentialist and biological discourses argue that women and men are biologically different, but 'naturally' fit together for reproductive purposes and, as such, heterosexual relationships must be the most 'normal' way of being. Even though there are many families in South Africa (perhaps most) that do not actually conform to a traditional nuclear family structure, Jackie Sunde and Vivienne Bozalek (1995) argue that a 'familist ideology' exists, which positions the traditional nuclear family (married mother and father with two children) as the most desirable family structure for ensuring psychologically and emotionally healthy individuals. This familist ideology extends from patriarchal and heteronormative assumptions about gender and sexuality where 'natural' and 'normal' is determined by biological and reproductive processes (Donaldson and Wilbraham 2013; Lubbe 2007). The 'Parental Leave and Benefits' policy of Rhodes University, whether meaning to or not, implicates a heteronormative understanding of 'the family' and this has implications not only for families headed by queer individuals or couples, but also for heterosexual individuals or couples who do not want to fulfil their roles as parents according to normative gendered notions.

The policy states that Rhodes University acknowledges that there exist 'different family patterns of our society' and that 'as an employer [they seek] to respect such differences through the provision of suitable parental benefits'. This acknowledgement is a positive step forward since, within the South African context, social factors, such as the death of biological parents due to HIV/AIDS and legislation allowing same-sex couples to adopt and parent children, have meant that traditional views and caretaking practices of 'the family' are being displaced as more 'non-traditional' families are formed (Lubbe 2007, 2008). As Sunde and Bozalek (1995: 63) argue: 'People's experiences of families in South Africa differ greatly according to their respective gender, race, class, cultural and age positions' and, as a result, 'one cannot speak about "the family" in South Africa as there are many family forms and hence the notion of "families" is more appropriate'. However, policies are never value-neutral, so while the policy claims to be inclusive of the needs of diverse family forms and sensitive to the needs of queer staff and students, the discussion that follows makes it clear that heteronormativity is not being deconstructed or challenged in the policy, but rather being reinforced and reproduced.

The policy goes on to say that it recognises 'the need to move away from an exclusive emphasis on the mother's role in child-rearing as this enforces gender stereotypes of women as primary caregivers and negates the potential role that fathers can play'. This statement implies that the policy aims to provide the opportunity for more egalitarian parenting structures, since heteronormativity promotes the notion of the mother (woman) as the primary caregiver taking on the majority of the responsibility for childcare, with the father playing a minimal role. While the policy offers the option of the father sharing the mother's leave in a clause later on, the initial benefit offered to the father is a mere two weeks, implying that Rhodes is doing very little to 'move away from an exclusive emphasis on the mother's role in child-rearing' and has rather reinforced heteronormative parenting structures, leaving little space for fathers to become more involved in the parenting of their children. Furthermore, the definition of partner is stated as being 'any person associated with the primary caregiver who has confirmed accepting shared responsibility for financial support of mother/child'. The primary caregiver is automatically assumed to be the 'mother' and the role of the partner is simply to provide 'financial support', reinforcing the heteronormative notion that a father's role is as the breadwinner, whose primary responsibility is to provide financial support, rather than emotional support, to the child.

The way in which the policy is structured further shows that 'partners' and alternative family forms are not the norm and this works to reinforce the othering of queer genders and sexualities. The terms used focus on 'mother' and 'women' first and 'father or partner', with 'partner' being placed second, reiterating that 'partners' are included, but the 'normal' structure of relationships or families are ones where there is a (female) mother and a (male) father. The clause stating that 'where both partners are employed at Rhodes

University for at least one year, they may make a choice as to who utilises maternity and paternity benefits' can be assumed to apply to same-sex couples. The way in which this is written implies that a same-sex couple must decide who is going to take on the role of 'mother' and who will take on the role of 'father'. The policy is literally asking same-sex couples to decide who the woman (mother) is and who the man (father) is, thereby expecting same-sex couples to structure their relationships in ways that conform to heteronormative understandings of gender. Perhaps this is not the intention of those who drafted the policy, but this is how it reads. If this is what the policy means in practice, it is extremely problematic and comes very close to reinforcing and reproducing anti-gay sentiments and stereotypes.

As mentioned earlier, a clause in the policy, which has received much praise from gender committees on campus, allows the primary caregiver/mother to give some of her leave to her partner. This is indisputably positive, as few other institutions in South Africa offer this benefit, so it is a step forward in addressing heteronormativity and acknowledging diverse family and parenting forms. However, it still reinforces heteronormativity as it others parenting and family structures that do not conform to mother and father, where the mother takes on the primary role of child-rearing. In other words, the nuclear family, where the woman takes the role of the primary caregiver, is still being promoted as the norm, the most 'normal' and desirable structure of parenting and families. However, in order to appear inclusive, clauses are included for those 'others' who do not quite fit into this norm. That the primary caregiver/mother has to 'give up' some of her leave is problematic, especially if there were birth complications and the woman needs time for recovery. Additionally, this benefit would only apply if both partners were employees at Rhodes University. In other words, a male partner employed by Rhodes University would only receive two weeks leave and not benefit from this clause if his female partner (or even male partner) was not employed at Rhodes University.

In order to challenge heteronormativity in this policy, the solution is to move away from merely attempting to include queer genders and sexualities into existing policies and structures and to radically transform how we understand gender. Rethinking gender and how policies promote and reproduce heteronormative gendered practices is essential because, by focusing simply on including and acknowledging sexual and gender diversity, we risk further inequality and unfair practices. For example, giving a lesbian couple benefits as two mothers (each being a woman and, therefore, receiving six months of maternity leave) may be seen as unfair when compared, for example, to the leave benefits afforded to a heterosexual couple where the man and woman receive vastly different benefits due to their sex. In other words, in order to ensure fairness, Rhodes University needs to ensure equality in terms of benefits afforded to women and men, regardless of the types of relationships they are in. It needs to start seeing 'the family' and parenting responsibilities as gender neutral and policies need to reflect this.

It is important to recognise that Rhodes University's 'Parental Leave Benefits' policy meets the minimum legal requirements, as set out in the 1995 Labour Relations Act and the 2002 Basic Conditions of Employment Act, with a few added benefits (for example, an extra two months of leave for mothers at the university's own expense). Attempting to restructure the policy to take into consideration the diversity of family and parental structures in South Africa is a complex and costly process. Thinking about the costs and practical implications associated with drastically transforming all policies where gender (and sexuality) is implicated is a legitimate concern and, as such, changing policy is not easy or by any means simple. However, it needs to be remembered that we inhabit an extremely heteronormative space and universities have the power to choose to replicate and reproduce heteronormativity or to transform, shape and influence thoughts and opinions about gender and sexuality. Jane Bennett and Vasu Reddy (2009: 240) agree, arguing that South African higher education institutions are 'key forces in the production of "professional" citizenship', but still 'construct gendered norms of sexuality (heterosexuality) which embed such citizenship into conservative notions of reproduction, sexual moralities, and respectability'.

If Rhodes University wants to claim that it is not heteronormative, it is not implausible to expect it to implement policies that aim to transform our understanding of gender and sexuality, rather than merely expecting queer individuals to conform to heteronormative values and morals in order to receive benefits and privileges (Bernstein 2001). How we understand equality in relation to queer genders and sexualities needs to move beyond simply assimilating queer individuals and couples into a system that was and still is designed to exclude them. We need to move away from viewing same-sex couples as *just like* heterosexual couples, as if heterosexuality is the norm. If Rhodes University does not want to undertake a commitment to changing heteronormative values and policies because expense and practicality takes priority over transformation and equity, the institution cannot feel insulted when it is accused of being heteronormative and not quite a 'home for all'.

Unfair discrimination: Who decides what is unfair?

The above critique of the current 'Parental Leave and Benefits' policy will not result in quick and effective change, not only because of the costs involved, but also because changing policy is never a quick process. If the institution is to rework the policy to be less heteronormative, this is going to require negotiation and numerous discussions on how best to proceed. At the recent *Imbizo* on gender held in October 2013, it was decided that the university would reconsider its current parental leave policy, acknowledging its heteronormative biases. Changing policy will be a significant step towards gender and sexual transformation and the recent decision to build gender-neutral/mixed-gender bathrooms is a further recognition that the gender binary that keeps heteronormativity alive needs to be deconstructed and challenged. However, changing policy is not enough. Despite South Africa's widely praised Constitution, which explicitly protects queer individuals, violence and discrimination is still rampant and increasing. We therefore need to acknowledge that changing policy cannot be seen as the only way to achieve transformation since social and cultural practices do not always mirror the values enshrined in official documents. We need to look at how Rhodes University deals with 'on-the-ground' heterosexism and prejudice against its staff and students.

The university has an excellent policy on 'Eradicating Unfair Discrimination and Harassment', which states: 'Behaviour stemming from racism, sexism, homophobia and harassment and vilification will be dealt with harshly' and the policy attempts to outline the 'institution's commitment to eradicating discrimination, harassment and prejudicial behaviour in order to provide an environment in which staff and students are able to work effectively and fully participate in University life'.[4] In my four years of working at Rhodes University in an academic position, I have witnessed a number of incidents where queer individuals have been affected by prejudiced attitudes and/or behaviour. In all of these incidents, the ways in which the university reacted worked to placate queer staff and students, but failed in actively challenging the attitudes and/or behaviour, which stem from heteronormativity. I want to present some of these situations to demonstrate the lack of engagement with issues affecting queer staff and students and also to provide recommendations for future incidents.

In 2009 I presented a paper on lesbian representations in the media at the annual postgraduate conference at Rhodes University. After I presented my paper, one of the audience members – a doctoral student – asked me who was going to protect the children, because children needed to be protected from gay and lesbian people. Days after the conference, this same individual confronted a friend of mine and asked how she could be friends with 'someone like' me and, a few weeks after this, my partner and friend were stopped in their car and this individual shouted another derogatory comment in relation to me. It was after this that I decided to lay a complaint and go through the official disciplinary channels of Rhodes University. In relation to the comments made at the conference, I was informed by a number of senior academics that charges could not be laid for this since it falls under the scope of 'academic freedom'. The second incident could not be prosecuted because it is based on mere 'hearsay'. Without the inclusion of these two incidents in the disciplinary process, however, the last incident made little sense and the student was found not guilty. This was upsetting and disappointing, but I understood the verdict until I received the report from the proctor. The proctor's report included a number of inaccuracies, such as mistaking the witness for the complainant, as well as statements that highlighted the biased and prejudiced attitude of the proctor himself. I contacted numerous senior academics and management and carefully stated all the issues in the report and requested that the situation be taken seriously and treated with urgency. Two senior managers met with my partner and I and stated that they understood my position and admitted that the report from the proctor was problematic. However, they also stated that there was little they could do because they did not want to interfere with the independence of the legal processes at Rhodes University. I was assured, however, that a similar situation would not happen again.

In 2011, a gay male student of mine was physically assaulted outside a popular nightclub in town and called derogatory names such as 'fag' and 'fairy' by a group of male students. He came to me for help and I suggested he pursue the disciplinary procedure route, which he did. During the process, he was met with narrow-minded comments by the lawyers in charge of his case. The students implicated were found guilty of the physical assault, but the derogatory comments were ignored. In the same year, a number of queer students were physically assaulted in a shopping complex and there were a number of incidents reported of 'gay bashing' in and/or outside of popular nightclubs in town. Two senior management staff met with a group of queer students and assured us that they cared and would find solutions to ensure our safety. These solutions included sending out an email stating the university's intolerance of this kind of behaviour and a meeting with the nightclub owners to get their input on ensuring that queer students and staff are welcome and protected in their venues. This latter solution included 'gay friendly flag' stickers stating: 'Rhodes University united against homophobia', which were to be placed on nightclub windows, as well as around campus.

Furthermore, a number of incidents have occurred during Pride Week over the past number of years, including the destruction of a wardrobe placed in the library quad for students to write comments in support of gay rights as well as, more recently, religious quotes from the Bible being placed over Pride Week posters judging queer students and stating that we need to ask God to save us. In both incidents, the dean of the Students' Division sent emails to the entire student body condemning this kind of behaviour. However, this year at almost the same time as the email was sent out, the Pride Week banner on the StudentZone website was replaced by an Israeli Apartheid Week banner. This may seem like a seemingly unintentional and harmless incident, but it does say something about how little importance is placed on queer issues at Rhodes University and on the experiences of our queer staff and students. Also, this was noticed by queer students and was the topic of discussion on various social media networks.

Rhodes University needs to take action and to deal seriously with the prejudice and discrimination faced by queer students and staff on campus and in Grahamstown. Hate speech needs to be dealt with harshly and should, under no circumstances, fall under the guise of academic freedom or freedom of speech. Hate speech is psychologically and emotionally harmful and its goal is to degrade and humiliate those believed to be inferior. Furthermore, hate speech goes against the very foundation of our Constitution, where the protection of human dignity and equality is placed over and above the freedom of expression and academic freedom (Van Wyk 2002). Tolerating hate speech in favour of academic freedom essentially constitutes prioritising the right to freedom of expression over one's constitutionally guaranteed right to protection against discrimination and prejudice and the right to human dignity and fair treatment. Furthermore, if hate speech is tolerated in any setting, Rhodes University is allowing and constructing spaces where prejudiced and harmful statements are allowed, tolerated and accepted with no repercussions. If a student is physically assaulted and anti-gay slurs are made, Rhodes University must ensure that those slurs are punished to the same extent as the physical beating. When our students are being attacked in bars and clubs in Grahamstown, our solution cannot simply be to placate the queer students and ask bar or club owners to place 'gay friendly' stickers in their establishment. While the intentions here may have been honourable, once again the strategy is of inclusion, rather than challenging the very ideology that allows these kinds of attacks to occur. Furthermore, as Catherine Fox (2007) argues, these 'safe space sticker' strategies imply that safe spaces can be constructed by putting a sticker on a window or a door and, as if by magic, queer individuals are suddenly safe from harm.

When incidents such as these are not treated with the seriousness they deserve, it has implications for whether students will report further incidents. As Andrew Walters and David Hayes (1998: 3) argue, 'threats and violence toward (perceived) homosexuals may not be reported by individuals on campus (students, staff, or faculty) because many persons suspect that administrations will be unsympathetic and unhelpful'. The way in which Rhodes University has dealt with the abovementioned incidents has meant that many staff and students do not feel they will be taken seriously. I, for one, will not report any further incidents and will not encourage students to do so either. Rhodes University needs to demonstrate an active engagement with prejudice and discrimination and implement proactive strategies to create awareness, while also promoting a culture that does not tolerate prejudiced behaviour or attitudes of any kind. The university must prove that those who do not abide by its vision and mission will not be tolerated, by ensuring that there are consequences for such behaviours and attitudes. In addition, this engagement and awareness-raising cannot be left to the queer staff and students or societies. The university must take responsibility for challenging and disrupting any form of violence, harassment or victimisation (Walters and Hayes 1998). Management and those with the authority and power to create change must be seen to visibly reject any form of oppression and this rejection needs to take the form of more than a few simple words uttered during orientation week or at graduation ceremonies.

Moving beyond inclusion and reaction

Instead of focusing on making queer staff and students feel included and comfortable at Rhodes University, we need to implement strategies and interventions that actively challenge heteronormativity (Francis and Msibi 2011). Challenging heteronormativity and its intimate connection to prejudice and discrimination will demonstrate that Rhodes University views *all* forms of oppression as intolerable and unacceptable (DePalma and Jennett 2010; Francis and Msibi 2011). If we want to do this and do it properly, however, it is going to require visible action that goes beyond simply trying to make everyone feel safe and comfortable. Furthermore, as others also argue in this book, perhaps we need to be making some people uncomfortable in order to achieve transformation and to challenge existing prejudices and ideologies. This, however, will require a constant engagement with 'questioning and redefining the language we use to talk about sexuality' (Shlasko 2005: 124) and gender in our policies and our curricula and how we deal with prejudice on campus. If our goal is transformation and we have the power to mould attitudes and change deeply entrenched beliefs, we have an obligation to disrupt heteronormative ways of thinking with which our students enter university. As educators with the ability to influence and transform ideas and beliefs in our classrooms, we need to find ways of addressing the 'silent and invisible underpinnings of normalcy' (Macintosh 2007: 35) that reinforce heteronormative ways of being as it is these unintentional and unreflective ways of speaking, reacting and teaching that serve to exclude and erase the experiences of our queer staff and students.

As a past student, an academic staff member, a researcher and a teacher, Rhodes University's heteronormative institutional culture influences my teaching practices, my curriculum development and my participation in staff and committee meetings. This influence is sometimes positive but, for the most part, its influence has implications for how safe I feel at Rhodes University as a black queer woman. This being said, I am still optimistic about the role I can play here at Rhodes University in creating a transformed institution that actively demonstrates its appreciation of diversity and is a 'home for all'. However, the role I can play means nothing if those in leadership positions cannot even acknowledge that there is a problem. We need proactive, reflexive and critical engagement with issues related to gender and sexuality in higher education and universities need to shift their focus from seeing transformation in terms of statistics and getting the numbers looking right (more black and/or women academic staff) to focusing on how a culture of heteronormativity is institutionalised in our policies, practices and discourses and how this culture affects the lived experiences of black and/or women and/or queer individuals. We have an obligation and a responsibility to transform the minds of our students and staff in order to develop future leaders who are able to promote a society that regards diversity in terms of race, gender *and* sexuality as essential for progress and transformation. This cannot be achieved if we ignore the ways in which heteronormativity entrenches and perpetuates itself.

Notes
1. The use of 'queer' in this chapter is used to refer to all sexualities, sexual practices and/or gender performances that do not fall under the description of normative.
2. The vision and mission statement can be found at http://www.ru.ac.za/rhodes/introducingrhodes/visionandmission/.
3. This policy and accompanying documents can be found at http://www.ru.ac.za/jobs/chooserhodes/lifestyle/parentalbenefits/.
4. This policy and accompanying documents can be found at http://www.ru.ac.za/studentzone/harassment/name,46762,en.html.

References
Bennett, J. and V. Reddy. 2009. 'Researching the Pedagogies of Sexualities in South African Higher Education'. *International Journal of Sexual Health* 21 (4): 239–52.
Bernstein, B. 2001. 'Symbolic Control: Issues of Empirical Description of Agencies and Agents'. *International Journal of Social Research Methodology* 4 (1): 21–33.
DePalma, R. and M. Jennett. 2010. 'Homophobia, Transphobia and Culture: Deconstructing Heteronormativity in English Primary Schools'. *Intercultural Education* 21 (1): 15–26.

Donaldson, N. and L. Wilbraham. 2013. '"Two Women Can't Make a Baby": South African Lesbians' Negotiation with Heteronormativity around Issues of Reproduction'. In *Home Affairs: Rethinking Lesbian, Gay, Bisexual and Transgender Families in Contemporary South Africa*, ed. C. Lubbe-De Beer and J. Marnell, 135–58. Johannesburg: Jacana Media.

Ferfolja, T. 2007. 'Schooling Cultures: Institutionalizing Heteronormativity and Heterosexism'. *International Journal of Inclusive Education* 11 (2): 147–62.

Fox, C. 2007. 'From Transaction to Transformation: (En)countering White Heteronormativity in "Safe Spaces"'. *College English* 69 (5): 496–511.

Francis, D. and T. Msibi. 2011. 'Teaching about Heterosexism: Challenging Homophobia in South Africa'. *Journal of LGBT Youth* 8 (2): 157–73.

Gevisser, M. 1994. 'A Different Fight for Freedom: A History of South African Lesbian and Gay Organisations from the 1950's to 1990's'. In *Defiant Desire: Gay and Lesbian Lives in South Africa*, ed. M. Gevisser and E. Cameron, 14–86. Johannesburg: Ravan Press.

Hames, M. 2007. 'Sexual Identity and Transformation at a South African University'. *Social Dynamics* 33 (1): 52–77.

———. 2012. 'Embodying the Learning Space: Is It Okay If I Bring My Sexuality to Class?' *Feminist Africa* 17: 62–81.

Lubbe, C. 2007. 'Mothers, Fathers or Parents: Same-Gendered Families in South Africa'. *South African Journal of Psychology* 37 (2): 260–83.

———. 2008. 'The Experiences of Children Growing up in Lesbian-Headed Families in South Africa'. *Journal of GLBT Family Studies* 4 (3): 325–59.

Macintosh, L. 2007. 'Does Anyone Have a Band-Aid? Anti-Homophobia Discourses and Pedagogical Impossibilities'. *Educational Studies* 41 (1): 33–43.

Posel, D. 2005. 'Sex, Death and the Fate of the Nation: Reflections on the Politicization of Sexuality in Post-Apartheid South Africa'. *Africa: Journal of the International African Institute* 75 (2): 125–53.

Shlasko, G.D. 2005. 'Queer (v.) Pedagogy'. *Equity & Excellence in Education* 38 (2): 123–34.

Sunde, J. and V. Bozalek. 1995. '(Re)presenting "the family": Familist Discourses, Welfare and the State'. *Transformation* 26: 63–77.

Van Wyk, Christa. 2002. 'The Constitutional Treatment of Hate Speech in South Africa'. Paper presented at the sixteenth congress of the International Academy of Comparative Law, Brisbane, 14–20 July. http://www.stopracism.ca/content/hate-speech-south-africa.

Walters, A.S. and D.M. Hayes. 1998. 'Homophobia within Schools'. *Journal of Homosexuality* 35 (2): 1–23.

7

Employing Safe Bets

Reflections on Attracting, Developing and Retaining the Next Generation of Academics

AMANDA HLENGWA

The imperative to transform South Africa's higher education system features strongly in policy briefs, informed by the principles of redress and social equity inscribed in the Constitution. South African universities are confronted with multiple challenges and, while each institution has the right to prioritise when deliberating how best to respond to certain imperatives given the institutional context, it is clear that the under-representation of women and black academic staff is of urgent significance across the system. This under-representation is largely a product of the colonial and apartheid regimes.

Higher Education Management System (HEMIS) statistics provided by the South African Department of Higher Education and Training are particularly distressing: black South Africans (including those formerly classified African, coloured and Indian) comprise around 90 per cent of the population and yet make up less than half of those employed as academics in South African universities (DHET 2012). While women academics are better represented than black academics, they comprise only 31 per cent of professors working in South African universities. If urgent attention is not paid to addressing the factors contributing to these figures, the achievement of meaningful social equity is unlikely.

This chapter explores what has emerged from a programme at Rhodes University aimed at producing and retaining academics expected to contribute to the agenda of transforming the South African academy (Badat 2009). Rhodes University is among a number of universities in the country that have, over a number of years, secured international funding designed to attract graduates from under-represented groups into the academy. The prevailing practice is that individual universities submit funding proposals to institutions such as the Andrew W. Mellon Foundation and the Kresge Foundation to support programmes aimed at strengthening the academy, with a focus on producing the next generation of academics. However, these programmes are drawn up by individual universities, whereas it could be argued that the challenge of identifying, encouraging and adequately supporting graduates into an academic career is systemic, requiring attention at a national level.

These programmes have been running for several years at Rhodes University as well as a few other universities and there are now plans to roll out such programmes to other South African public universities. In 2009 Higher Education South Africa (HESA) commissioned a national working group to, as the foreword puts it, 'examine the current literature and institutional case studies on building the next generation of academics' (HESA 2011), resulting in a proposal for a national programme. The proposal refers to the 'next' generation, as opposed to the 'new' generation, to indicate that the focus is on 'individuals who are currently not academics or on a trajectory towards a career in academia' (HESA 2011: 1).

This chapter focuses on Rhodes University's Programme for Accelerated Development (PAD), of which I am a product. Given that the proposed national intervention is modelled closely on the Rhodes University programme, there is a need for a careful interrogation of its shortcomings and successes. However, I should clarify that this is not a comprehensive evaluation of the PAD. It is also not aimed at providing a detailed discussion of the concept of institutional culture in general, something that Louise Vincent and Samantha Vice do in their contributions to this collection (see Chapters 1 and 2). Rather, it draws on my own personal reflections, as well as those of five other academics who have benefited from the programme in order to outline tentatively some of the strengths and weaknesses of the programme. In particular, I argue that many of those appointed as part of this programme are 'safe bets' in the sense that, while they are members of designated groups, they are culturally similar to the majority of those already at Rhodes University. It is hoped that the insights offered here could be useful considerations for institutions once the proposed national strategy is approved and ready for implementation.

Programme for Accelerated Development (PAD)

PAD positions are advertised nationally. Successful candidates are offered a three-year contract, with the understanding that there is a possibility of the post becoming permanent after the three-year period is completed. All PAD lecturers are assigned a mentor within their department and jointly the lecturer and mentor construct a developmental plan, framing the goals for the three-year period. This developmental plan takes into account what level of qualification the lecturer has achieved, from which an appropriate workload and support activities are determined. Development plans are tailored to suit the needs of each PAD lecturer. However, there are some generic features, such as a reduced teaching load, which is increased gradually each year. Support to enhance teaching and learning practice is offered through modules in the Postgraduate Diploma in Higher Education (PGDHE).[1] Lecturers in the PAD are required to complete a minimum of two modules of the PGDHE if they begin with a Master's degree and to complete the entire PGDHE if they have already obtained a doctoral degree. PAD lecturers still pursuing PhDs will already be registered for a qualification and therefore unable to concurrently register for another qualification.

Substantial research time is apportioned to PAD academics. The development plan also provides them with opportunities to become acquainted with institutional structures and practices in order to become active, participating members of departmental, faculty and university functions and committees.

Over the three-year period of the programme, mentors and mentees review the progress of the mentees against the goals set in the development plan and produce four reports, two in the first year and one annually thereafter. These reports are submitted to the institutional co-ordinators of the PAD, the dean of the relevant faculty and the vice chancellor, and constitute a formal review platform, encouraging commentary.[2] There are also quarterly lunches hosted by the institutional co-ordinators, which create an informal reporting platform where lecturers and their mentors are provided opportunities to share their experiences.

Reflections on the PAD programme

I now explore some of the multiple mechanisms at play that account for the experiences of some lecturers forming part of Rhodes University's PAD, from which tentative conclusions are offered that may be helpful for those implementing the proposed nationwide programme, as well as for others introducing similar programmes in South Africa and further afield.

As mentioned earlier, I am drawing here on my own experiences and on those of five other PAD academics. To avoid compromising participants, I omit their names. The six women academics whose experiences are discussed here are at various stages of their academic careers.[3] The interview questions focused on the aims of PAD, which generated a discussion with each colleague inviting reflections of their experiences of the PAD.

Drawing on our reflections, I explore the extent to which the employment of PAD academics has resulted in transformation of the institution. I am particularly interested in examining my assumption, based on my own experiences as a PAD academic, that PAD academics are 'safe bets'. For the purposes of the present discussion, a 'safe bet' is an individual from a designated group who helps the university to improve its equity statistics. However, in addition and perhaps more significantly, a 'safe bet' fits with relative ease into the prevailing institutional culture and hence is unlikely to challenge prevailing exclusionary cultures.

Being a 'safe bet'

It seems reasonable to assume that individuals working at established universities will wittingly or unwittingly tend to perpetuate established cultures. They would therefore presumably tend to prefer to employ those who do not challenge established cultures.

As I mentioned above, I am a 'safe bet'. I am a black woman, so my presence at Rhodes has helped to improve the equity profile of the university – the aim of the PAD – but I worry that, given my middle-class status and privileged educational background, my presence does not challenge the status quo. At Rhodes University, white, middle-class men are disproportionately represented.[4] Given my background, it could be expected that I would not fit in. It is therefore curious that colleagues at Rhodes University frequently and voluntarily comment on how well I 'fit in'. This bothers me, for I was presumably supported in order to challenge institutional inertia, but in actual fact I am, it seems, giving the status quo a veneer of acceptability. What is it that enables me to 'fit in' in an institutional culture dominated by white, middle-class values?

Drawing on Pierre Bourdieu's (1986) well-established ideas related to forms of capital, it could be said that I possess the kind of cultural capital that enables me to fit in. This can be attributed to my private and Model C schooling, my Master's degree from a prestigious Australian university, as well as the fact that, in many ways, I was brought up in a home dominated by white, middle-class ways of being. I embody the language, accent and mannerisms prevalent within the institution. The result is that I do not typically experience interactions with my colleagues and students as alienating or demeaning. And this is deeply discomforting to me in light of the bewildering realities faced by some of my black colleagues (see, for example, the contributions from Minesh Dass, Natalie Donaldson and Thando Njovane in Chapters 4, 5 and 6 of this volume).

Reflecting on my affirming experiences of the PAD, I was intrigued to investigate how many PAD lecturers had similar experiences to mine and if the evidence would confirm or challenge my growing suspicions that, despite the institution's espousing transformation goals, candidates selected into the programme are 'safe bets' and hence are, by and large, not actually making much of a contribution to the transformational imperatives allegedly guiding the PAD programme.

'Safe bets': What is at stake?

In order to ascertain whether the practice of employing 'safe bets' is widespread, five of my PAD colleagues were asked questions aimed at finding out whether they fitted the description of 'safe bets'. In my view, the five colleagues interviewed qualify as 'safe bets' because they have the necessary cultural capital aligned to the university's institutional culture. For example, one commented: 'In the interview they could hear that I sounded like them.'

A common factor is that all except one have undergraduate and/or postgraduate qualifications from Rhodes University. The one exception obtained her qualifications from a comparable institution. All five interviewed colleagues considered Rhodes University an institution that shared their understanding of the academic project, which is why they chose to pursue an academic career there. 'I worked at another institution,' one of the PAD candidates stated. 'I did not like it there and I resigned after eight months. I kept in touch with the [Rhodes University] head of department who knew I was interested in working in the department here at Rhodes.' Because most of the respondents had studied at Rhodes, they could anticipate what an academic career at Rhodes University would entail, having observed academics they wished to emulate in their respective department as well as having been exposed to teaching as tutors and guest lecturers prior to their appointments in the PAD. Thus when the opportunity of the PAD came along, they already had a strong sense they were pursuing an academic career of the sort offered at Rhodes University. One of the candidates stated: 'I knew I would come into academia. I was a student here, tutored students like me and the staff in the department knew me.'

The advantages to employing 'safe bets' are evident: there are benefits to both the institution as well as the candidates. However, there are also drawbacks. If we want to bring about genuine transformation, universities such as Rhodes University cannot limit themselves to employing only 'safe bets'. Arguably this practice has the effect of protecting the prevailing institutional culture with minimum disruption.

Once the proposed national programme to develop the next generation of academics for the South African higher education context is approved, it is expected that institutions put in place similar strategies where they do not already have them. However, institutions in a similar predicament to Rhodes University will need to rethink the level of mentoring and support that will need to be provided to those who are not 'safe bets', if they genuinely wish to attract and retain academic staff who do not possess the relevant status-quo-perpetuating cultural capital.

'Safe bets' and the element of surprise

I have sketched how employing 'safe bets' can be problematic. However, it would be a mistake to assume that 'safe bets' simply and only support institutional inertia. This was evident in the PAD candidates' responses to the direct question of whether they perceive themselves as 'safe bets'. One commented: 'No! I grew up having to work for everything, grew up in apartheid South Africa.' Another said: 'I do not see myself fitting into Rhodes University at heart, never into the whiteness of the culture.'

A revealing tension is expressed here, a tension that could potentially have a transformative effect. 'Safe bets' do not unproblematically inhabit the white world embodied in institutions such as Rhodes University. On the one hand, we do 'fit in' and we are, relatively speaking, comfortable working there. On the other hand, we are not comfortable with this comfort. We feel that it is somehow inadequate. This tension at the heart of 'safe bets' is potentially creative.

As one of the PAD lecturers makes clear: 'I can see that it is a struggle that I am so culturally radical, more than they imagined or picked up on in the interview.' The lecturers spoke of how they have taken opportunities in departmental, faculty and institutional forums to raise pertinent questions, challenging heteronormativity, social exclusion, patriarchy and other aspects of institutional culture. These 'safe bets' have thus played some role in transforming the institution and have not simply perpetuated the status quo.

Conclusion

This brief exploration of one programme aimed at increasing diversity at one South African university makes it clear that the ability of such programmes to transform our institutions can be undermined when those who are culturally assimilated are employed. The very point of such programmes is to help transform a given higher education institution, but such an aim is undermined when those selected for such programmes do not sufficiently challenge the status quo.

However, it also reveals that even those who are apparently culturally similar can play some role (although perhaps a fairly limited one) in shifting aspects of universities' institutional cultures. If the intent of initiatives such as the PAD is to 'transform the historical and social composition of the academic work force' (Badat 2009), these programmes need to strongly consider moving beyond only employing 'safe bets'. Continuing to focus on employing 'safe bets' places in jeopardy the goal of substantially transforming South African higher education institutions.

Notes

1. This qualification attracts lecturers across the university campus and is not aimed solely at lecturers in the PAD.
2. Institutional co-ordinators are based in the university's Centre for Higher Education Research, Teaching and Learning (CHERTL), where the expertise in academic development is located.
3. Male academics who were part of the PAD were approached, but were unavailable at the data collection stage.
4. According to the 2010 Rhodes University Digest of Statistics, out of 357 permanent academic staff on campus, 177 are white males. White female academics follow as the next represented group at 110. Collectively male and female African, coloured and Indian representation number only 70.

References

Badat, S. 2009. 'Producing, Transforming the Social Composition of, and Retaining a New Generation of Academics'. Keynote address at the Higher Education South Africa: Developing the Next Generation of Academics Workshop, Rhodes University, Grahamstown.

Bourdieu, P. 1986. 'The Forms of Capital'. In *Handbook of Theory and Research for the Sociology of Education*, ed. J. Richardson, 241–58. New York: Greenwood.

DHET (Department of Higher Education and Training). 2012. 'Staff Tables for All Institutions'. http://www.dhet.gov.za/Structure/Universities/ManagementandInformationSystems/Staff/tabid/472/Default.aspx.

HESA (Higher Education South Africa). 2011. *A Generation of Growth: Proposal for a National Programme to Develop the Next Generation of Academics for South African Higher Education*. Pretoria: HESA.

PART III

PATHWAYS

8

Race and Justice in Higher Education
Some Global Challenges, with Attention to the South African Context

LEWIS R. GORDON

As this chapter emerges from a discussion of race in higher education in the South African context, it may bode well to begin with some observation about the pernicious history of race and class in South Africa. The separation of the two, as Oliver Cox (2000) observed in the American context, is not workable primarily because so much of American racism was premised on the proletarianisation of people of African descent. As South African apartheid was heavily modelled after the American system of Jim Crow, it stands to reason that South African racialisation was also linked to the proletarianisation of the country's black population. Although there were certainly genocidal wishes in this process – that is, the hope for a future white utopia devoid of black and brown peoples – the reality was that the colonial history of the country depended on a cheap labour pool. For example, Cape Town was, among many other things, a slave colony and it was able to thrive as such because of the high availability of such labour from nearby countries and from the large island of Madagascar (see Frederickson 1981 and PBS 2010). Thus, along with the colonial disputes over indigeneity and settlement were also those of displacement, forced servitude and anxieties wrought from a world maintained precariously on boundaries forged by social practices of exclusion and systemic violence.

The development and maintenance of the institutions constitutive of such practices of exclusion and regiments of control, especially after their formalisation in 1948, depended upon limiting education except for small groups whose main purpose was race mediation. The circumstance was, much as Mahmood Mamdani (1996) describes in *Citizen and Subject*, the reservation of citizenship for a small portion of the population and the cultivation of a relationship of rule for the remaining majority. Education was thus highly controversial except for the ideological advancement of such a system – a perverse pedagogy and production of propaganda that rationalised racial inferiority of black and brown peoples. The need for mediators, however, required offering the illusion of more to those willing to play such a role and apartheid schemes of permissible achievement followed.

None of this, however, emerged in a vacuum, which the apartheid South African government and the white minority to whom it was beholden eventually learned, as a future without trade was threatened by the anti-apartheid movements that culminated in the illegalisation, although not social elimination, of the system by the 1990s. South Africa was not simply a racist society with a racist governing system; it was also an economy in which the system had expectations of a high standard of living for the citizens who mattered versus the rest of its population. Thus, in spite of the totalitarian efforts of the apartheid regime, necessity dictated varieties of exceptions to its rule, especially with regard to its status as a *modern* state, and higher education became a consideration for a trained workforce in some institutions and the production of knowledge in others.

South Africa's similarities to the United States of the past it admired and imitated also took form in the telos through which white supremacist states were organised. As white supremacy valorised itself as the guardian over an infantile world of colour, it also at times admitted its proponents' naked desire for profit and service. South Africa's history thus also became about the cultivation of a cheap labour force in the service of a racial consumer group. The latter wanted to eat their proverbial cake and have it, too, so their godlike status in South Africa needed affirmation outside as well. It has always struck me how 'hungry' many white South Africans are for recognition in the upper echelon of white power abroad – especially in the United Kingdom and the United States. They have something to prove, so to speak, perhaps to demonstrate that all the privilege they had received was, at the end of the day, worth it because they were somehow meritorious, somehow more deserving. Such talent, under many schemes of justice, should be rewarded, which, when thus granted, is also redemptive.

In addition to the right of consumption, white South Africans then had access to becoming an educated managerial force whose labour capacity, laterally valued, was well situated in a global hierarchy. While educated and professionally trained white labour had access to the global labour economy, the pressures on the South African economy by way of sanctions and international outcry came to a head in the events that culminated in the elections of 1994 and the de jure elimination of apartheid and the new South African Constitution that took its place. For many across the world, the momentous character of those monitored elections offered the promise of a new day, one of dignity offered by faces black, brown, red, golden and white facing each other as equals. Such a promise meant, as it did in the United States, a demand on the institutions most connected with opportunities, namely, those devoted to education. Thus, the issue of race and class came to the fore in demands for the transformation of the South African cheap labour force, as a consumer group worthy and with dignity, into one that could reap the benefits of becoming an educated lateral group – a people on the same playing field, a people who are, in a word, 'equal' to the working force in European and North American countries. The problem, however, is that post-apartheid South Africa has adopted a programme in which that group is not 'needed' as an educated working force, but only as an endless supply of cheap labour, driving down its value, which, given the now global movement of that human commodity, renders them seemingly obsolete. The argument for the transformation of their lives, then, depends on transcending the specificity of South Africa and addressing a larger global problem, which is the waste of human potential in our times. Simply put, those with most access to educational opportunities are not necessarily the most talented.

The global situation is worsened, however, by social, technological and environmental upheavals that have placed old problems on new terrain. As global relations became increasingly tailored for the interests of those with the most capital, the illusion of self-sufficiency as one of its guiding mantras and the breaking down of regulations and protections for the vulnerable that are its consequence have had the effect of kicking up a hornet's nest. The disarray has its markings everywhere in disrupted economies, forced migration, the radicalisation of old systems of exploitation – for example, the rise of de facto if not de jure enslavement – and economies built upon social and biological death.[1] Race, as a site of vulnerability since its inception in medieval Iberia, is caught in this regime of death in multiple ways, as it has always been with mechanisms of exploitation. As Frantz Fanon observed more than half a century ago, there is a tendency, when it comes to matters of justice and desert, for those at the racialised bottom to arrive on the scene of opportunity 'too late'. Across the globe, black subjects are offered promises of de jure equality with the proviso that conditions for de facto equality are reduced at best and dismantled at worse.

The impact of these considerations on education, especially higher education, has been enormous and perhaps catastrophic. Part of this is because although educational achievement often leads to prosperity and a higher quality of life, the promise of bare labour was never its actual purpose. There is thus a radical and revolutionary element to the expansion of humanistic education, especially for people who were expected to devote their lives exclusively to servitude, as Antonio Gramsci observed in his reflections on the humanities in the twentieth century. The movement from servant (tool) to desiring agent (consumer, client) requires drawing upon reflective capacities that echo the dichotomy of subject and citizen.

There is an imperative at work if the avowed goals of equality and democratisation of societies such as South Africa and the United States, both heavily weighed down by histories of racism, are to ring true. Not only must racial discrimination with regard to access to higher education be overcome, but the racial dynamics at the core and in the content of such institutions must also be addressed. This challenge requires, however, dispelling a variety of misconceptions at work. The first is to do with the fundamental question of access as one moves up the ladder of levels of education – the well-known qualifications debate. The second requires addressing the conundrum of education in a world of neo-liberal and neo-conservative market fundamentalist demands on the purpose of knowledge.

The 'qualifications' debate

No issue addresses the question of access mentioned above more than the hotly debated one of affirmative action. Affirmative action has been under assault in the United States since the 1970s and has pretty much been eradicated there since the 1990s. It is taking similar paths in South Africa and many countries across the globe in which there are historic patterns of discrimination, whether on the basis of race, religion, sex or other considerations such as physical or mental disabilities. Although severely weakened from transformed policies, aided by robust academic and juridical resistance over the course of the past three decades, there is a persistent belief on the part of many critics, and even many proponents, that it is the prevalent policy of selection in countries such as the United States and the United Kingdom, in addition to South Africa. Though many institutions have either remained as white or become whiter, the belief in a loss of white opportunity persists primarily because of increased access, best exemplified by such shining examples as the president of the United States and the recent three presidents of South Africa that emerged from the foundational years of affirmative action policies in the case of the former and a historic transformation of the Constitution in the case of the latter.

There is a fact that trails, some would say stains, every person of colour who now occupies spaces previously reserved exclusively for whites: if it were not for affirmative action policies, she/he would not have been admitted into the selected educational institution or place of employment, regardless of how high her/his credentials. This admission reflects a fundamental problem with affirmative action as it poses a great threat to what could be called 'white privilege', as the context today is one mostly of white access over most others – namely, it works.

I had the opportunity to reflect out loud on this aspect of affirmative action in a discussion at the Race and Higher Education roundtable in Grahamstown, which played a key role in occasioning the volume in which this chapter appears, when I asked: 'Are there no mediocre white people in South Africa? Is every white person hired, every white person offered admission to institutions of learning, excellent?'

My rhetorical question was premised on what many highly achieved (and many not-so-highly achieved) black people know: the myth of legitimated white supremacy is the subtext of the 'qualifications' narrative that accompanies debates on affirmative action. Perhaps nothing exemplifies this more than the recent American presidential elections. The disparity between Barack Obama and his opponent, and the extraordinary breakdown of race and geography, which we could call the 'geography of race', reveals qualitatively and quantitatively how a slightly above average white man whose entire campaign was premised on a misrepresentation of reality would fare against an extraordinary black incumbent. That there was a time that Obama would not have stood a chance even to be elected for a first term makes this achievement a change, as was the case of Nelson Mandela before him. But the geography of race revealed a divided nation along mostly racial lines with white populations having more geographical space than people of colour.[2] This is a phenomenon that is nearly global with regard to concerns of race. The concentrated demographics of urban centres reveal multiracial regions of dense populations. Black and other dark-skinned populations in white-dominated countries tend to live where numbers of people are most dense. Although different parts of Africa face additional dynamics with regard to race and the rural/urban divide, the fact remains that large acquisitions of land and resources tend to be in fewer hands in most parts of the world and those hands tend to be lighter in complexion on both sides. The referendum from Obama's victory is unavoidably a statement from those who have to work with access to less to those with such and opportunities for more. A subtext of affirmative action has always been this basic point: could sharing occur without loss? And the normative question is, at the end of the day, are historic and continued structures and practices of exclusion justified? If not, are efforts toward their transformation normatively legitimate?

Bernard Boxill (1992), in his classic *Blacks and Social Justice*, offers a detailed engagement with the labyrinth of theoretical arguments unleashed against the legitimacy of affirmative action as a social remedy. Each more complicated than the last, these arguments reflected their proponents' failure to address the basic historic and human element at the heart of affirmative action as a response. Justice, for the critics, was premised on abstract moral subjects devoid of historic specificity and living difference of flesh and blood. While Boxill's goal was to demonstrate that a better conception of justice would respond to the very real exclusion and suffering of black people, he found himself also discussing the near callous comfort with which critics could live with the continuation of such a condition, but be outraged by any impact on the lives of whites, especially the more elite and privileged among them. Boxill was identifying the bad faith that underlies mainstream or establishment treatments of social justice for blacks. His faith in social justice leads to an expansive hope, for the belief in the capacity of justice to overcome the contradictions of normative social practices. Although not his intent, Boxill identified an important problem at the heart of any effort at justice. No theory of justice will be adhered to where the humanity of the excluded and the brutalised is brought into question.[3] The rejection of that precious human element may at first seem absurd since blacks and other people of colour are, after all, human beings. But that is the nature of bad faith: its investment in a pleasing falsehood for the sake of avoiding a displeasing truth.[4]

In addition to what many, not only in North America, but also the rest of the Americas and perhaps globally, consider to be the displeasing truth of the humanity of blacks, other communities of colour and indigenous peoples is also for *their* critics the displeasing truth about justice, at least as conceived of in the contemporary West, namely, its limits. I will not focus on this problem here, but its concern is a subtext of what follows.[5] What most people of colour and historically excluded groups experience is the task of what to do in a world when justice is not enough, when there is a paradox of what I have elsewhere called 'unjust justice and just injustice' (see L.R. Gordon 1995, 2014).

Our discussions at the Race and Higher Education roundtable led to my writing an opinion piece for *truthout.org*, which was reprinted in a variety of contexts, including the Thinking Africa special supplementary edition of the *Mail & Guardian* (L.R. Gordon 2011a). A striking response to that essay was the international outpouring of letters I received that were rich with stories of how either highly qualified and often overqualified people of colour were passed over for opportunities readily available to their white counterparts. Was affirmative action necessary for those people of colour's advancement? While the answer is 'Yes', there is an additional truth. Was investment in white supremacy necessary for less than stellar whites to be promoted? I think the question answers itself.

Many whites, however, often miss an additional aspect of social investment in white supremacy and I am using the word 'investment' intentionally: whiteness, under such a scheme, functions as a special kind of credit or capital. It is offered, as such, as meeting the requirement of human access, pretty much like a human credit rating. In fact, whiteness means a good human credit rating. Non-whiteness has degrees of lesser rating, which means that one has to offer much more to receive the benefits of social expectations such as, for example, justice.

Affirmative action, which brought people of colour to the table to learn first-hand about the level of performance of their white predecessors and contemporaries, stimulated a reflection on standards in many institutions not only in the United States and South Africa, but also across the globe.[6] As more people of colour began to meet inflated standards, what was being concealed were the low standards available to many whites who preceded them (think of the days of the 'gentleman's C' at some elite institutions of higher learning) and no doubt many who continue to join them as presumed agents of excellence (see Katznelson 2006).[7]

So, what is the truth about the qualifications narrative, the claim about having to lower standards for the admission of people of colour, especially blacks? It masks racial hegemonic mediocrity, which we shall call the first premise of white privilege: to be mediocre with impunity and without social stigma. One would think for blacks and others the opposite would apply – mediocrity with deserved disdain – but that is not the case. The situation for other groups, especially blacks (because treated in anti-black societies as the most distant politically and biologically from whites), is of degraded excellence through *presumed mediocrity*, as Fanon (1967) showed.[8] Thus, achievement (often in the form of being proverbially twice as good) or failure (which unfortunately also includes simply being just as good, in addition to being below average) both amount to a form of failure, *being black in the first place*.

There is, however, another truth with which to contend. There are few social systems that depend on excellence to function. Most of the services we rely on to get through our lives depend on average levels of performance. The norm is, by definition, not the exception, whether by that is meant excellence (above the norm) or wanting (below the norm). Nearly a decade ago, I wrote an essay entitled, 'Critical Reflections on Three Popular Tropes in the Study of Whiteness', in which I argued against a dimension of the discourse on white privilege in cases of what could properly be called entitlements or basic human needs (L.R. Gordon 2005a). A reason for white defensiveness regarding that conception of privilege is a concern for being guilty about having access to things that most, if not presumably all other human beings want – security, health, education, shelter and a society committed to the conditions for one's self-esteem and basic dignity. Privilege, I argued, pertains to things that are more luxuries or, simply, undeserved rewards without social objection. The general advantages available to whites as a function of white supremacy and anti-black racism properly belong to the latter. The rewards lavished on many whites in the modern world have not, however, been based on merit. What many people of colour discovered upon entering those previously closed corridors was not white superiority but, for the most part, white mediocrity. What also baffled them was the seeming inability for many, including some people of colour, to admit what was right before their eyes. It is as if there is a cognitive incapacity to see white mediocrity. The credit rating of whiteness is simply too high and the access it offers makes whiteness a form of capital that is still well worth having.

I have elsewhere examined this phenomenon as institutional bad faith, where a social world facilitates believing (and seeing) what its prized members prefer to believe (L.R. Gordon 1995).

To preserve a system of white supremacy, there must be investment in the notion that blacks and other groups of colour fall short (have a lower human credit rating and thus are not viable as capital but useful, as history attests, when made into property for others, as in the case of slavery). While it is unlikely that every member of a group exemplifies excellence in her/his vocation, what is not brought up is the black and brown people who were excluded on the basis of their excellence. The prevailing view in predominantly white institutions about such candidates is fear about whether such candidates are 'controllable'. Although I mentioned blacks and other people of colour, this concern of controllability is almost exclusively reserved for blacks and especially so for black males.[9]

Women often fall under the rubric of affirmative action as well. The success of affirmative action is evident with regard to reducing exclusion on the basis of gender, but, as is also clear, it is so primarily for white women, although both South Africa and the United States have been making progress with the inclusion of women of colour.[10] Black and brown women are harder cases to discuss in terms of their controllability, but in recent times, the presumption of their being more docile and controllable, with all the sexist connotations, has found a home with gender, where it remains dormant until women seek positions of leadership. There are still glass ceilings at those levels. The reader could think through how these concerns will unfold at the highest echelons of representation in the countries most relevant to this discussion. (Countries such as China and Japan have correlates worth considering, although the highest authorities are not white.) There are exceptions, but in truth *real power*, which means not what is seen in public but behind closed doors, the *power behind power*, remains categorically male and white.

Keeping institutions white and predominantly male is not only about tests and evaluating dossiers. It is also maintained through creating unnecessary obstacles, rationalised as important criteria. Consider the story of James Weldon Johnson, the famed novelist and songwriter of, among other great works, 'Lift Every Voice and Sing', known as the 'Black National Anthem', whose work I have discussed elsewhere. Johnson was also a lawyer. He became one the way Abraham Lincoln became a lawyer – he took the bar examination. In the past, it did not require a law degree. It did not even require a Bachelor degree. All that was required was passing the bar examination. Doing so meant that one had mastered the required understanding of the law to practise it.

Johnson was principal of the now famous Stanton College Preparatory School in Jacksonville, Florida. He showed up to take the state's bar exam in 1897.[11] Seeing he was black, and realising there was no rule stating that blacks could not take the exam (since it was presumed no black would dare show up to take it or *could* take and pass it), he was permitted to undergo the examination. As it became clear that he knew the law, his examiners inflated the standards and tested him at several times the expectation of the white candidates. One of the examiners left the room out of protest in the face of the possibility of a black man meeting the criteria. Reluctantly, the others capitulated and he was sworn in as a member of the Florida bar (see Johnson 2008: 143). Other blacks followed in droves.

Although degrees in law existed at various institutions of higher learning for nearly a millennium, they were not required to sit before the bar. This changed as black and brown membership increased. First, there was the requirement of a Bachelor of Law. Since many blacks could not afford to go to college, that reduced a significant number. But since there was a growing black middle class, even with American apartheid, more began to meet that criterion. So, the American Bar Association then required postgraduate study. To sit for the exam, a candidate must now have completed law school, which generally means three years of study *after completing an undergraduate degree*. In effect, seven or more years of investment in higher education became the criterion to sit before the bar. The stratagem was effective: the number of blacks 'qualified' to take the bar examination plummeted.[12]

This story of increased obstacles is also one of great social costs. If one considers the damage to institutions of legalised white supremacy done by the small cadre of blacks who met the additional criteria, imagine what would have happened if their ranks were larger. Mandela studied law, but what might have happened if he had been joined by a large number of comrades who were not only armed with the knowledge of law, but also with the credentials to act on it?

Law is but one example, but there are many cases across a variety of professions, disciplines and activities, ranging from political participation to sports. The resources devoted to excelling in many fields are invariably stacked in favour of whites, often from childhood through to adolescence and early adulthood. The demise of public investment in North America and Europe, and the effort to make such policies the model for other nations, pretty much assure the demographic elimination of many groups of colour and especially blacks. A stark example is the impact such policies have had on jazz music. Although an African-American art form, the elimination of music programmes in predominantly black schools has led, in effect, to the privatisation of music education. The result is an increased whitening of the face of jazz (and, for that matter, those who actually play musical instruments) and, additionally, a decline in the black audience for the music since it is an art form that requires some ongoing relationship with its performance, which increasingly prices out many black populations. The same applies to a decline in public investments in other areas of the arts, sciences and even physical education, in spite of the stereotype of the black athlete. Although there are blacks who manage to achieve access to the limited resources available, the overwhelming circumstance is one of abrogated societal responsibility for developed infrastructures in favour of, as the prison industries across the globe attest, *disaffirmative* action in the form of a punishing state and civil society (see Alexander 2010; Comaroff and Comaroff 2006; Gordon and Gordon 2009).

What a genuine commitment to affirmative action would demand under circumstances such as the ones outlined here is not only the insistence of inclusion, but also a critical reflection on the purposes of the articulated criteria and a commitment to the material and socio-cognitive conditions by which more just arrangements could be made possible. Such requirements should be created for the healthy function of a society's institutions, which will entail just practices of exclusion. But, as we know, in a society committed to injustice, it is very easy to create unjust practices of distinction and elimination. In the words of Boaventura de Sousa Santos (2007: xviii): 'This much is expressed in the idea, widely shared by activists, that there will be no global social justice without global cognitive justice.'

So, we come to a fundamental problem with affirmative action for beneficiaries of white privilege who seek further comforting about their condition. Its existence is the admission of continued racism and sexism. If the system is not just, how, then, could their benefiting from it ultimately be so?

In countries such as South Africa and the United States, the bad faith language of denial has hijacked the language of affirmative action. For instance, the expression 'past discrimination' dominates debates on the subject. If racial and gender discrimination were aberrations of the past, it would mean that no overseer of criteria today is motivated by racist and sexist goals. It would mean there is no racial or gender discrimination, which would make the use of race or gender as criteria for access unjust. Yet, as we know, the language of 'reverse discrimination' emerged in the United States in the 1970s.[13] Such language turned the tables on the situation. In effect, it stimulated a reactionary movement that treated discrimination as a reality ultimately faced only by white males (and more recently, white females) precisely through denying the continued existence of racism and sexism at work in unmonitored processes of selection and what could be called, drawing on the work of Jane Anna Gordon and Vincent Beaver, the production of vulnerability (see J.A. Gordon 2012; Beaver 2012).

The anti-affirmative action group in the United States perversely found its version of Rosa Parks in Abigail Fisher, who filed a Supreme Court case against affirmative action practices at the University of Texas in Austin. The university's admissions policy was as follows: state resident applicants who were ranked in the top 10 per cent of their high school's graduating class received automatic offers of admission. Those in the lower percentile were considered on an accumulative ranking score that took other criteria into consideration, including athletic ability, community service and race. There are parallels between Fisher and Allan Bakke, whose case occasioned the rallying cry of 'reverse discrimination': they both have more options than most black people and expect to get even more at the expense of blacks and other racial minorities. The bottom line is that they have an important commodity – indeed, racial capital – that every black person and most people of colour lack: whiteness.[14] It is a leveraged term so prevalent that to bring it to the fore would be redundant in terms of the many advantages already offered in an anti-black society. The additional problem with their position – and most anti-affirmative action arguments, as we have seen thus far – is that it depends on a hidden premise: the erroneous view that racism no longer exists. Although there has been much progress on racial matters by way of individual achievements of people of colour in historically anti-black societies (such as the South African and United States' presidencies), the structural realities persist and in some cases have worsened. If there were no racism, affirmative action would make no sense. Thus, part of the effort to eliminate affirmative action is a social denial of empirical reality.

What is also crucial is that the denial of persisting racism leads to an additional presupposition of intrinsic black under- or disqualification. Recall that Fisher's overall academic record placed her below the 10 per cent of Texas residents offered automatic admission to the university. Beyond this point, admissions officers expected other factors (such as being an excellent athlete) to come into play. Even where race was brought into consideration, by virtue of the majority population already being white, there would still have to be other considerations since presumably under-represented racial minorities would be competing with other members of their own group as well. More than one black or Latino being considered means something other than her/his race would have to be taken into account, once race or ethnic identity has been established.

Now what is curious is that while Fisher did not see herself as less qualified because of falling below the 10 per cent group of Texas residents offered automatic admission to the University of Texas, she was interestingly enough not charged with underqualification in public discussions and critique, while the blacks and other racial minorities within that group were charged as such by the opponents of affirmative action. This disparity is proof of how whiteness as capital functions. That Fisher *had (and continues to have) this capital* already made her claim of discrimination silly: her complaint was about being required to offer more, after producing less with the advantages she already had and continues to have. But the blacks and racial minorities *in the top 10 per cent group*, in fact, those *in the top 1 per cent group*, also faced what those outside the top 10 per cent group faced: the presumption of their illegitimacy. *This* was not Ms Fisher's problem, at least in terms of her colour. In terms of her gender, however, she could have made a case, but then she would have been *affirming* the need for affirmative action. As everyone who studies the changing demographics of institutions of historic exclusion knows, no group has benefited more from affirmative action than (white) women. Ironically, she *needed* affirmative action, as misconceived, to evade the reality of her own limitations. The distorted conception of affirmative action as an unjust remedy blocking the path of white entitlement, where every white is supposedly meritorious, becomes an invested narrative of national *ressentiment*.[15]

Ms Fisher's response to this critique could no doubt be similar to those of many white immigrants to the United States, including those from countries such as Australia, Canada and South Africa: she was not personally responsible for the conditions that led to the disadvantages faced by racial and ethnic minorities in the United States. It is similar to the arguments waged against reparations for legalised slavery, even though slave masters had received reparations for the loss of their human chattel in many countries across the globe. We could extend this argument beyond recent white immigrants to a form of metaphysical immigration, namely, that of being born at a different time. Why, asks the current generation of young white students and professionals, should they be penalised for the actions of their ancestors? Many of them are neither racist nor a willing beneficiary of racial and other forms of unjust acquisitions of wealth. And then some would simply argue that the status quo is not a racist or unjust one.

Bearing responsibility

A major problem with such views is that they overpersonalise social responsibility. Such arguments forget that the revenue for a government's responsibility will come from everyone under its jurisdiction. This includes citizens and residents, whether permanent or temporary. Thus, it is not only whites who bear the responsibility for enslavement and continued racial injustice. It is ironically a burden shared by those who have been historically victimised or oppressed by such activities and institutions. Who else bears responsibility for a government that has behaved badly? Karl Jaspers (1965) identified and discussed this problem well in *The Question of German Guilt*, a misleading title since the actual German is simply *Die Schuldfrage*, the question of guilt, blame or responsibility.[16]

Jaspers addressed all these issues – including metaphysical immigration (checking out, so to speak) – ironically in the context of bearing the responsibility of rebuilding the German university system in the midst of reconstructing the society. He pointed out that while one's 'innocence', even one's fighting against the injustices of an unjust society, makes one less, perhaps even not, morally culpable, it does not follow that one is without *political* and *legal* responsibility. The tragedy of irresponsible government and, even further, an unjust society, is that it is the people who carry the onus of responsibility. This is a familiar double burden for black people and most, if not all, indigenous peoples: they face the burden of fighting for justice and the shared burden of bearing the costs for the remedies posed, even for them.

We come to an observation made by Fanon. Although he detested violence, as his former student and friend Alice Cherki (2006) reminds us in her poignant portrait of his life and thought, he did not shy away from speaking the truth about tolerated violence and injustice under colonial regimes and the strange logic of what he called the 'Greco-Roman pedestal' of supposed moral objections against decolonial efforts (Fanon 2005: 11). Since colonialists regarded colonialism as just, how could they be expected to see decolonisation as anything but unjust? If the ongoing efforts needed to maintain colonialism were considered just, how could they be considered violent? This became a charge made against efforts to dismantle colonialism. And relatedly, if the exclusion of colonised people were considered just, would not their inclusion be considered unjust? Even worse, the appearance of such people was considered more than unjust. It was considered violent.[17]

Fanon argued that the effort to demonstrate non-violent change was futile. By this, he did not mean that one should aim to be as violent as possible. His point was a negative one: the only way to satisfy the expectations of non-violence was to be ineffective at practices of social change. We forget that Martin Luther King, one of the apostles of non-violence, was considered violent in his day. When he marched with fellow protestors against American apartheid, it was not the police officers who set Alsations on them, not the hordes of whites who stoned them, not the firefighters who sprayed them with water at a force capable of stripping skin, not the gangs who lynched many of them, it was not those people and agents of state power that were considered violent. What supporters of the status quo 'saw' was violent black people, against whom the society was being protected.[18]

The situation is familiar to many in South Africa. There are those who praise South Africa for making the transformation to a supposedly post-apartheid society non-violently. Yet, the many blacks (in the Black Consciousness conception) and their supporters who were killed, tortured and imprisoned, the many protestors harmed, the tanks, the guns, the dogs, the 3.00 a.m. knocks on the door, the many instances of trauma make such an assessment mystifying; do none of these people count?[19] What is hidden in this misguided notion, as in what is suppressed about racism and sexism in the anti-affirmative action rhetoric of reverse discrimination and qualifications, is this: in a white supremacist state, violence is only recognised if it is waged against whites.[20]

So, the hysteria about crime, about insecurity, in South Africa, is similar to the same in the United States and a growing number of countries gripped by growing states of insecurity. Even when the actual figures of violent crime declined, incarceration of blacks was high in South Africa and the United States because there was in effect the criminalisation of a people (see Alexander 2010; Comaroff and

Comaroff 2006; Davis 2003). As violent appearance, black visibility was criminalised (see L.R. Gordon 2004).

An odd feature of postcolonies is that criminalisation of black populations does not require white institutional leadership. In so-called black countries, the phenomenon exists and is colour-dependent, where darker-skinned blacks are the most criminalised. The reasons for this are manifold, but most amount to the near isomorphic relationship between closed social options and skin colour as a legacy of racialised slavery and colonialism in the midst of postcolonial environments heavily invested in keeping capital in the hands of the former governing population.[21]

The correlation between anti-affirmative action and the preservation of colonial institutions of exclusion and violence emerges because both rely on the same things – racist states and civil societies. In fact, 'uncivil society' becomes the *inclusion* of the black and, where at issue, indigenous masses – see Mamdani (1996) and Comaroff and Comaroff (2000).

Two ideological considerations

Stacking the decks in favour of whites (or those who function as such in their social location) is a consequence of two prevailing ideologies of state function (or dysfunction) in recent times – neo-conservatism and neo-liberalism. Together, these twins move to the right of centre on rationalisations of reality devoid of verification and rigour of analysis. Particularly with regard to race, their proponents work more through fictional and often mythic tropes than reality supported by empirical evidence. Where white income is typically twelve times that of blacks (and ironically even more so in many predominantly black countries), whites complain about being at a supposed disadvantage and point in their countries to the miniscule number of affluent blacks as an indication of excessive achievement. If there are no impediments to black progress, there must be something *in blacks* curtailing them. The neo-conservatives thus offer portraits of blacks as depraved, diseased, deviant, delinquent and intellectually deficient. The correlated disciplinary rationalisations of these tropes are black people as problems of criminal justice studies, health and education.

The specific correlates are studies of crime, AIDS and intellectual deficiency. The effect is manifold. It is theodicean, where the society or the nation is idolised as a god without responsibility for good and evil. The United States and the entire modern Western tradition become without fault and the plight of the many whose labour and lives were fodder for its emergence not only suffer from their own supposed inherent deficiencies, but also from an apparent lack of gratitude for the privilege of having some part in this self-congratulatory portrait. It thus attempts also what De Sousa Santos calls 'epistemicide', which he describes as the cognitive side of genocide, in an effort to achieve what Michael Tillotson recently formulated as 'resistance to resistance', a form of political nihilism in which the will to fight is wiped out of a people (De Sousa Santos 2007; De Sousa Santos, Nuens and Meneses 2008; Tillotson 2011).

There are many contradictions and double standards of the neo-conservative position, including its proponents' lack of memory of the role they played in creating the circumstances they criticise. The decimation of public institutions from the Reagan and Thatcher administrations onwards, for instance, created dysfunction on a scale that made it appear foolish to seek public solutions to problems of the common weal (see Handler 1995, 2004). At the same time, the bloated military budgets of the United States and some of its allies are premised on the use of public funds for private interests. We could call this what it is: welfare for the rich. That black interests tend to be linked to a viable public infrastructure made blacks a marked enemy of privatisation. In some instances, blacks were collateral damage, but in most cases, they were in the direct line of fire, as the policies of criminalisation and structurally produced poverty in countries such as the United States and South Africa attest.

The neo-liberal position is not as overtly blatant as the neo-conservatives'. While they share the neo-conservative fetishising of privatisation, they are also concerned with preserving some semblance of human rights and democracy in the process. Thus, they are compelled to offer an alternative to the neo-conservative mantra of pathological blackness and cultures of deviance. Instead, they present a conception of democratic life premised on individualism, which makes the collective needs of disenfranchised black, brown and indigenous populations illegitimate. Privatisation demands an engagement with these groups as neo-liberals continue the neo-conservative attacks on public infrastructure. For neo-liberals, such populations were at first more collateral damage. As it became clear that disenfranchised groups' interests rested on a model of democracy premised on group or collective rights, neo-liberal critics waged a war on them in the insidious language of being concerned about their ultimate interests *as individuals*. This assault, ironically, received its greatest support in what at first appears to be perhaps the most paradoxical effect of previous struggles – the changed hue of higher leadership in South Africa and the United States.[22]

Germane to the question of white racial capital and affirmative action, this new leadership faces a stark contradiction: loving Mandela and Obama does not require having the same sentiment towards black people. White normativity and privilege could be preserved through making them 'exceptions' to the rule in a world where black failure is the norm. Their existence can thus be subverted, ironically, for the preservation of a racist system, however noble their individual intentions may be. This has been a difficult problem of black achievement from the moment anti-black racism emerged. Such blacks face having to succeed, even where their success is undermined as their being exceptions to a rule. Mandela and Obama did not get rid of white supremacy, as the overwhelming evidence of decline in black communities well into the second decade of the twenty-first century attests, but we have a sense that the world would be much worse off without them (see Alexander 2010; Tillotson 2011).

There is also the irony of the situation of each black person who manages to scrape through and rise in a system premised on black suppression. There will always be objections to the presence of such people, as the uproar in response to the emergence of a paltry black middle class across the globe reveals.[23] Where millions of affluent whites do not occasion a raised eyebrow, the existence of thousands – not even a million – of rich blacks in countries with populations exceeding 40 million people, such as South Africa or

Brazil or Colombia, in addition to the United States, leads to outcries with often hypocritical concerns about *class*. There are even objections about where such affluent blacks live. A Brown University study of race and domicile provided an answer: for the most part, affluent blacks live in predominantly black and brown neighbourhoods with lower overall opportunities (Logan 2011). And why is this so? In the end, affluent whites, although welcoming the *idea* of integrated neighbourhoods, prefer to live in segregated places in practice. Even white lower-middle-class and working-class people have access to neighbourhoods with more resources and possibilities of accrued wealth than many blacks with higher incomes. None of this is news to black middle-class people. As with the affirmative action debate, the truth here could be denied only through closing one's eyes to the continued practice of racism at institutional levels.[24]

This is not to say that there is no excellence among rewarded whites. History offers ample evidence of such.[25] It is to say, however, that, as with every group, high performance is by definition a virtue of those who are devoted and talented. The odds of a *people* manifesting such characteristics without extraordinary cultural investment are very low. But as Anna Julia Cooper (1998) showed in her provocative essay, 'What Are We Worth?', far too much is invested in those who fail to meet such traits in white supremacist societies. Very little is put towards those who, with few incentives, produce more. Could one imagine what proper social investments, especially with regard to opportunities in higher education, in the people who are resourceful enough to survive in the shacks of South Africa, the *favelas* of Brazil, the slums of India and the ghettos and reservations of the United States could mean for the future of humankind?

To make some headway on these matters demands, then, bringing to the fore the truth about the development of institutional opportunities in the so-called post-racial and post-apartheid world in which we now live. It requires admitting the onus of past victories is the next stage of struggle, a reality that, unfortunately, never fails to arise, but whose battle must be waged, however weary our souls may be because, as many of us in higher education know and those who sacrificed their lives to make access to it possible knew, what is at stake is no less than humanity's most precious resource, in whose potential is, in the end, the future of all.

Such a goal at this point seems more like a courageous dream. Imagine a South Africa in which the proverbial 'poors', large in number, hungry for opportunity, have access to the conditions for the cultivation of their talents. People so resourceful at survival could offer much to the future of South Africa, which raises the question of what South African institutions of higher education could be, if they were to take seriously the needs of the country's disenfranchised populations. Such a task requires rejecting an abstract model of higher education, where professors fiddle while the nation burns. It means taking seriously that education is always situated in conditions of pressing needs and, as the term 'education' itself means to lead out, which has associations with growth, it means, as well, that institutions of higher learning need to educate themselves on what these challenges signify for a country whose constitutional rhetoric extols an inclusive conception of that powerful word: the 'people'.

Notes

1. For recent discussion of this development, see J.A. Gordon's (2012) paper on enslavement. For an earlier formulation, see Bales (1999).
2. See '2012 Presidential Election Electoral Vote Results Map and County-by-County Popular Vote Map': http://freedomslighthouse.net/2012-presidential-election-electoral-vote-map/. For discussion of correlations between race and land ownership, see Gilbert, Wood and Sharp (2002) and Campbell (2012).
3. I explore this consideration in L.R. Gordon (2014).
4. For elaboration, especially in the context of anti-black racism, see L.R. Gordon (1995).
5. I do so, however, in L.R. Gordon (2014).
6. See, for example, Darity (2005), which offers empirical data and analysis of affirmative action in the contexts of England, Ireland, India, Malaysia, South Africa and the United States.
7. A C is a grade of 'average' performance. As no one questioned the elite's right to be at those institutions, they simply needed to complete their degrees. The C meant their work was satisfactory to award the degree.
8. For discussion of this problem, see L.R. Gordon (2005b).

9. This is so for many reasons in this stage of global capitalism and its investment in the production of vulnerable populations. The empirical data regarding black males are overwhelming. For lucid and frank discussion of the data, see Alexander (2010) and King and Smith (2011).
10. For discussion, see 'Affirmative Action: A Dialogue on Race, Gender, Equality and Law in America' in the American Bar Association's *Focus on Legal Studies* XIII (2) (Spring 1998). http://www.americanbar.org/publications/focus_on_law_studies_home/publiced_focus_spr98gender.html.
11. This once all-black and now mostly black high school is the only public school in the United States to have been in the top five (and four times) in the *Newsweek* rankings since 2000. The presumption of large numbers of blacks being disastrous for school performance persists, however (see Salter 2006).
12. Although I focus on blacks here, the presence of people of colour, such as Native Americans and Latinos, in the American Bar Association, has a history with a similar logic. For many discussions, see various issues of *La Raza Law Journal*, especially 12 (2) (2001), which features, among many illuminating articles, an influential introduction by Francisco Valdes, 'Insisting on Critical Theory in Legal Education: Making Do While Making Waves'.
13. Principally through the United States Supreme Court case *Regents of the University of California v. Bakke* (1978).
14. I say 'most' because there are people of colour in the United States who are white in other countries – for example, many white Latin Americans become people of colour in the United States. The status of some Eastern Europeans, for example, brown Serbs and people from the various countries from the former Soviet Union, while not black, could be one of questionable whiteness.
15. On ressentiment in the American context, I encourage readers to consult Ephraim (2003). For discussion, see my review essay (L.R. Gordon 2011b).
16. The subtitle is, properly translated, 'from the political liability of Germany'.
17. A visit to the Civil Rights Museum in Memphis, Tennessee, and the Slavery Museum in Liverpool, England, should dispel any doubts about this observation. Nearly every serious study of slavery and various systems of apartheid also attest to the double standard. See Gutman (1978), but also Guthrie (2003) where the author examines the history of black resistance and struggles for freedom being treated as forms of mental illness.
18. For discussion of civil rights activists as, in effect, monsters, see Gordon and Gordon (2009: Chapter 4).
19. Blacks were, simply, enemies of the apartheid state. Blackness was a political identity. The most influential formulation of this conception of Black Consciousness is Steve Bantu Biko's *I Write What I Like* (2002) and, for discussion, see Alexander, Gibson and Mngxitama (2008).

20. For elaboration, see my colleagues' and my chapters in *Biko Lives!* (Alexander, Gibson and Mngxitama 2008) and Gibson (2011).
21. The phenomenon in black postcolonial states is so rampant that Fela Kuti and Bob Marley even wrote songs about it, 'Sorrow, Tears, & Blood' (1977) and 'Burnin' and Lootin'' (1973) respectively. The situation is well chronicled in the literature on criminalisation in predominantly black countries; for example, see Comaroff and Comaroff (2006) and Mbembe (2001). For a recent study of dark-skin criminalisation and police brutality in Jamaica, see Bell (2011).
22. For more discussion, see Gordon and Gordon (2009: Chapter 4).
23. Much of this uproar emerges from disingenuous class rhetoric through which expressions such as 'truly disadvantaged' and 'underclass' emerged. In spite of claims about class over race, the odds of being poor continue to be so if one is born in a world that is more dark than light, as nearly every recent study on poverty has shown. For more discussion, see Darity (2005) and Handler (1995, 2004).
24. An illusion overlooked in the recent presidential elections is the construction of 'red' (Republican) zones or regions and 'blue' (Democrat) ones. The actual geographical terrain of the latter appeared quite small and that of the former is vast. Yet the figures add up to nearly 50/50, which raises the obvious: 50 per cent of the population is living in dense or compact setting over small geographical territories. The rest simply have more space and, by implication, not only more property, but perhaps also greater access to it since the pressures of demand are reduced over such vast territories. Urban living is simply more expensive than suburban or rural living. So, the sociological pressures and other factors – for example, living in proximity to difference – entail very different demands and capacities for wealth.
25. In a radio interview on this topic, I was asked to name an institution that functions according to the thesis of excellence in diversity I put forth here. The National Air and Space Administration (NASA) is an excellent example. Given how high the stakes were, that institution genuinely sought the most capable people they could find and that extraordinary community was and continues to be a diverse one. It is unfortunate that it is among the institutions targeted for reduced federal funding in spite of its being a fragment (0.6 per cent as of 2008) of the federal budget.

References

Alexander, A., N. Gibson and A. Mngxitama, eds. 2008. *Biko Lives! Contestations and Conversations.* New York: Palgrave.

Alexander, M. 2010. *The New Jim Crow: Mass Incarceration in the Age of Colorblindness.* New York: Free Press.

Bales, K. 1999. *Disposable People: New Slavery in the Global Economy*. Berkeley: University of California Press.

Beaver, V. 2012. 'Alienation and Vulnerability in the Philosophy of Jean-Paul Sartre'. PhD diss., Temple University, Philadelphia.

Bell, D. 2011. 'Ode to the Downpressor: A Psychological Portrait of Racism, Classim, and Denial in (Post)Colonial Jamaica'. Phd diss., Pacifica Graduate Institute, Carpinteria.

Biko, B.S. 2002. *I Write What I Like: A Selection of His Writings*, edited by Aelred Stubbs C.R. Chicago: University of Chicago Press.

Boxill, B. 1992. *Blacks and Social Justice*. Revised edition. Lanham: Rowman and Littlefield.

Campbell, J. 2012. 'Who Owns Land in South Africa?' *Council on Foreign Relations*. http://blogs.cfr.org/campbell/2012/07/19/who-owns-the-land-in-south-africa/.

Cherki, A. 2006. *Fanon: A Portrait*. Translated by Nadia Benabid. Ithaca: Cornell University Press.

Comaroff, J. and J. Comaroff, eds. 2000. *Civil Society and the Political Imagination in Africa: Critical Perspectives*. Chicago: University of Chicago Press.

———. 2006. *Law and Disorder in the Postcolony*. Chicago: University of Chicago Press.

Cooper, A.J. 1998. 'What Are We Worth?'. In *The Voice of Anna Julia Cooper: Including 'A Voice from the South' and Other Important Essays, Papers, and Letters*, ed. C. Lemert and E. Bahn, 161–87. Lanham: Rowman and Littlefield.

Cox, O.C. 2000. *Race: A Study in Social Dynamics*. New York: Monthly Review Press.

Darity, W. 2005. 'Affirmative Action in Comparative Perspective: Strategies to Combat Ethnic and Racial Exclusion Internationally'. http://www.schwartzman.org.br/leituras/Darity%20Affirmative_Action_Comparative_Perspective.pdf.

Davis, A.Y. 2003. *Are Prisons Obsolete?* New York: Seven Stories Press.

De Sousa Santos, B. 2007. 'General Introduction: Reinventing Social Emancipation: Toward New Manifestos'. In *Democratizing Democracy: Beyond the Liberal Democratic Canon*, ed. B. de Sousa Santos, xvii–xxxiii. London: Verso.

De Sousa Santos, B., J. Nuens and M. Meneses. 2008. 'Introduction: Opening up the Canon of Knowledge and Recognition of Difference'. In *Another Knowledge Is Possible: Beyond Northern Epistemologies*, ed. B. de Sousa Santos, ix–lxii. London: Verso.

Ephraim, C.W. 2003. *The Pathology of Eurocentrism: The Burdens and Responsibilities of Being Black*. Trenton: Africa World Press.

Fanon, F. 1967. *Black Skin, White Masks*. Translated by C. Lamm Markmann. New York: Grove Press.

———. [1963] 2005. *The Wretched of the Earth*. Translated by C. Farrington. New York: Grove Press.

Frederickson, G.M. 1981. *White Supremacy: A Comparative Study of American and South African History*. Oxford: Oxford University Press.
Gibson, N., ed. 2011. *Living Fanon: Global Perspectives*. New York: Palgrave.
Gilbert, J., S.D. Wood and G. Sharp. 2002. 'Who Owns the Land? Current Agricultural Land Ownership by Race/Ethnicity'. *Rural Conditions and Trends* 17 (4): 55–62.
Gordon, J.A. 2012. 'Theorizing Contemporary Practices of Enslavement'. http://www.scribd.com/doc/185968288/Theorizing-Contemporary-Practices-of-Slavery-Gordon#download.
Gordon, J.A. and L.R. Gordon. 2009. *Of Divine Warning: Reading Disaster in the Modern Age*. Boulder: Paradigm Publishers.
Gordon, L.R. 1995. *Bad Faith and Antiblack Racism*. Atlantic Highlands: Humanities International Press.
———. 2004. 'Philosophical Anthropology, Race, and the Political Economy of Disenfranchisement'. *Columbian Human Rights Law Review* 36 (1): 145–72.
———. 2005a. 'Critical Reflections on Three Popular Tropes in the Study of Whiteness'. In *What White Looks Like: African-American Philosophers on the Whiteness Question*, ed. G. Yancy, 173–93. New York: Routledge.
———. 2005b. 'Through the Zone of Nonbeing: A Reading of *Black Skin, White Masks* in Celebration of Fanon's Eightieth Birthday'. *C.L.R. James Journal* 11 (1): 1–43. http://www.jhfc.duke.edu/wko/dossiers/1.3/LGordon.pdf.
———. 2011a. 'The Problem with Affirmative Action'. *truthout*, 15 August. http://www.truth-out.org/problem-affirmative-action/1313170677. Reprinted in *Pambazuka News*. http://pambazuka.org/en/category/features/75787. Reprinted also as 'Affirmative Action Meets White Mediocrity', *Mail & Guardian*, 26 August – 1 September, Thinking Africa: Special Supplement: 1 and 3.
———. 2011b. 'Charles Wm. Ephraim's *Pathology of Eurocentrism*'. *Antigua-Barbuda Review of Books* 4 (1): 4–11. Reprinted in *C.L.R. James Journal* 17 (1): 231–8.
———. 2014. 'Justice Otherwise: Thoughts on Ubuntu'. In *Ubuntu: Curating the Archive*, ed. L. Praeg and S. Magadla, 10–26. Pietermaritzburg: University of KwaZulu-Natal Press.
Guthrie, R.V. 2003. *Even the Rat Was White: A Historical View of Psychology*. Second edition. Boston: Allyn and Bacon.
Gutman, H. 1978. *The Black Family in Slavery and Freedom: 1750–1925*. New York: Pantheon Books.
Handler, J. 1995. *The Poverty of Welfare Reform*. New Haven: Yale University Press.
———. 2004. *Social Citizenship and Workfare in the United States and Western Europe: The Paradox of Inclusion*. Cambridge: Cambridge University Press.
Jaspers, K. 1965. *Die Schuldfrage: Von der politischen Haftung Deutschlands*. Munich: Piper. Available in English as *The Question of German Guilt*, with a new introduction by J.W. Koterski, S.J., translated by E.B. Ashton. New York: Fordham University Press, 2001.

Johnson, J.W. 2008. *Along This Way: The Autobiography of James Weldon Johnson*. New York: Penguin Classics.

Katznelson, I. 2006. *When Affirmative Action Was White: An Untold History of Racial Inequality in Twentieth-Century America*. New York: W.W. Norton.

King, D.S. and R. Smith, 2011. *Still a House Divided: Race and Politics in Obama's America*. Princeton: Princeton University Press.

Logan, J. 2011. 'Separate and Unequal: The Neighborhood Gap for Blacks, Hispanics and Asians in Metropolitan America'. *US 2010 Project Report*. http://www.s4.brown.edu/us2010/Projects/Reports.htm.

Mamdani, M. 1996. *Citizen and Subject: Contemporary Africa and the Legacy of Late Colonialism*. Princeton: Princeton University Press.

Mbembe, A. 2001. *On the Postcolony*. Berkeley: University of California Press.

PBS (Public Broadcasting Station). 2010. *Slave Ship Mutiny*. Documentary. http://www.pbs.org/wnet/secrets/episodes/slave-ship-mutiny-watch-the-full-episode/756/.

Salter, K. 2006. *Schooling and the Politics of Disaster*. New York: Routledge.

Tillotson, M. 2011. *Invisible Jim Crow*. Trenton: Africa World Press.

Valdes, F. 2001. 'Insisting on Critical Theory in Legal Education: Making Do While Making Waves'. *La Raza Law Journal* 12 (2) (2001): 137–58.

9

Thinking Outside the Ivory Tower
Towards a Radical Humanities in South Africa

NIGEL C. GIBSON

> Was my freedom not given to me then in order to build the world of the *You* (Fanon 1967a: 232)?

> No attempt must be made to encase man, for it is his destiny to be free ... I want only this: That the enslavement of man by man must cease forever. That it be possible for me to discover and to love man, wherever he may be ... It is through the effort to recapture the self and to scrutinize the self, it is through the lasting tension of their freedom that man will be able to create the ideal conditions of existence for a human world (Fanon 1967a: 230).

At a Rhodes University graduation ceremony, the vice chancellor at the time, Saleem Badat, called on graduates to put their knowledge and expertise to work 'for the benefit of society at large' through 'ethical conduct, impeccable integrity, visionary endeavour, selfless public service and commitment to people and responsibilities' (2011: 7). Such a graduation ceremony address has become commonplace today and would fit with many English-speaking liberal universities and colleges whose mission statements articulate a common 'truth' of the postmodern age, where the grand ideas of social change have not only been replaced by more the pragmatic idea of 'civic engagement', but the 'ethical' is called 'conscious capitalism' and something akin to social entrepreneurship is viewed as the only realistic alternative to Margaret Thatcher's smug comment that 'There Is No Alternative' to neo-liberal capitalism. In such a context, we are told that the best we can hope for is to address structural inequality and structural violence through the promise of self-commodification. The irony of the power of such a purely capitalist ideology in the context of the mind-boggling centralisation of wealth is not lost on its critics, but its hegemony means that the spaces for what Edward Said (2002) names an oppositional and *critical* humanism have become increasingly constricted.

Thus the critique of humanities education – the question of its value, indeed worth – is framed by the global neo-liberal capitalist context. The increasing corporatisation, marketisation and instrumentalisation of higher education modelled on functional business and corporate needs, with university 'trustees' like boards of governors implicitly or explicitly measuring the value of education on quantitative assessment and corporate business models. The value of education, at least as it is marketed to and understood by students, is not a career but a market advantage, which in the language of human resources is nimble, flexible and technically proficient. The humanities offer little alternative to their decline; their value is reduced to a set of 'critical thinking' skills to enhance a pre-professional degree and digitalised humanities is proffered as the cutting edge.[1] Thus corporatisation of the university has a logic that continues to reduce all academic units to measurable quantifiable outputs. This management model sits alongside an increasing need to brand and market 'innovation', research and global relevance and to reproduce it at every level of the university corporation – from advertising (for example, how often the words 'excellent', 'outstanding' and 'innovation' appear in Rhodes University's vision and mission statement – see Rhodes University 2014) to teaching evaluations and long-distance education.[2]

In this context, how much is Frantz Fanon's critique of the colonised intellectual, schooled in the 'narcissistic dialogue' of the colonial universities, still valuable today? Fanon, the psychiatrist from Martinique who joined the Algerian Revolution, argued in *The Wretched of the Earth* that among this educated group, 'western values remain essential . . . and in the back of his mind st[ands] a sentinel on duty guarding the Greco-Roman pedestal' (1968: 46–7). In a sense, the sentinel is the humanities, which has for its basis the eternal belief – even among liberal critics and some Marxists – that the European metropole is the authentic heir of the Greco-Roman pedestal and, as such, is *the* standpoint for all human thought and the measure of all human development. Fanon's critique has often been repeated. Indeed, the critique of humanism is the standard fare of postcolonial studies, though often only discursively.[3]

Standing behind colonial humanism was the power of the colonial state, backed by the colonising regime. In purely political terms, the desire of many African nationalist parties during the anti-colonial struggle to take over the colonial state signalled the inevitable defeat of the liberation movement. In other words, access to the state (from the national to local level) literally became the monetary pay-off and thus, at the same time, a deadly game. The patronage and the corruption that such a politics engenders become difficult to miss.[4] Fanon makes this patently clear. Believing that the colonial nation-state – an expression of colonial power and its ideology, based on bourgeois property rights and mediated by religious and secular conceptions of Africans as subhuman – could be taken over and at best reformed, the nationalist parties made a fatal mistake. Paraphrasing Audre Lorde (2007: 112), the master's tools cannot be used, even if the master has left: 'They may allow us to temporarily beat him at his own game, but they will never enable us to bring about genuine change.' For Fanon, the mistake marks a dividing line between national liberation and nationalism, between the people and the nationalist elites. It is in this context that Fanon says we must leave Europe. But why?

More literal than Walter Benjamin's (1969: 256) argument that 'there is no document of civilisation that is not at the same time a document of barbarism', Fanon is talking about the traumatic reality created by systematic dehumanisation. Europe never stops talking of humanism, he says, even as it murders humans everywhere. Yet for him there is no purely theoretical answer; it is not a question of simply rejecting European thought, but rather rejecting its unconscious and uncritical reproductions. And thus, leaving Europe is to turn away from Eurocentrism, although not simply to reject all of European thought, and to turn over a new leaf that is anti-racist and practical. The true reality of the nation, the pauperisation inherited from colonial domination and reframed in the neo-colonial present, has to be rigorously criticised.

Rethinking the university

If we extend Fanon's critique to the postcolonial university, it is necessary to begin socially, to refocus our mandate towards the human, towards human kindness and dignity, towards human welfare and rehumanisation (Fanon 1968: 312, 314). What form might such humanistic reflection take? The remarkable 1 600-page, two-volume collection *Reclaiming the Human Sciences and Humanities through African Perspectives* (Lauer and Anyidoho 2012) has already gone some way towards addressing this question across the disciplines. The first chapter, Claude Ake's 'Social Science as Imperialism', written more than 30 years ago, remains timely and well worth rereading in the context of deontologising Africa and thinking about it as a site of epistemological resistance to the pervasive 'consultancy culture' of World Bank paradigms and funding sources that dominate research.

To return to Rhodes University's mission statement, what does 'proudly affirms its African identity' mean? It sounds like little more than a slogan from South African Airlines. 'Shifting the geography of reason' is also metaphorical, in the original sense of metaphor as transfer, and here the transfer bears the almost unconscious weight of Europe's racialised common sense and speaks directly to the problem of intellectuals and the inculcation of class and racial syndromes that concerned Fanon.[5] In South Africa, the university is an institution established to reproduce colonial ideology. Any critical politics of pedagogy and curriculum must also include its geography, its location and buildings, its accessibility, gates, barriers and dividing lines (literal and figurative) as well as its classrooms; challenging the very structures of the university (its disciplines, academic ranks, administration, exams, grades and daily culture, including all its social-spatial relations). Because colonialism is totalitarian, Fanon argues that it inhabits every relationship and every space and every institution. Thus the university as reproducer of reification has to be thoroughly reconsidered (and like the state) not simply taken over. Fanon argues that during the liberation struggle the university has to be cast aside and those who had benefited from a university education have to put this knowledge to use in the popular struggle. Knowledge and expertise not only benefits the struggle, but are produced in the critical evaluation of the struggle's needs.

But what happens after colonialism negotiates a withdrawal? Even where colonialism has been defeated and forced out, Fanon did not envision business returning to normal. Doctors and engineers, for example, become essential to benefit and build the new society and Fanon envisions them as socially committed professionals, which means working directly with liberated communities and thereby breaking with elitist syndromes learned in the university. Ethical conduct is based not on an external relationship or clientelism, but is a living and equal relationship. Such a notion of 'selfless public service' (Badat 2011) may seem far away from where we are today. I am not denying that such commitment does exist and that such work is being done. Indeed, in the interstices of the university, almost unintentional (from a strategic planning point of view) new spaces can open up, allowing critical thought and social engagement, yet these too often remain isolated, middle-class and gated spaces. How does a university education, aware of its privileges, foster the conditions for critically and socially engaged thinking to come about?

The post-apartheid university (a place that continues to rely on cheap custodial labour) implicitly reflects structural inequalities and, as far as it focuses on global relevance, also reflects policy paradigms and funding guidelines as the real or imagined global frame imposed on it.[6] I am not suggesting there is no room to manoeuvre, but to do so requires conscious counterhegemonic action, without which the university passively, if not actively, recreates global hierarchies on a local level. In other words, analyses of the nation often repeat the hierarchies of the geography of reason: poor communities, outsiders to the university, are subjected to research and researchers – whose goal is to provide a non-governmental organisation with a report or to publish an academic paper, often without even checking with the people who are 'researched', thereby repeating the (colonial) anthropological practice where poor people become simply reified and thus viewed as unthinking and inert objects of study. Thus, to be socially responsible, universities need to actively challenge the same class divisions from which they are produced and what Fanon called the 'intellectual alienation' (1967a: 224) it reproduces. There needs to be a constant return to the questions: what is the liberation struggle and what are its aims? These questions, often reduced to celebratory sound bites or anecdotes, require serious research and also popular engagement with what ordinary people want South Africa to be, which can lead to humanistic and inclusive, rather than technicist and elitist, discussions about the nation's geography, resources, ecology, land and, most of all, its people.[7] However, the post-apartheid university currently reflects South Africa's limited transition from apartheid. In some respects, despite the undeniable fact that the university reflects the partial deracialisation of apartheid spaces, it remains a middle-class space. The university continues to reproduce itself as an elite and often, at best, technicist space. In such a context, discussions of what Fanon called the reality of the nation, even those critical of corruption and delivery failures, are framed by a technicist idea of 'development' and 'service delivery' (see Pithouse 2011), which creates fundamental barriers between experts and communities of people in the townships and informal settlements. To make meaningful connections with people marginalised and peripheralised from political society is not at all easy and a commitment to social activism outside a funded research production frame is often seen as counterproductive to any research.

Where does the project of South African liberation stand twenty years into neo-liberal capitalism? Not only in terms of what Michael Watts calls the 'violent geographies of fast capitalism' (cited in Nixon 2011: 7), but also in its production of inequality expressed by gated communities and in the lived experience of the often wilfully unseen poor of the country, those who do not count, and are not meant to count; those subject both to the violence of the state and what Rob Nixon calls 'slow violence', not the spectacular violence of the media, but the long, slow violence over time and space. 'The long dyings', he writes, whose casualties are 'out of sync' with civil society (2011: 9).

In reality who are we?

Fanon (1968: 250) begins 'Colonial Wars and Mental Liberation' in *The Wretched of the Earth* with an existential evaluation: 'Because it is a systematic negation of the other person and a furious determination to deny the other person attributes of humanity, colonialism forces the people it dominates to ask themselves the question constantly, "In reality who am I?"'

This is a question that continues to be asked in post-apartheid South Africa, even if does not take this form, even if it is not always heard. But when heard, it can catch the imagination for a moment, upsetting the arrangements of the here and now, even when those arrangements have been heretofore absolutely unquestioned and taken for granted. The question is not simply an existential exercise that emerges out of a cloistered philosophy seminar, but out of what S'bu Zikode (2013) from the Durban shackdwellers' movement, Abahlali baseMjondolo, calls 'dark spaces', from the thinking of those who are not supposed to think for themselves. Hearing such questions from such spaces – where living is reduced to immediate animal needs, places of non-being and of non-existence – becomes an epistemological challenge. It is a challenge that can be dismissed, of course (as illegitimate, unruly and so on), but it speaks directly to the issue of a radical humanities. For example, in August 2013, in response to a continuing water crisis in the Makana Municipality, the vice chancellor of Rhodes University wrote an open letter to the mayor and other public figures, demanding that the crisis be addressed (Badat 2013). The letter underlined the importance of the university to the local economy, while drawing attention to the situation in the townships and informal settlements, where some people had been without water for months. Badat concluded: 'We feel we are being treated like second-class citizens, which is not acceptable in our hard fought for and won democracy. So we are now mobilising in defence of our constitutional rights as citizens.'

President Zuma's office immediately sent a team to assess the situation. But members of the Ethembeni informal settlement found this response profoundly unacceptable. Badat's open letter helped to create some media attention, opening up space for others outside to be heard. Thandeka Ndlovu pointed out in an interview in the *Sunday Times*: 'We've been here [in the informal settlement] since 1993 and our taps were installed in 2003, but there is hardly any water in them' (Skiti 2013). She continued with a philosophical question of profound import because it upset what is considered normal: 'Is it because they are better than us that Rhodes gets listened to?'

Asking the question of how equal are we in the eyes of the government criticises an emancipation limited to enfranchisement, but it also demands an answer. 'We are supposed to be living in a democratic country, a country of justice, a country where everyone should be treated [equally],' argues Bandile Mdlalose (2013), Abahlali baseMjondolo's former general secretary, and yet

> for the poor this country is a democratic prison. We are allowed to vote for our prison warders and managers but we must always remain in the prison. We must remain in silence when our shack settlements are illegally destroyed leaving us homeless. We must remain in silence when we are forcibly removed to transit camps that are only fit for animals but not for people. We must remain in silence when we are told to return to Lusikisiki or taken to human dumping grounds far outside the cities. We must remain in silence when we are threatened, beaten, shot and killed. The politicians think that when we refuse to be silent, and when we resist repression, they can silence us by throwing some meat at us. After all these years they think that we are dogs. We are not dogs. We are people. We will continue to rebel until we are treated as human beings.

While politicians see such questions as a threat, these questions at least require engagement from the university.[8] How can the university purport to teach values and include ethical practice without engaging with questions of human worth? How can we think something different, which serves the people, in Fanon's sense, and encourages spaces for intellectual exchanges, self-education and self-organisation that recognises thinking outside the ivory tower?

Towards radical humanities?

So far this questioning seems to have little to do with the humanities and one might wonder why it should since the birth of the humanities is connected with racism and colonialism. Indeed, the study of English literature as a subject in the curriculum was developed and tested in the colonies before it became part of the national curriculum in the metropole.[9] The development of the humanist disciplines in Britain could not be separated from the colonial project and, as Gauri Viswanathan (1989: 3) argues, the institutionalisation of literary education enabled 'the humanistic ideals of the enlightenment to coexist with and indeed even support education for social and political control'.[10] The 'rights of man' meant propertied white European men (see Trouillot (1995: 76).[11] The universalisms of the French Revolution of 1789, with the declaration of human liberty, fraternity and equality, would soon have to be silenced in response to the struggle for freedom in Saint-Domingue (Haiti). It was unthinkable that these revolutions had been fought on behalf of blacks (82).

If European civilisation and its best representatives, to quote Aimé Césaire (2000: 54), 'are responsible for colonial racism', how can the humanities possibly be exempt? Like Césaire, Fanon was critical of how the European conception of the human passed itself off as universal, the end-all and be-all of human knowledge. Behind its normalisation was an ethics based on the absolute violence of colonial racism. Enlightenment secularisation was intimately connected with the biologisation of what was considered human. The biologisation and dehumanisation of black people, developed alongside the systematic violence and mass extinction of the slave trade, continued as its enduring legacy. To repeat, if Europe's concept of humanism is intimately connected with racism, colonialism and the subjugation of others, who by definition are not human, where does this leave the humanities?

Radicality is about getting to the root of the problem and if the root is 'man', the problem is human liberation. This is why Fanon rejects Europe, but at the same time does not reject the project of human freedom. He is not interested in mimicry, but in finding a new element, one that is both excluded and embedded in the modern world (see Gilroy 1993). For Fanon, the damned of the earth are such an element. The problematic is how could such marginalised people play a creative, rather than simply reactive role in politics? In *The Wretched of the Earth*, Fanon argues that human consciousness is not simply a passive effect of material conditions, but is best understood through action and by action he means conscious activity. 'Let us decide not to imitate Europe,' Fanon (1968: 314) argues, because the project of human freedom depends on conscious action not reaction. 'Let us try to create the whole man,' he says, 'whom Europe has been *incapable* of bringing to triumphant birth' (313; emphasis added). Engaging with the best of its thought, Fanon concludes that Europe had failed in the task to realise the project of human freedom:

> All the elements of a solution to the great problems of humanity have, at different times, existed in European thought. But *the action of European men has not carried out* the mission which fell to them, and which consisted of bringing their whole weight violently to bear upon these elements, of modifying their nature, of changing them and finally bringing the problem of mankind to an infinitely higher plane (1968: 314; emphasis added).

Far from following European history, which would simply reinscribe the colonial project, it is a question, Fanon argues, of 'starting a new history, a history which will have regard to the sometimes prodigious theses Europe has put forward' (1968: 314; see also Hansen 2011). The new history would have regard for ideas of freedom and equality in as far as it includes everyone, 'the whole of humanity', he writes in *The Wretched of the Earth*, which 'Europe has been incapable of bringing to triumphant birth'. We need to create a new history, a new direction, which does not drag human beings towards mutilation.

Indeed, Fanon understood that bourgeois Europe was, in fact, built on 'stratifications, and bloodthirsty tensions . . . racial hatred, slavery, exploitations and . . . genocide' (1968: 315) from its beginnings. The French Revolution declared 'the rights of man' – freedom and equality as grounding universals – and the sans-culottes challenged the concreteness of those declarations in calls for economic and social equality, thereby questioning, at the very birth of bourgeois freedom, the real content of its humanism and infusing it instead with new radical (namely human, in the sense of the etymology of radical as going to the root of the problem) content; the same can be said of the Haitian Revolution (1791–1804) in the French colony of Saint-Domingue, which encouraged the French convention to abolish slavery. And yet bourgeois humanism would only go so far, making sure that there would be no 'rights of man' in the Caribbean. The Haitian Revolution was 'unthinkable' because it was unreasonable. It was unreasonable because it shifted the geography of reason and challenged the rigid racial ontological divide structuring being and nonbeing (see Gordon 1997: 29). The idea of including everyone was unthinkable; the idea of including everyone was unreasonable. It was unreasonable because blacks could not be imagined as fully reasoning and thus not fully human.[12] Michel-Rolph Trouillot (1995: 82) continues:

> *The events that shook up Saint-Domingue from 1791 to 1804 constituted a sequence for which not even the extreme political left in France or in England had a conceptual frame of reference.* They were 'unthinkable' facts in the framework of Western thought ... The Haitian Revolution was unthinkable in its times: it challenged the very framework within which proponents and opponents had examined race, colonialism and slavery in the Americas.

It was unthinkable within the 'the range of possible alternatives' (Trouillot 1995: 82). In other words, it was unthinkable in the context of abolitionism (which was gaining ground in England) because the revolution defied 'the terms under which the questions were phrased ... not only because it challenged slavery and racism but because of the way it did so' (82, 87).[13] Thus, Trouillot concludes: 'The Haitian Revolution was the ultimate test to the universalist pretensions of both the French and American revolutions ... And they both failed' (82, 88).

When Fanon says that all of humanity must be included, it is not simply a quantitative evaluation, following European history and 'carrying the torch that was already waiting for this historic change'

(Fanon 1967a: 134). Rather, it suggested a radical shift in thinking derived from action and the very form of revolt suggested by Trouillot (1995: 88): 'Not only was the revolution unthinkable ... it was also – to a large extent – unspoken among the slaves themselves. By this I mean that the revolution was not preceded or even accompanied by an explicit intellectual discourse.' But there is thinking, even if only '*at the limits of the thinkable*' (emphasis added), even if such movements from practice cannot be thought without developing new categories (see Fanon 1968: 316). And so, out of these revolts, new ideas can be formed: that thinking human needs and a society that could fulfil them is possible.

Thandeka Ndlovu's question about human worth articulated in the interview in the *Sunday Times* (mentioned above) as such is an expression of this movement from practice. Grounded in experience, she asks the most basic, but human of political questions, which thereby can open up new avenues for thought. This thinking is a source for a radical humanities, understanding that the struggle for human freedom is, as Said (2003: xxx) put it at the end of his life, 'long and often interrupted'.

Thinking the unthinkable in the present situation

Fanon and Steve Biko both went to medical school.[14] Both had a critical attitude towards their educations. Biko was critical of how higher education created elitist attitudes towards African culture and day-to-day and often hidden acts of resistance against apartheid. To challenge this elitism, the black consciousness South African Students' Organisation (SASO) created 'formation schools', with SASO students going to work with people in rural communities. Far from a community-service programme – though some believed it was about bringing consciousness to the masses – it became a programme of conscientisation of all the participants. Rick Turner, who had been schooled in existential philosophy and New Left Marxism of the 1960s in France, and who was then teaching politics at the University of Natal in Durban, also proffered a programme of conscientisation, challenging anti-apartheid white students' complicity with apartheid by working directly with the emerging black trade union movements.

Likewise, Fanon (1968) writes of anti-colonial intellectuals using their education against the very system that had educated them by putting it to work in 'the service of the people'. The work, argues Lewis Gordon, 'demands a critical, reflective relation to one's epistemic efforts ... premised upon recognition of the constant threat of bad faith' (1995: 18–19).

Returning to the question of a radical humanities, the issue of creating space begins with a negative: Gordon (2006: 4) reminds us that the term 'discipline originally meant "to educate" ... [but] the emergence of the disciplines has often led to the forgetting of their impetus in living human subjects', resulting in a kind of 'disciplinary decadence ... [and] the ontologising or reification of a discipline'. Thus, 'the disciplines' became a theodicy, 'a system complete on all levels of existence ... description ... and prescription ... of all there is, can and ought to be' (2000: 31). Standing in the way of the *human* being, theodicy stands in the way of any revolt against it. There seems no way out. Thinking with Fanon, Gordon adds, the others (namely the majority of people, the outsiders and pariahs who inhabit dark spaces) 'live the contradictions of this self-deception continually through attempting to live this theodicy in good faith'. It is these contradictions that offer an answer and become the work of the humanities. We could add in a Gramscian sense of the praxis of philosophy (Gramsci 1971: 405) that the radical humanities engage with these lived experiences of self-deception. The philosophy of praxis, Gramsci argues, is a 'consciousness full of contradictions', elevated 'to a principle of knowledge and therefore of action'. Ideas of freedom and equality are expressed in 'every stirring of the multitude'.

Struggles for freedom have enormous and radicalising effects on their participants, on society and on discourses of education. Not only are histories rediscovered and revised, but also historiographies are challenged and the unthinkable becomes thinkable. Local struggles are rewritten from below; new literatures, philosophies and cultures are celebrated and become part of works in progress with communities and people who had hitherto been considered outside or absent of culture, thought and history. But the conservatism of the disciplines and the 'academy' has often meant that the project of education's liberatory mission is soon on the back foot and the initial transformative character of new fields of study becomes professionalised and reified. The corporate work of 'disciplinary decadence' (Gordon 2006: 4) professionalises education, diverting it from the practical tasks of social justice. Fanon's existential commitment to radical humanism and concomitantly to structural change concerns his practice as a physician. In the penultimate chapter of *The Wretched of the Earth*, what he articulates as the 'important theoretical problem' is a typically humanistic one relating to self-study, self-reflection and self-criticism of one's 'epistemic efforts'. He writes: 'It is necessary at all times and in all places, to make explicit, to demystify, and to harry the insult to humanity that *exists in oneself*' (1968: 304; emphasis added). Fanon's thought expresses, in a sense, an optimism of the human will *qua* thinking subject, namely an optimism in the thinking of those objectified and dehumanised by the system. And there comes a time, he argues, when people wonder, was liberation worth it? Life seems to get more, not less, difficult. This is articulated in numerous ways on an almost daily basis in South Africa. Additionally, there is also the brutality that is becoming increasingly apparent, marked by the massacre of miners at Marikana in 2012, by the increasing number of political shootings (see Bruce 2013), ethnically organised violence and violence against women and children.

Fanon understood that the struggle for liberation also breeds pathologies, psychological disorders, traumas and stresses created by extreme situations, which can last a lifetime. One cannot help but notice the tragedy. This is especially apparent in *A Dying Colonialism*, which Fanon (1967c: 26) prefaces with a critique of the brutality of revolutionary violence: 'We condemn with pain in our hearts, those brothers who have flung themselves into revolutionary action with almost physiological brutality that centuries of oppression give rise to and feed.' The tragedy is concretised by a quote from a Swedish newspaper's report of a child of seven, marked by deep wounds made by steel wire that bound him and whose eyes were forced open while French soldiers raped and killed his sisters and parents. 'Does anyone think,' Fanon asks, 'that it is easy to make this child forget both the murder of his family and his enormous vengeance?'

Fanon forewarns further tragedy: 'No revolution can with finality, and without repercussion, make a clean sweep of well-nigh instinctive modes of behavior' (1967c: 113). Psychological health is intimately connected with what Fanon calls the second struggle for liberation.

According to his colleague and biographer, Alice Cherki (2006), Fanon considered working full time as a psychiatrist and also undergoing psychoanalysis after Algeria's independence. This did not mean he was going into private practice; it was a political commitment to work with those damaged during the struggle, but also a recognition of the slow violence of its aftermath and that psychotherapy had to be a continual process. Trauma, in other words, which is manifested in myriad ways, also offers a window into society and becoming human (in the most social and creative sense) and is a continual process. The trade union militant and anti-apartheid activist Ma (Emma) Mashinini expresses this in her autobiography, *Strikes Have Followed Me All My Life*. Physically and mentally traumatised from a six-month detention, much of it incommunicado, she found it hard to speak about her experiences. After visiting a psychotherapist, she writes: 'Psychotherapy for us Africans is something very new. I never thought that a normal person, not suffering from anything, would go for psychiatric treatment ... [but] I began to think that many people would benefit from treatment' (1991: 113).

If a strong woman such as Mashinini finds this trauma hard to speak about, what about the rest of society? Is this not part of the work of radical humanism? In other words, there is a magical thinking that after liberation everything will go back to normal and the mental scars of oppression will be miraculously lifted. In reality, there is no going back, but also what is called liberation is only a first step. Postcolonial society is a political society because liberation is unfinished. Thus, Fanon would not be surprised that now, twenty years after the formal end of apartheid, people continue to experience trauma and relive countless sufferings. The socio-economic inequality (mass unemployment and structural pauperisation, which are almost taken for granted) and political corruption that undergird trauma are intimately connected to why Fanon signals a second struggle for liberation. As he points out in *Black Skin, White Masks* (1967a), the mind is absolutely essential for imagining and realising a liberated society. Mashinini, who knows full well the importance of collective action, concludes her book, written well before the end of apartheid looked possible: 'May we once concentrate on the minds ... Let us think about a better society' (1991: 114).

It is not enough for education (as a liberal education claims) to be a transformative experiential process. Indeed, a notion of education as transformative is recognised in the rhetoric of individual entrepreneurship – education as the key to success, or 'where leaders learn' as the Rhodes University logo puts it, with its unquestioned assumptions. Rather, the goal of radical humanities is, while aware of limits imposed by social conditions, to help to create a social consciousness and a socialised individual – a social individual, rather than a selfish individual. Can this be realised without addressing the structural/spatial contradictions of the university inherited from apartheid? The university as elite space, a privileged place where philosophical questions are asked from the comfort of the bubble, is an expression of 'bad faith'. Gordon explains: 'Bad faith is the denial of sociality ... The irony of sociality is that although it is a world of others, it is a world of replaceable others ... they are not simply here or there; they are achieved' (2000: 78–9). Sociality, like Fanon's notion of a new humanity, includes everyone.

Fanon is not concerned with educating the educated elites, but with creating new spaces, where the worth of those countless people so often excluded and repeatedly told of their worthlessness is taken seriously. In this context, a radical humanities is about animating ideas and a new way of listening, helping in the creation of 'fully conscious men and women' (Fanon 1968: 197).

Notes

1. The decline includes the elite universities in the United States. See, for example, the front page article in *The New York Times*, 'Interest Fading in Humanities, Colleges Worry' (31 October 2013).
2. On 'excellence', see Readings's (1997) chapter 'The Idea of Excellence', which he likens to the emperor who has no clothes, arguing that excellence has no intellectual reference point. There are many books on the modern corporate, globalised university, but his remains essential and critical reading. The perfect

labour is thus a contingent faculty; precarious labour as some sociologists might argue, rehired on the basis of evaluation and need and fired at will. It is the reality in the United States and the United Kingdom and if South Africans desires the university to become like Harvard, it is the image of the future. See Bouquet and Nelson (2008).

3. Spivak's (2012) notion of 'strategic essentialism' is one pragmatic attempt to find practical space, that is, to oppose essentialist discourses, but strategically be open to essentialist formulations.
4. The daily news of corruption is normal in South Africa. It is taken for granted as the *raison d'être* of politics. For example, a protest at the Kennedy Road shack settlement in Durban against the mayor's delivery of meat parcels to the poor – we need a house not meat – was put down to the frustration of non-ANC residents who did not receive a goody bag by a police spokesperson (Naidoo and Khoza 2013).
5. 'Shifting the geography of reason' – see http://www.caribbeanphilosophical association.org/. I use 'unconscious' here since transference is an essential opening to the unconscious in Freud's own remarkable psychic shifting of the geography of reason. I use the term 'syndrome' following Fanon, ironically. See Fanon (1967b), 'North African Syndrome'.
6. 'Global relevance' understood as a gated space for global elite circulation and recognising the importance of 'Americanisation' (and corporatisation) to global relevance.
7. I am thinking of the 'ordinary' in a critical sense or, in Gramsci's terms, 'good sense', rather than common sense, simply reflecting ruling ideology. Fanon explains that such a discussion about the future must be profoundly dialectical, grounded in the reality of the people and aware of the 'discouragement which has been deeply rooted in people's minds' (1968: 193–4).
8. For example, see the African National Congress's response to housing protests in Durban, which they argue are organised by a 'third force' (Memela 2013).
9. See, for example, Johnson's *Shakespeare and South Africa* (1996).
10. I am reminded here of the continued importance of Said's remark in *Orientalism*, that the study of history, literature, and so on (the humanities) is political and that its political significance includes its 'pretended suprapolitical objectivity' (2003: 10). Therefore the first order of teaching humanities, he argues, is to emphasise that critique includes socio-economic and historical contextualisation.
11. Indeed, framed by colonial rule, the study of humanities took on a caste character, promoting the idea of Empire and natural hierarchy. This instrumentalist idea of education is thus not new, but deeply embedded in the humanities and became intimately connected with the ideological work of dehumanising African human beings.

12. Hegel's conception that Africans were children in *Philosophy of History* was simply the normative expression.
13. It is worth remembering that while reparations have not been paid for Britain's vast slave trade, the British Parliament did agree to pay compensation to slave owners in 1833.
14. Black doctors and black teachers were needed by the apartheid regime and by the 1970s these students became a key constituency in the Black Consciousness Movement.

References

Badat, S. 2011. 'Rhodes University 2011 Graduation Ceremonies Address'. 7–9 April. Rhodes University, Grahamstown.

———. 2013. 'An Open Letter to Makana from Rhodes University'. http://activateonline.co.za/an-open-letter-to-the-mayor-the-municipal-manager-and-the-makana-municipality-councillors-from-rhodes-university.

Benjamin, W. 1969. 'Theses on the Philosophy of History'. In *Illuminations*, 253–64. New York: Shocken.

Bouquet, M. and C. Nelson, eds. 2008. *How the University Works: Higher Education and the Low-Wage Nation*. New York: New York University Press.

Bruce, D. 2013. 'A Provincial Concern: Political Killing in South Africa'. *SA Crime Quarterly* 45 (September): 13–24.

Césaire, A. 2000. *Discourse on Colonialism*. New York: Monthly Review Press.

Cherki, A. 2006. *Fanon: A Portrait*. Ithaca: Cornell University Press.

Fanon, F. 1967a. *Black Skin, White Masks*. New York: Grove Press.

———. 1967b. *Toward the African Revolution*. New York: Grove Press.

———. 1967c. *A Dying Colonialism*. New York: Grove Press.

———. 1968. *The Wretched of the Earth*. New York: Grove Press.

Gilroy, P. 1993. *The Black Atlantic: Modernity and Double Consciousness*. Cambridge: Harvard University Press.

Gordon, L.R. 1995. *Fanon and the Crisis of European Man: An Essay on Philosophy and the Human Sciences*. New York: Routledge.

———. 1997. *Her Majesty's Other Children: Sketches of Racism from a Neocolonial Age*. Lanham: Rowman and Littlefield.

———. 2000. *Existentia Africana: Understanding Africana Existentialist Thought*. New York: Routledge.

———. 2006. *Disciplinary Decadence: Living Thought in Trying Times*. Boulder: Paradigm Publishers.

Gramsci, A. 1971. *Selections from the Prison Notebooks*. London: Lawrence and Wishart.

Hansen, W.H. 2011. 'Frantz Fanon and the European Intellectual Tradition'. In *Political Culture, Cultural Universals and the Crisis of Identity in Africa*, ed. R.T. M'Bayo, 25–52. Lewiston: Edwin Mellen Press.

Johnson, D. 1996. *Shakespeare and South Africa*. New York: Oxford University Press.

Lauer, H. and K. Anyidoho. 2012. *Reclaiming the Human Sciences and Humanities through African Perspectives*. Accra: Sub-Saharan Publishers.

Lorde, A. 2007. *Sister Outsider: Essays and Speeches*. New York: Crossing Press.

Mashinini, E. 1991. *Strikes Have Followed Me All My Life: A South African Autobiography*. New York: Routledge.

Mdlalose, B. 2013. 'The Housing List versus the Death List'. 30 October. http://abahlali.org/node/13034/.

Memela, M. 2013. 'Abahlali and Opposition a Third Force'. *The Witness*, 17 October. http://www.witness.co.za/index.php?showcontent&global%5B_id%5D=108219.

Naidoo, M. and A. Khoza. 2013. 'We Want Houses Not Meat'. 27 October. http://www.iol.co.za/news/politics/we-want-houses-not-meat-1.1598064#.VFjoxChQ0UU.

Nixon, R. 2011. *Slow Violence and the Environmentalism of the Poor*. Cambridge: Harvard University Press.

Pithouse, R. 2011. 'The Service Delivery Myth'. *The South African Civil Society Information Service*. 26 January. http://sacsis.org.za/site/article/610.1.

Readings, B. 1997. *The University in Ruins*. Cambridge: Harvard University Press.

Rhodes University. 2014. 'Vision and Mission Statement'. http://www.ru.ac.za/static/policies/vision_mission.html.

Said, E.W. 2002. *Reflection on Exile and Other Essays*. Cambridge: Harvard University Press.

———. 2003. *Orientalism*. New York: Vintage.

Skiti, S. 2013. 'Town up in Arms over Water Crisis'. http://www.timeslive.co.za/sundaytimes/2013/08/25/town-up-in-arms-over-water-crisis.

Spivak, G.C. 2012. *Outside in the Teaching Machine*. New York: Routledge.

Trouillot, M-R. 1995. *Silencing the Past: Power and the Production of History*. Boston: Beacon Press.

Viswanathan, G. 1989. *The Masks of Conquest: Literary Study and British Rule in India*. New York: Columbia University Press.

Zikode, S. 2013. 'Abahlali and "the Politic of Blood"'. Speech at Rhodes University, 13 October. http://www.youtube.com/watch?v=nA8hVAY5anY.

10

Towards a Decolonial Analytic Philosophy
Institutional Corruption and Epistemic Culture

PAUL C. TAYLOR

The idea of institutional culture has long featured prominently in the transformation agenda for higher education in South Africa. The connection is straightforward: the burden of transforming a society so that it no longer reflects apartheid-era values and structures is essentially bound up with the process of tearing up the roots that apartheid put down in the society's total way of life. Something like this will be true of all the institutions in South African society, but perhaps nowhere more crucially than in higher education.

Higher education is crucial in this regard because it represents a particularly difficult and important case for the transformation agenda. It is important for perhaps obvious reasons, not least because of the role that it plays in developing the next generation of citizens. If a post-apartheid society is to have the productive and responsible citizens essential to democratic life, tertiary institutions must interrupt the operation of apartheid-era habits and practices and help to cultivate new ones.

The importance of the tertiary sector makes the difficulty of the case all the more acute. Contemporary higher education institutions are often, as Clark Kerr (2001: 1–34) rightly remarked, 'multiversities', doing their work at the intersection of a variety of different and not obviously related purposes and stakeholder communities. This means that there may be not one, but *many* institutional cultures in need of transformation. Students (especially students in residence), administrators, academics and support staff are distinct groups with different 'underlying assumptions and practices' (Soudien et al. 2008: 11), though they also interact to constitute the culture of the institution as a whole. And these groups will take some of their cues from the wider cultures in which they participate – the cultures, say, of young people, workers, managers and scholars.

In the light of the complexity of the problem of institutional culture in higher education, it is important to approach it as clearly as possible. Studies of the problem often equate it with problems of management style or social inclusion at particular universities and they often distinguish these from questions of 'epistemological change', which is what happens when transformation efforts focus on issues such as the curriculum (Soudien et al. 2008: 36). The problems of inclusion and institutional climate are, of course, real problems. And the preference for these problems over questions of epistemology may simply be provisional, a way of acknowledging the limits of time and resources and of temporarily deferring an important task (as in Soudien et al. 2008). But the routinisation of this deferral effectively confines the idea of institutional culture to questions of inclusion. And this in turn threatens to obscure important connections to the transformation agenda.

In what follows I argue – or, better, I develop, because the basic point should need less argument than elaboration – that university cultures are shaped in part by the 'epistemic cultures' of the wider institutions that sustain professional scholarly communities (Knorr-Cetina 1999). Using a reading of the community that I know best, the one comprising Anglo-analytic professional philosophers, I argue that the cultures of communities such as this can inhibit the work of transformation, epistemological and otherwise, in ways that have little to do with the merits of the relevant arguments and evidence. And attending to the particular mode of inhibition allows us to read the problem of institutional culture in post-apartheid spaces – that is to say, in spaces including, *but not limited to* South Africa – as a problem of institutional *corruption* and to propose both theoretical and practical ameliorative interventions.

Philosophy as an institution

Most often, when we speak of higher education institutions we have in mind particular universities. We have in mind the specific constellation of objects and relations that answers to a name such as 'Rhodes University' or 'Pennsylvania State University'. However, the operations of certain broader institutions, not associated with specific universities, are also essential to higher education, as we know it now.

I am thinking, as noted above, of academic intellectual communities, which are crucial to the training, certification and ongoing edification of the people to whom we entrust the intellectual component of the higher education world. These communities are enduring, structured social forms and as such satisfy the definition of 'institution' that one finds in theoretical sociology. As Rom H. Harré (1979 cited in Miller 2012) puts it, an institution is 'an interlocking double-structure of persons-as-role-holders ... and of social practices involving both expressive and practical aims and outcomes'. In terms of this approach, universities exemplify the more concrete institutional form that we call the 'organisation', with its governing documents and duly certified leaders. But the constituent members of these organisations also belong to the more far-flung institutions that have grown up around particular modes of intellectual practice and disciplinary inquiry.

As indicated above, my concern here is with one of the many institutions that help to structure the practice of professional philosophy. These institutions are defined by the structured interactions of scholars, texts, ideas and practices within and across various geographic boundaries. Each has constituent professional organisations, such as the Philosophical Society of South Africa, the British Philosophical Association and the American Philosophical Association. I am interested in the institutions that link the geographically distinct spaces that this list of organisations partially marks out. This is the world created by the overlap of anglophone philosophy and analytic philosophy, the world that prefers Kripke and Kant to Ranciére and Husserl and that typically does its work in English. It is the world that venerates places such as Princeton, Cambridge and the University of Cape Town, prizes texts published by Oxford and Cambridge and sends students, scholars and ideas circulating relatively freely between the United Kingdom, the United States, Australia and South Africa.

What is interesting about this Anglo-analytic world for my purposes – or about the part of it with which I concern myself here, the part that dominates philosophy in the United States and South Africa – is that it is remarkably monochromatic and male. It is a little difficult to come by the numbers that would substantiate this claim, but for reasons that actually make the point. The main professional associations in these countries have mostly declined to prioritise the sort of data gathering that would make clear just how much the profession still resembles its apartheid-era incarnations. But some more and some less ad hoc efforts by various members of these communities have provided some information.

As of December 2011, the 50 philosophy departments in the United States regarded most highly by the influential *Leiter Reports* assigned only 22 per cent of their tenure-stream appointments to women. In 2009, only 30 per cent of the philosophy doctorates awarded by universities in the United States went to women (Van Camp 2011). In the same year, less than 5 per cent of the doctoral degrees went to 'traditionally under-represented' groups, with only 2.48 per cent going to African-Americans (APA 2013).

The numbers appear to be roughly similar in South Africa, though it is difficult to evaluate because the numbers are even more elusive. Based on an informal scan of the membership rolls of the Philosophical Society of South Africa, it appears that the organisation has 139 members. Around 100 of these are men and all but 15 or 20 seem to be white (Samantha Vice, personal communication, 10 October 2013).

If this were a different sort of piece of writing, I would do more with these numbers. For one thing, I would get more of them and sift through them more carefully. But that is work for someone more skilled in quantitative methods than I am. Another thing to do with these numbers, something more amenable to the gestures I can make, would be to frame them better, by noting some countervailing trends. For example, the American Philosophical Association has recently become serious about collecting demographic data and seems to be genuine about acting on the picture of the field that emerges. In addition, the United States numbers have got marginally better in recent years and in any case do not tell the whole story. Alongside the numbers, one has to consider, among other things, the increased diversity of the Association's governing bodies, beginning with the election of scholars racialised as black and brown (Kwame Anthony Appiah and Linda Martín Alcoff) to the presidency of the American Philosophical Association's eastern division. Similarly, the numbers in South Africa seem poised to improve as well, with concerted efforts to recruit black graduate students appearing to bear fruit.

These real and important developments aside, the quantifiable disparities still remain. And they remain despite explicit attempts, which have met with some success, to welcome and cultivate students and faculty from traditionally under-represented populations. In the light of the persistence of these disparities and my determination to give them a role here, it is important to be clear about the picture into which I mean to insert them.

I offer the numbers above simply to set the stage for a wider inquiry into the world that can produce and sustain such numbers. Legal and ethical sanctions in the United States and in South Africa now preclude the kind of explicit exclusions that would once have easily explained these disparities and I mention, for the sake of argument if nothing else, the sincerity of the efforts people in both spaces have made to overcome the legacies of past exclusions. In the light of these sanctions and efforts, why does philosophy still look the way it does? To introduce the term I use to mark the failure or absence of transformation: why does it remain to some degree *unreconstructed*?

There is no shortage of ways to answer this question. One might appeal to implicit bias at various points, from grading and advising students to hiring and promoting faculty staff. One might appeal to the workings of the stereotype threat, also at various points, beginning with student performance on the standardised exams that we use in the United States to sort our graduate applicant pools. One might suggest that Anglo-analytic philosophy's resolute indifference to the issues of the day tends not to recommend it to people – routinely, but of course not always or only from under-represented populations – for whom the issues of the day are issues of the utmost ethical and existential import. (This resolve has, thankfully, been weakening in recent years.) One might suggest finally, with Anita Allen-Castellito, that smart young people from these under-represented populations might rationally conclude that there are better and more lucrative things for them to do, especially if doing philosophy means not only losing a lawyer's income, but also taking on the burdens of navigating a space still in the early stages of transformation (Yancy 1998).

Others have made these arguments and I have on occasion joined them. But my aim in this chapter is to work towards another kind of answer, or to chart a somewhat different path to the answers. I mean to connect the question of philosophy's resistance to transformation to the discussions of institutional culture, but to do so, as I suggested above, without reducing those discussions to reflections on issues of management and human resources. The transformation of philosophy depends on an engagement with the epistemic cultures of its constitutive institutions. And one route to this engagement runs through the thought that the problem of institutional culture is, in at least some cases, a problem of institutional corruption.

Institutional corruption

I am encouraged to think that the idea of institutional corruption may be of use here because of the many interesting uses to which it has recently been put in other contexts. I am thinking in particular of the work generated and supported by the Edmond J. Safra Research Lab at Harvard University, in its multi-year project on institutional corruption, carried out under the direction of Lawrence Lessig. Following Lessig (2013: 2), institutional corruption exists where 'a systemic and strategic influence which is legal, or even currently ethical ... undermines [an] institution's effectiveness by diverting it from its purpose or weakening its ability to achieve its purpose'. There are conceptual puzzles to settle here, some of which grow out of worries about how to identify an institution's purpose. But indulging in these worries would take us too far afield of the main point of this chapter. The main outlines of the approach are clear enough and there are surely some clear cases of institutional purpose – institutions with governing documents, for example, or clear fiduciary duties.

The case for invoking the idea of specifically institutional corruption is to account for the gap between garden-variety individual corruption, on the one hand – exemplified most clearly by individual malfeasance – and, on the other hand, phenomena that seem similar, but lack the easy markers of individual misbehaviour. To use an example that is common in the literature: consider the difference between simply bribing a government official and making a campaign contribution. One is illegal, the other is not, but they can be structurally quite similar. And one of them, the latter, may be baked into the electoral system in such a way that the distortions it introduces into the processes of political deliberation become features instead of bugs. When this happens, as most would argue it has in the United States, the relevant institution can be said to have become institutionally corrupt, however lofty a ranking its home country enjoys in the world corruption indices.

Money-related conflicts of interest may give us the clearest cases of institutional corruption, but they are not the only ones. It is important to worry about the impact of industry funding on pharmaceutical research, for example, but researchers (academic researchers in particular) are often swayed by a variety of non-financial interests. Richard Saver (2012: 468), a scholar of interest conflicts in medical research, puts it this way:

> Investigators may be swayed by the prospects of enhanced reputation, professional honors and prestige, access to power, and general 'glory-seeking'. Social relationships formed in the research process, ranging from collegial to competitive to hierarchical, also create pressures and can compromise the actions of investigators, journal editors, peer reviewers, and other key stakeholders. In addition, intellectual or political predispositions can bias research conduct.

Saver's point generalises beyond scientific research and may in fact be more relevant in fields such as philosophy, where there is less opportunity for financial gain. In these spaces, it is important to account for the impact of relationships, reputation, esteem and 'intellectual predispositions' – call this last one 'ideology', in something like the sense developed by Marie Newhouse (2013). These factors may systematically divert truth-seeking or knowledge-producing institutions from their purposes. This is where the prospect of institutional corruption becomes most relevant to Anglo-analytic philosophy.

Philosophy corrupted

Applying this idea of corruption – as it has so far been formulated – to the institution of philosophy makes sense only if the institution has specific purposes. But what might those be? There are surely some obvious candidates. The practice of philosophy – not speaking yet of the institution or its constituent organisations – has long identified itself with such lofty goals as the pursuit of truth, or the plumbing of intellectual, ethical and existential depths that the exigencies of daily life, or of more specialised inquiry, cause us to overlook. Philosophy, in this sense, is concerned with what more than one introductory text refers to as the 'big questions' or, as I will put it here (to remain non-committal in choosing between wisdom, knowledge, truth and the rest), 'deep insight'.

The professional institution that claims to have this practice at its core embraces these purposes, while also embracing others. Professional philosophy *as an institution* has at least three purposes besides the time-honoured objectives of the practice. It aims (1) to produce a steady supply of people who can help students to learn to entertain the big questions – call these 'lecturers' and 'professors' and call this reproduction of the institution 'persistence'; (2) to expand and deepen the conversations and debates undertaken by professional students of the big questions – call this 'research' and (3) to help its practitioners, in particular its junior participants or students, to achieve more productive, harmonious or intelligent relationships with the conditions of their lives than they otherwise would – call this 'self-knowledge'.

If quests for deep insight, persistence, research and self-knowledge are among philosophy's purposes, philosophy in a state of institutional corruption would complicate its own pursuit of one or another of these goals. It might evade the ethical and existential questions that many people find particularly vexing. In this and other ways, it might deny itself access to populations of students who might become its next generation of advocates and practitioners. It might be less than helpful to the junior participants it does attract as they seek to orient themselves to the world of their experience. And it might do all these things even as its researchers burrow ever deeper and more inventively into the subjects they do take up.

My sense is that this is precisely the state in which Anglo-analytic philosophy finds itself. A systematic influence has undermined and still undermines the institution's ability to fulfil its purposes. The influence is mediated not by money, but by considerations of esteem, reputation, scholarly propriety and the like. These considerations operate in ways that are peculiar to the self-conceptions, modes of practice and ways of being – the elements of culture – that define the institution. And these cultural elements not only follow from philosophy's unreconstructed condition, but also block critical consideration of this condition.

One way to pursue this thought might be to consider the refrain that one commonly hears among practitioners of liberatory and critical modes of philosophy. Scholars of feminist and queer theory, critical race theory and so on have all seen or heard The Question: 'This is all very clever, but is it really philosophy?' People in other, more traditional fields also face this question, of course. But the policing effect of the question – and of its corollary assertion, 'That's not an interesting question', to which I will return – multiplies when the area under suspicion is marked by the stigma of gender or racial difference.

As with my gesture at demographic data above, there are richer stories to tell about The Question and complicated abstract frameworks that might be invoked in the telling. But I would like to take a different approach; I would like to consider the refusal of one of these frameworks and then consider how we might respond to this refusal.

Why 'postcolonial analytic philosophy' names an empty set

Postcolonialism is not a going concern in Anglo-analytic philosophy. This may not need demonstration, but a few words in the right direction might be useful. I started to think about combining, or juxtaposing, the analytic and the postcolonial around 2010, at which point, according to one authority, 'a spate of new work on empire in political theory and the history of political thought' had been ongoing for about a decade (Pitts 2010: 211). Up to that time, the journal *Philosophy and Public Affairs* had only one reference to anything postcolonial – in a footnote from an article in 2009. The article is fascinating and touches on the sorts of things that should interest anyone interested in postcoloniality. But the one reference to anything like postcoloniality as such is only a gesture at the idea that states in the contemporary overdeveloped world might have 'postcolonial duties'. The authors do not develop or define this locution (Ypi, Goodin and Barry 2009: 133, note 72).

The situation is even worse in the venerable and somewhat less resolutely analytic journal *Ethics* – the situation is worse, I should say, if one thinks this indifference to the postcolonial as such is a problem, a thought that I confess not to have demonstrated yet and that I do not entirely endorse. (I do, however, largely, or almost, endorse it. This will become clearer.) Going back as far as the thirties – a bit of overkill, to be sure, since the idea of the postcolonial did not take root even in the places where it has taken root until well after this – I can find only six proper references. All but one of these uses the term in passing, either to describe some specific place, such as Algeria after 1962, or 1954, or to refer generally to theorists who are concerned with such places, such as Frantz Fanon. The remaining article is Thomas McCarthy's (1992) long review essay of recent currents in anthropology, which could hardly avoid the idea. As in McCarthy's piece, some of these pieces are knowledgeable enough, which is to say that occurrences of 'postcolonial' and its cognate terms happen in passing not because of indifference or ignorance, but because they are not entirely germane to the subjects of the articles. Which goes to my point: one can imagine these authors, some of them, saying more about the postcolonial, but not really in this space. I take this to be the moral to draw from the fact that all of these references, without exception, appear in *book reviews*, that essential, but lightly regarded artefact in our professional world.

I conclude from this quick and dirty scan of the literature that postcoloniality is not on the agenda or even on the radar of Anglo-analytic philosophy, even among scholars concerned with subjects – such as global justice – that seem to point towards it. I will soon ask whether this is a bad thing and what to do about it. A first step in that direction, though, would be to say a little more about what this blind spot obscures.

Why 'postcolonial analytic philosophy' is an oxymoron

As I use the term, postcoloniality refers to a specific social condition and to a certain awareness of or orientation towards that condition, which has to do with the social and political challenges that face inhabitants of societies formerly locked into modern relations of colonial dependence. In the sense I have in mind, the United Kingdom and Jamaica are both postcolonial societies, though we tend to think of only one of these in that way; perhaps the way to credit this impulse is to say that both face postcolonial conditions, while only one has in the modern period *been* a colony and had to build its present and future in the aftermath of having been colonised.

So to refine further: there are postcolonial societies in the sense of having to organise themselves 'after colonialism'. However, as we know from various forms of contemporary theoretical discourse, 'post' talk is not only about temporal succession. It is also about repudiation, what Appiah (1993: 156) calls 'space-clearing'. It is, more than this, about temporality, about the intertwining of nostalgia and ambivalence that comes with leaving a known past, however problematic, for a future that remains shaped by that past, but is in some ways opposed to it. The 'post' in 'postmodernism' and 'postcolonialism' and the like should put us in mind of 'posterity' and of all the anxieties and tensions that come with the thought of parents acting over time to shape – but not determine – their children and the world their children will inhabit.

In one sense, postcoloniality has to do with a set of specifiable conditions, but in another sense it has to do with specific tensions that come with these conditions – that come, more precisely, with the burdens of being shaped by just these conditions, while nevertheless seeking distance from them. A moment's reflection on some of these tensions will flesh out the idea a bit more. Modern colonialism was an intersectional project: it mobilised, manipulated, shaped and reshaped the meanings and practices that we refer to in ideas such as race, gender, sexuality, nation and class. You will know where I am headed with this: the various supremacist projects that helped to make the world we now inhabit – privileging white, propertied, heterosexual men over other kinds of people, robustly imagined as other *kinds* – were intimately bound up with the projects of turning places such as Cambodia and Haiti into resources for colonial metropoles.

With all of this in place, we can say that postcolonial *theory* or scholarship has to do with a specific critical project. Postcolonial theory endeavours to highlight the continued influence of colonial meanings and institutions on our practices, beginning with and never straying far from the practices of self-making. Modern colonialism was, as much as it was anything else, a complex regime for the formation of certain kinds of human subjects. It was a system for making selves that would imagine the world and their places in it in ways that fit with, say, the co-optation of white labour with visions of imperial adventure and with the expropriation of black, brown and red land and labour through arguments about savagery and civilisation. Postcolonial theory means to excavate and uproot the workings of this regime.

There are a variety of reasons for the failure of postcolonial thought to take root in Anglo-analytic philosophy. At least some are narrowly sociological and have to do with a philosophical aversion to the poststructuralist resources and thinkers that inform and advance the postcolonial project. This quarrel between philosophy and English, or between analytic and continental thought, bears on my subject here, but is sufficiently distant that I want to bracket it and move on.

The more interesting factor, I think, is that postcolonial thought is precisely about something that Anglo-analytic philosophy typically refuses itself: self-excavation or, more precisely, critical self-excavation in relation to historical and cultural conditions. Remember that the roots of the analytic project lie in thinking about thinking as such, as mediated by thoughts about language as such, both considered in abstraction from their cultural contexts. Analysis gained traction as a professional project in the 1950s and, in the United States at least, has the run of a tertiary sector that was being cleared of Marxists and socialists. It was a virtue of the project – a professional virtue, contributing to the professional viability of its practitioners in a Cold War context – that it had nothing in particular to say about culture or society, or nothing in particular to say about particular cultures or societies.

Some of this institution's architects and participants, such as Bertrand Russell and Michael Dummett, have had a great deal to say about what we might broadly call 'social ethics' and have acted on the convictions expressed by their words. But these convictions have been at best tenuously related to their considered philosophical convictions, as Russell happily noted. And even when someone in the grip of the project did have something philosophical to say – someone such as John Rawls, say – the wider world of political and cultural conflict somehow dropped out of the account. (This, like the demographic profile of the profession, has changed recently, in ways I will come to.) Rawls, of course, had principled philosophical reasons for virtually ignoring the anti-colonial, anti-racist and other struggles that were raging precisely when *A Theory of Justice* appeared. These reasons have since come in for serious scrutiny and lie beyond the scope of my argument here. My point is that the forces, the cultural forces, that rendered the subjects of non-ideal theory invisible also support unreconstructed philosophy's contentment with itself and its imperviousness to the burdens of transformation.

The point so far is that the same aversion to self-critique and self-excavation (along with other aversions) that blocks philosophy's access to postcolonial modes of reflection has also supported a refusal of metaphilosophical curiosity and sociological sophistication about the profession's place in the postwar, post-apartheid landscape of the higher education enterprise. And this refusal has sustained a kind of indifference to the ways in which the features of this landscape were reflected in the institution itself.

What this means in theory: phenomena such as white supremacy, patriarchy and Empire have typically not been cognisable philosophical problems. As a result, the problems and questions that these concepts mark have not been seen as philosophically 'interesting' – *even when they bear on the profession's prospects for carrying out its mission*. And philosophical interest in this sense, as an attribute of a scholar's research programme, a department's teaching mission or a student's intellectual aspirations, is the key to career advancement, scholarly reputation and the other non-material factors that influence the behaviour of participants in the institution of philosophy.

What this means in practice: it was until recently fairly easy for people, even those of goodwill, to conclude that good philosophy just is good philosophy; that there is no interesting, philosophically interesting, story to tell about how the arbiters of good philosophy came to be the arbiters; that the homogeneity of the population of good philosophers is a function of factors beyond the purview of philosophical reflection, as are the free choices of students, the asymmetric capacities of various populations or the blameworthy but, again, philosophically uninteresting failure of political authorities to do the right things. In this unreconstructed philosophic idyll, sensitivity to some of the more pressing 'big questions' of a post-apartheid world marks a *lack of intellectual seriousness*. The fact that engaging with these questions is a key to connecting with a great many potential stakeholders and to achieving anything worth calling 'deep insight' in a world that makes Mandelas and Obamas and that also makes them necessary, is, in the idyll, beside the point.

Towards a decolonial analytic philosophy

I am happy to be able to end this chapter on an optimistic note. Anglo-analytic philosophers now feel more acutely than ever before that participation in an unreconstructed institution is untenable. Even better, we now have access to resources that enable a degree of self-excavation and self-criticism. The emergence of behaviour science now enables people with aversions to discourse theory and ideology critique to tell richer stories than they otherwise could have about structured, behind-the-scenes influences on individual choices. (These get framed in terms of implicit biases and cognitive heuristics, instead of in terms of ideology and discourse. But no matter, at least for now.) The availability of these richer stories creates space for a virtue-theoretic engagement with the burdens of habituation and cultivating character. And these resources get taken up into the ethical common sense of the post-apartheid world, which holds that virtue, in individuals and institutions, is incompatible with invidious discrimination on grounds of social identity.

The combination of implicit bias research, virtue theory and ambient egalitarianism does not, however, add up to a postcolonial analytic philosophy. For one thing, the language of the postcolonial is, as noted above, intimately bound up with specific theoretical resources and professional circuits of debate and exchange. This fact need not be grounds for the sort of aversion that philosophers typically feel, but it should have some bearing on the choice of vocabularies in framing a project that has yet to take root in the field. For another thing, and as important decolonial theorists have pointed out, postcolonial theory has its own aversions and heuristics to uproot, beginning, one might argue, with its insistence on Eurocentric resources and frames (Mignolo 2007).

Instead of taking on the baggage that comes with the invocation of postcoloniality as such, I think of the encouraging developments discussed above in relation to the idea of decoloniality. And in deference to the distance still yawning between these encouraging developments and a truly decolonial mode of inquiry, I think of them not as contributions to an Anglo-analytic mode of decoloniality, but as halting first steps *towards* a decolonial approach. (This moves me to think further of a 'philosophy after apartheid', but working out that formulation is beyond the scope of this chapter.) This movement has at least three manifestations on the ground. First, subfields such as race theory, Latino/a philosophy, Africana philosophy and feminist theory have become increasingly prominent and professionally viable. Second, the demographic data seems to be trending in the right directions. And third, participants in the institution continue to make the right noises about change and inclusion and they continue to support initiatives that are consistent with these noises.

These changes are encouraging, but they are not enough. In order for Anglo-analytic philosophy to deal responsibly with the burdens of transformation, it must deepen its resources for self-critique. It must, first of all, take on board some account of post-racialism as a racial project. That is, it must take account of the way ambient anti-racism and well-meaning tolerance of new and 'radical' subfields can coexist with, and even hasten, the reformulation of racial privilege and hierarchy. I mean this as a point about professional practice, not as a point about the possible space for theory. The institution of philosophy must reckon with the compatibility of tolerance and ghettoisation. It is not enough to cultivate students and scholars from under-represented populations or to create space in which individuals are free to do oppositional and liberatory work. This is not enough, more clearly, if the recruitment and the space-making are simply layered over old assumptions about what is philosophically interesting and who is philosophically adept, assumptions that will then play themselves out in judgements about hiring, promotion, publication and so on. Toleration is not identical to transformation.

Real transformation must settle deep into the practices and habits that define the institution. I mean to have suggested that this cultural transformation must begin, for institutions organised around particular modes of inquiry, with the practices that define an epistemic culture: with the processes of professional legitimation and subject-formation that tacitly, and sometimes explicitly, define what counts as good, interesting philosophy. Reconstruction in this sphere will help make room, has already to some degree *made* room, for participants from under-represented populations, for whom certain 'uninteresting' questions are often more grave than any others.

Consolidating and building on this partial transformation will somewhat paradoxically require a turn back to the more obvious considerations of institutional culture change. Philosophy will have to take more seriously the burdens of empirical self-inventory — gathering and analysing data on its participants and practices — and carefully tending the opportunity structures and entry pathways that define its constituent organisations. Transforming our pictures of the profession and the states of affairs our pictures mean to capture is an essential step towards reconstructing the habits that organise our structures of professional legitimation. And this is, in turn, essential to making philosophy a resource for transforming the tertiary sector as a whole, rather than a hindrance.

The project of transforming higher education in South Africa (and elsewhere) requires that we attend to the burdens of transforming the epistemic cultures that converge on our universities. To be sure, each university has its own peculiar challenges, challenges that derive from, among other things, its distinctive history, mission and community. But each university also connects, through its faculty if in no other way, to the wider institutional contexts of specific disciplinary formations. As inhabitants of both contexts, as citizens of university communities and of scholarly communities, the members of the professoriate must take the lead on this phase of the transformation agenda.

References

APA (American Philosophical Association). 2013. 'Minorities in Philosophy'. https://c.ymcdn.com/sites/apaonline.site-ym.com/resource/resmgr/Data_on_Profession/Minorities_in_Philosophy.pdf.

Appiah, K.A. 1993. *In My Father's House*. New York: Oxford University Press.

Harré, R.H. 1979. *Social Being: A Theory for Social Psychology*. Oxford: Blackwell.

Kerr, C. 2001. 'The Idea of a Multiversity'. In *The Uses of the University*, fifth edition, 1–34. Cambridge: Harvard University Press.

Knorr-Cetina, K. 1999. *Epistemic Cultures: How the Sciences Make Knowledge*. Cambridge: Harvard University Press.

Lessig, L. 2013. 'Foreword: "Institutional Corruption" Defined'. In *Institutional Corruption and Pharmaceutical Policy*, ed. M. Rodwin, special issue of *Journal of Law, Medicine and Ethics* 14 (3): 2–4.

McCarthy, T. 1992. 'Doing the Right Thing in Cross-Cultural Representation'. *Ethics* 102 (3): 635–49.

Mignolo, W. 2007. 'DELINKING: The Rhetoric of Modernity, the Logic of Coloniality and the Grammar of De-Coloniality'. *Cultural Studies* 21 (2): 449–514.

Miller, S. 2012. 'Social Institutions'. In *The Stanford Encyclopedia of Philosophy*, ed. E.N. Zalta. http://plato.stanford.edu/archives/fall2012/entries/social-institutions/.

Newhouse, M. 2013. 'Ideology, Partisanship, and Scholarship'. *The High Horse*, 8 April. http://thinktankproject.net/?p=277.

Pitts, J. 2010. 'Political Theory of Empire and Imperialism'. *Annual Review of Political Science* 13: 211–35.

Saver, R.S. 2012. 'Is it Really All about the Money? Reconsidering Non-Financial Interests in Medical Research'. *Journal of Law, Medicine and Ethics* 40 (3): 467–81. http://onlinelibrary.wiley.com/doi/10.1111/j.1748-720X.2012.00679.x/abstract.

Soudien, C., W. Michaels, S. Mthembi-Mahanyele, M. Nkomo, G. Nyanda, N. Nyoka, S. Seepe, O. Shisana and C. Villa-Vicencio. 2008. 'Report of the Ministerial Committee on Transformation and Social Cohesion and the

Elimination of Discrimination in Public Higher Education Institutions'. http://us-cdn.creamer media.co.za/assets/articles/attachments/21831_racism report.pdf.

Van Camp, J. 2011. 'Tenured/Tenure-Track Faculty Women at 98 U.S. Doctoral Programs in Philosophy'. http://www.csulb.edu/~jvancamp/doctoral_2004.html.

Yancy, G. 1998. 'Anita Allen'. In *African American Philosophers: 17 Conversations*, ed. G. Yancy, 163–228. New York: Routledge.

Ypi, L., R.E. Goodin and C. Barry. 2009. 'Associative Duties, Global Justice, and the Colonies'. *Philosophy & Public Affairs* 37: 103–35.

11

The Countercultural University

PEDRO TABENSKY

Each generation must out of relative obscurity discover its mission, fulfil it, or betray it (Fanon 1963: 205).

As they place consumer civilization in judgment, denounce bureaucracies of all types, demand the transformation of the universities (changing the rigid nature of the teacher-student relationship and placing that relationship within the context of reality), propose the transformation of reality itself so that universities can be renewed, attack old orders and established institutions in the attempt to affirm human beings as the Subjects of decision, all these movements reflect the style of our age ... (Freire 2005: 43).

The teacher talks about reality as if it were motionless, static, compartmentalized, and predictable. Or else he expounds on a topic completely alien to the existential experience of the students. His task is to 'fill' the students with the contents of his narration – contents which are detached from reality, disconnected from the totality that engendered them and could give them significance. Words are emptied of their concreteness and become a hollow, alienated, and alienating verbosity (Freire 2005: 71).

In this chapter, I defend the view that we cannot ignore the influence that our modes of being and perceiving have on our epistemic projects, meaning that academics should be critically responsive to these modes. Our modes of being and perceiving are a function of the worlds we happen to be born into, our 'thrownness' as Martin Heidegger (1996) puts it, so they are not something that can typically be changed by a simple act of will. Changes in consciousness, in modes of being and perceiving, are far harder to achieve than changes in specific epistemic commitments that are relatively unattached to our passions, to what moves us at our core. Our modes of being and perceiving are recalcitrant and hence changes can only be expected to happen slowly and effective changes in our modes of being and perceiving – changes in consciousness – cannot typically come about in the relatively straightforward way that beliefs tend to change in the light of evidence.[1] This means that we need to think about understanding in a way that is not purely intellectual and academics need to adjust their work as researchers and teachers in the light of this insight about the nature of understanding.

The cultures of our academic institutions and of our specific disciplines are deeply informed by the broader social spaces in which we happen to be immersed. Academic cultures, which are expressive of broader historical cultures, play a key role in shaping and, typically, safeguarding the modes of being and perceiving that define academic work at any given moment, be it in the Scholastic period where church and thought were inseparable or in the contemporary era where students are increasingly becoming clients and academics are there to serve the interests of the market. The style and content of our academic pursuits is shaped by the prevailing mood of the times, so understanding – arguably the key aim of any academic project – cannot be divorced from critical engagement with the prevailing cultures that shape the style and content of our academic pursuits. So the academic project is inseparably an ethical and political project, in addition to being an epistemic one, inseparably an intellectual project and one that aims to transform – within the bounds of possibility – our modes of being and perceiving, our consciousnesses.

In this chapter I describe two pedagogical experiments I have been involved in, in order to illustrate one way in which the shift could occur between solely teaching students to engage critically with specific subject matters so that they become 'experts' and engaging with students in a way that will help to bring about changes in consciousness.

I agree in broad outline with Paulo Freire's (2005) conception of the relationship between thought and action. To understand, properly speaking, is to orient oneself towards the totality of existence in a virtuous manner, that is, with properly formed ways of being and perceiving. In this respect, the ancient idea of academic work, of philosophy more specifically, is closer to being correct than is the contemporary highly professionalised idea where knowledge is separated, indeed alienated, from an orientation towards the totality of existence. For the ancients, intellectual work was an inseparable part of the wider project of living virtuously, living an integrated life, where thought, affect and behaviour are in harmony with one another. This is what it meant to live virtuously and a philosopher was understood to be a lover of virtue, of *phronesis* rather than merely *sophia* (of virtue generally, rather than merely intellectual virtue).

Typically, academic institutions function as replicators of the status quo, but they need not and more often than not should not function in this way – certainly not exclusively. And, given the substantial epistemic role played by our modes of being and perceiving, it is the epistemic responsibility of academics to think about their academic projects as inseparable from the project of helping to build a virtuous academic culture, a culture that guides the formation of appropriate modes of being and perceiving. To work to foster such things is often, dare I say typically, to work against that grain, to promote a countercultural academic environment. This approach to the academic project is missing from the global university, as well as from the South African university.

Because the academic project is so intimately tied up with our modes of being and perceiving, it follows that the academic project must be understood as a leadership project, where academics aim through their work – and particularly through their teaching – not merely to transmit the facts and to teach students to think critically within the boundaries set by a given ethos – a given collective mode of being and perceiving – but also to refine and transform their modes of being and perceiving, their total orientation towards reality in a way that promotes virtuous living. To transform this is to have an influence on how students act, but also to play a significant role in the formation of what could be characterised as their navigational apparatus, their way of orienting themselves in social (and natural) reality, their modes of being and perceiving.

Modes of being and perceiving

One thing that flows from previous contributions to this volume, although the matter is not for the most part explicitly discussed, is that understanding cannot be reduced to intellectual understanding; more specifically, understanding within certain fields is, to a significant extent, a function of our modes of being and perceiving, our largely inherited ways of being and perceiving. To put things in slightly different terms: understanding requires critical engagement with the consciousness of the times. Our consciousness is historical.

Let me illustrate my concerns with an example from my own discipline, philosophy. A standard implicit misconception pervasive among analytic philosophers (as opposed to postcolonial theorists or feminists as Paul Taylor argues in Chapter 10 of this collection) is the idea that we ideally ought to aim at what I would call epistemic puritanism. By this I mean the view that our grasp of reality should and, indeed, ideally could be quite independent of the historical contingencies or structural social conditions that form our ways of being and perceiving.

As mentioned above – and this is a central theme of his *Being and Nothingness* – Heidegger argues that we are thrown into this world or, similarly, as Hans-Georg Gadamer (2006) discusses – a central theme of his *Truth and Method* – prejudice is the starting point for any understanding, the total worldview that is a condition for the possibility of all thinking. By 'prejudice' he means something more positive than the standard understanding of the concept; he means something like prejudgement.[2] Prejudice is the background for all understanding such that, without it, understanding would be impossible, which is to say that any attempt at understanding is grounded in prejudice. This background delimits the sphere of inquiry and determines the character and style of the epistemic agent and the products of her/his intellectual work.[3]

That this is so is evidenced by the facts that history has a logic, that worldviews unfold in time in ways, I should add, that are never under the control of specific agents (history is permanently doing its work, but the direction of its unfolding is always a mystery, which helps to explain why it can only be told retrospectively). One central reason why history unfolds, rather than merely changes, is that the ground (the domain of prejudice) is the starting point of all historical movement. Any future state is a reaction to a previous one, which explains why the logic in question is the logic of the narrative. In post-apartheid South Africa, the specific problems we are dealing with in South Africa today are precisely post-apartheid problems. South Africans from all groups – including their institutions – are grounded in post-apartheid ways of being and perceiving.

Our mission, in any given epoch, as Franz Fanon (1963: 205) puts it in one of the epigraphs at the beginning of this chapter, is to respond to our historical legacy, to understand it and work against the grain or act as custodians – depending on the character of the specific legacy – of the world into which we have been thrown. To imagine, as epistemic puritans do, that we can somehow grasp the world ahistorically, is a myth. Our quests for understanding always have a historically contingent starting point from which all possible pursuits of understanding must commence. This is why we are 'thrown' into the world. We cannot escape the current of history, although we can influence its course.

Prejudice is inescapable precisely because all action, thought and affect is grounded in it, but there are more or less salutary approaches that we can have towards the backdrop. One aspect of the more salutary approach is that which defines the genuinely critical and virtuous epistemic agent. This individual engages critically with the backdrop and, by doing so, is able to contribute to changing what needs to be changed. Any proper attempt to understand is a transformative act. Understanding must be differentiated from mere clarification. To come to understand, properly to understand, involves making a contribution to shifting our ways of being and perceiving. In this regard, understanding involves the collective work of creating the conditions for changes in consciousness. Properly to work to increase our understanding involves working to shift the ground of understanding, rather than merely working uncritically within a tradition (as analytic philosophy largely did during apartheid and not only there) (see McCumber 2001).

Gadamer (2006) understood all too well that there are severe limits to how much this backdrop – the epochal ethos, one could say – can be changed by solitary individuals. Genuine shifts take time and are always and necessarily a collective effort. But the collective effort is not typically managed from a controlling centre, nor does it typically involve high levels of co-ordination. It is always unclear what ideas will stick and what it is that will loosen recalcitrant schemes. No one, in this regard, can be expected to be the author of history, which is not to say that individuals cannot influence history's unfolding. The problem is that individuals have only limited influence over the trajectory of the future, which is one important reason, from an epistemic point of view, why individuals should be working together to help to bring about the right sorts of cultures. It is because history has this level of autonomy that we can say that the future takes care of itself. History, one could say, writes itself. This points to the stark limits of human agency. There is no way of knowing in advance what course history will take and any changes require a collective effort and, because we never know the precise direction of the unfolding, hope.

But it is not issues of agency or hope that I wish to focus on in this chapter. Rather, what the above all-too-brief discussion aims to do in the context of the purpose of this collection is to highlight the shortcomings of the misguided idea of epistemic puritanism. But why am I concerned in the context of a collection on institutional culture in universities with taking issue with epistemic puritanism? I want to show to what extent our epistemic wonderings are grounded in prejudice, in our ways of being and perceiving, ways of being and perceiving that all people, by virtue of the fact that they are thinking creatures, have inherited and to what extent this legacy plays a central role in determining the content and character of our academic concerns. So, if academics are genuinely committed to understanding, they must understand understanding in non-puritanical terms and this non-puritanical understanding calls for a way of understanding the academic project that is sensitive to the influence of our specific socio-historical conditions. These conditions are the ground upon which universities rest and so, if we are genuinely committed to understanding, we must work to understand the constraints imposed on us by our institutional cultures. We must be genuinely committed to understanding the constraints that our modes of being and perceiving place on academic production. To understand, in this sense, cannot be separated from genuine engagement with the cultures that inform our academic practice. Such separation would be a clear sign that we are not taking our academic work seriously, or that we are failing properly to understand it.[4]

Institutional cultures matter a great deal, for they are a function of our collective modes of being and perceiving and strongly influence our modes of being and perceiving, our modes of understanding, our sensibilities and interests, our styles of being. Institutional cultures, one could say, frame our specific concerns, delimit them and set the terms of the debates that we chose to engage in, or regulate the distinctive character of the debates. And specific institutional cultures cannot be understood in isolation from a 'total way of life' (an ethos), to borrow from Taylor's contribution to this collection. Specific institutional cultures are expressive of these total ways.

Teaching: Two pedagogical experiments

In this section, I focus on teaching and on how to transform it in the light of the above understanding of understanding. I discuss two particular interventions that I have been involved in at Rhodes University and show to what extent academics need to rethink our pedagogical practices in a way that will help to make universities into consciousness-transforming places.

In Chapter 10 of this volume, Taylor argues: 'If quests for deep insight, persistence, research and self-knowledge are among philosophy's purposes, philosophy in a state of institutional corruption would complicate its own pursuit of one or another of these goals.' Clearly this comment applies to academic work generally and not merely to philosophy. If academics more generally aim, as they should, to further understand their roles as teachers, they need to be cognisant of the modes of being and perceiving that mark out their student body as inhabitants of a given ethos. We need to complicate the way in which we interact with our students if we are genuinely committed to fostering an ethos of 'deep insight, persistence, research and self-knowledge'.

Proper understanding was, to the ancients, a virtuous orientation towards the world, a virtuous mode of being and perceiving. This is something that was lost with the advent of the specialisation of intellectual production. With the movement towards specialisation, understanding was severed from its existential moorings and the expert took the place of the wise. One cannot deny the importance of specialisation, but one must also acknowledge its very negative aspect: the tendency to privilege disembodied modes of understanding in the academy. This privileging is not a necessary offshoot of specialisation – although it fits comfortably with it – so there is room for revision within a framework that privileges specialisation.

One thing that points to deep problems in the contemporary global academic project – and South Africa is no exception – is that increasingly universities are being understood by students as instruments for 'success', where success is measured narrowly in terms of wealth and social standing. The value of understanding is increasingly seen as instrumental to these self-serving aims. This is not to suggest that universities are, for the most part, responsible for actively promoting the ethos from which these approaches to studying flow, but universities are certainly not doing enough to combat it and hence they are complicit in the production of self-serving greed. The contemporary global university is operating principally as a caretaker of prevailing cultures, prevailing styles of being and perceiving. Students (and certainly they are not alone) are the mouthpieces of their times and if academics genuinely value 'deep insight, persistence, research and self-knowledge', they must challenge this passive relationship to our shared ethos, our shared styles of being.

Our typical students are not holding these views primarily because they are intellectually committed to them. They hold them because their modes of being and perceiving have been distorted by the problematic ethos that defines our times. Understanding, as discussed above, cannot merely be understood as an intellectual activity. Rather, more generally, to understand is to pursue virtue, the right sorts of habits of intellect and character (from which ways of being and perceiving flow), so education ought to be understood as virtue education. This contrasts markedly with the almost complete focus on disciplinary expertise. But it does not amount to a rejection of expertise. Instead, this approach acknowledges that expertise is always embedded in an ethos that needs to be understood and engaged with if we are genuinely committed to disciplinary excellence.

Teaching accounting ethics

I have set out my general concerns above. Now I move on to show one way in which universities could come to operate as countercultural institutions – challenging the ethos that defines their modes of being – rather than being the caretakers of the status quo. In the next section, I discuss another way that flows from the first.

As mentioned above, understanding hangs on understanding how individual epistemic undertakings are rooted in 'total ways of life'. Because what we are dealing with here are modes of being and perceiving – which flow not so much from intellectual commitment as from relatively recalcitrant habits of being and perceiving – relevant interventions must be of the sort that can help to transform such habits. Habits, as the ancients, most famously Plato and Aristotle, taught us, cannot be changed by argument or discussion alone, or at least not for the most part. We need to be able to change the soil upon which understanding grows. Thus, we need to radically rethink some of our pedagogical practices so that they come to have an impact on aspects of the mind that are not, for the most part, changed by the standard lecture/tutorial format – aspects pertaining to modes of being and perceiving.

The results of the accounting ethics courses that I taught were not as good as I would have liked, but what I did there set the ball in motion for a far more promising intervention that I am currently piloting and that I discuss in the next section. It was clear to me from the outset that the aims of teaching ethics to accounting students cannot be the same as those that guide the standard approach to teaching ethics to philosophy students. Rather than promoting theoretical expertise of the different ethical theories available in the literature, the aim guiding the teaching of accounting ethics was to encourage accounting students to be ethical, rather than simply to become acquainted with ethical theories. It was also clear to me that standard approaches to teaching accounting ethics could not work. What students are missing is not so much the capacity to recognise right from wrong. The point is rather that their ethical commitments are being short-circuited by other concerns that float in the air of the times and that form our modes of being and perceiving. The aim of a course such as accounting ethics was to show students how to be ethical, how to live an ethical life, to help to transform their modes of being and perceiving so that they can act genuinely as effective and properly motivated agents of change.

This largely involves showing students to what extent being ethical actually matters to them, from their own point of view. Aristotle rightly thought that one can only show people how to be ethical – virtuous, to be more precise – if they are to some extent already there. The point is to show students how most (or merely more) fully to be ethical by showing them, as seen below, to what extent being ethical matters to them personally. And, perhaps, in this context the word 'teach' is inadequate, which is why I have surreptitiously moved from 'teach' to 'show'. A better description would perhaps be to create the conditions where students experience an ethical conversion, where the idea of a conversion is understood as a reorientation of what is known by them at some level all along. The aim should be, following mystical traditions to some extent, a kind of enlightenment.

The point of accounting ethics is to encourage ethical behaviour in the accounting profession, rather than simply to get students to become knowledgeable about ethical theories. For this reason, I began my accounting ethics courses by asking students to write their eulogies. I informed students what a eulogy is, but I did not tell them what the point of the exercise was, for that would increase the chances of getting students to tell me what they thought I wanted to hear. The results were expected, but interesting nevertheless, especially because of what the exercise showed students. I wanted to surprise them, to get them indirectly to tell me the extent to which they already thought that ethics is central to their lives. Almost all students who did the exercise – irrespective of class, race or cultural background – wrote pretty much the same eulogy. Other academics (who took over the course from me) asked students to do the same exercise and the results were much the same. I estimate that 300–400 students were asked to do the exercise and, with the exception of no more than a handful, all of them claimed to want to be remembered as ethical human beings who made a difference to the lives of others and, if perchance they mentioned wealth, it was almost always thought of as an instrument for helping others.

These results are particularly interesting given that, it is fair to assume, most students who choose to study accounting do so not because they are passionate about the discipline – although many claim to enjoy the challenges – or because they are committed to social change, but because they are strongly motivated by the prospect of affluent lifestyles.

What I think this exercise shows is to what extent we share a common understanding of what matters most in life. Eulogies are meant to be celebrations of the lives of the departed, highlighting the features, actual or perceived, that the author of the eulogy thinks are most praiseworthy and that show that the life of the deceased was a worthwhile one in the eyes of all those whose opinions are taken to be correct by the author. A eulogy expresses what is taken to have mattered most to the deceased and, centrally, what matters most to those present at the funeral. It expresses a shared understanding of what matters most. The eulogy exercise illustrates not only, broadly speaking, that there is a shared ethic, but it also shows that what makes life praiseworthy is primarily its ethical dimension.

So, how do we reconcile what originally motivates the typical accounting student to study accounting with what they express in their eulogies? This is the question that guided the course and a general account of student attitudes is worth noting. Some students, a minority, responded very positively to the exercise and started to reconsider the commitments that contradict those expressed in their eulogies. Other students, probably most, experienced the reconciliation efforts as a personal threat and became hostile. Why did they become so? It is reasonable to surmise that this was because two incompatible domains of value were sitting side by side in their minds and I was encouraging them to recognise the incompatibility and to experience a kind of conversion that would have put a dent in their aspirational ambitions. This would, in all likelihood, mean giving up their deeply held desires for wealth and status and pursuing a far more uncertain path that would be consistent with their own stated priorities. A successful accounting ethics course would function to show students that when it comes to choosing life paths, considered risk-taking is typically worthwhile.

I do not think the course succeeded in achieving its aims because I do not think an isolated course in what is, in all other senses, a mainstream accounting curriculum – a curriculum deeply expressive of the market-driven status quo – can really challenge students' modes of being and perceiving. At some level, I knew this all along, but it became increasingly clear to me that the aims simply could not be achieved without substantial curricular change, something the accounting profession generally, and certainly the Department of Accounting at Rhodes University, is not ready to embark on – in part because of the tight control that the governing body of the profession, the South African Institute of Chartered Accountants, has on curricular issues.

But, notwithstanding the problems, the insights drawn from the eulogy case are, I think, important. What it shows is that we share a common ethic, which at some level, we hold to be of deep importance, but other things get in the way of living in accordance with our own deeply held primary commitments. This, I surmise, is one locale where an ethos – say, the contemporary global ethos that flows to a significant extent from neo-classical economics – can do its nasty work. It splits us and, by doing so, it allows for the possibility of ethically mediocre or deeply pernicious behaviour and, by motivating a split, it warps the mind.

The aim of the course was to show students to what extent the ethical life is where one is all there with oneself, in addition to being the life that, all things considered, the great majority of us, in our more reflective moments, would wish to live. The ethical life is one where intellect, affect and behaviour are in harmony. This insight is as old as philosophy. In this sense, the ethical life is the life that is integrated, the life of integrity.

This fact about our ethical-psychological lives is, I think, important for our purposes because it makes the task easier for the educator to show to what extent it is always deeply disadvantageous to be unethical. Not only is unethical living bad because it is unethical, but it is also bad because it involves bad faith (self-deceit), born out of a breakdown of integrity.

It is arguable that there may be circumstances in which bad faith is warranted – not in the sense that someone in bad faith could justify her/his bad faith, but in the sense that an outsider could interpret a pattern of behaviour as being in bad faith, but still recognise that this is the best state for someone to be in given the circumstances – and I am sympathetic to this view. But nobody could justify being in bad faith to her/himself; nobody could possibly willingly be in that state, for we are unable knowingly to hold a falsehood, for to have a belief is to hold that belief to be true.

Existential conversations: Leadership, virtue and the academic project

To reiterate something mentioned above, the virtuous life is a life of integrity, a life where thought, affect and behaviour harmonise with each other. This insight, which draws its inspiration from my experiences with accounting students as well as from Plato and Aristotle, is what led me to think of a more ambitious intervention that is currently being piloted at the Allan Gray Centre for Leadership Ethics, based at the Department of Philosophy at Rhodes University. The aim is that what is now a pilot will become a university-wide intervention that will potentially help to turn Rhodes University into a countercultural university. If this project is successful at Rhodes, it could potentially be exported to other institutions of higher learning.

I named the pilot project 'Existential Conversations'. I recruited around twenty student volunteers who were involved in this experiment throughout 2013. There were two groups and each group met for one two-hour session per week during term times. Many of the students who formed part of these groups were student leaders in one form or another and one aim of the conversations was to reflect upon how the students could better take up this role. Another aim of the conversations was to show students – by creating opportunities for them to discover things through guided introspection – the central role that integrity plays in their own lives. Existential conversations are meant to show students how central ethical living is to their lives from their own point of view. Among other things, I describe the eulogy case and we discuss many issues ranging from discrimination, corruption and career choices to the purpose of life, all in order to show how it is that integrity, or its lack, function in our own lives in a concrete and deeply personal way.

Following Freire's lead, I position myself as a facilitator of a learning process, rather than as an 'expert'. Many examples are brought to the table, including the cases of Nazi criminals, such as Franz Stangl and Adolf Eichmann, and professional cyclist Lance Armstrong's epic fall from grace, in addition to race politics on campus in Grahamstown (where Rhodes University is located) and nationally. We discuss how it is that everyday psychological defences operate to allow individuals such as Stangl, Eichmann and Armstrong to convince themselves that their own unjustifiable behaviour is justifiable, thus showing how bad faith (and ignorance) can have a deleterious effect on integrity. The focus on the ethico-psychological make-up of these individuals reveals how banal evil can be, helping to support the thesis most famously associated with Hannah Arendt (2006).

We also discuss benchmark social psychological experiments, such as the classic and controversial Milgram experiment, the Stanford prison experiment and the Good Samaritan experiment (see Zimbardo 2008).[5] These three experiments, and others, help to show to what extent commonplace human tendencies can lead us to act corruptly.[6] We also, for instance, discuss a piece by Amélie Rorty (2001), which shows how psychological mechanisms can operate to buy us solace at the price of integrity. Someone, for instance, who is professionally ambitious, could hide the fact from herself that her success has come at an extremely high ethical price. Often, if not always, those who commit the most ghastly acts imaginable fancy themselves to be moral crusaders. This can only happen because we have the ability to hide the obvious from ourselves when the price of an epiphany is high in the economy of the psyche. The above cases help to show the central role that integrity plays in our lives and they also help us to see to what extent maintaining and perfecting integrity is hard work. And, centrally, to what extent it is deeply worthwhile, even if laborious work.

There are abstract and concrete ways of understanding appropriate action. Existential conversations are meant to show to what extent the ethical is something that should be of concern to students in a very concrete and deeply intimate way. That said, I do not think enough has been done yet to bring about ethical conversions among most participants. One thing that was missing from the existential conversations was concrete action. Again, following insights that are as old as the field of ethics, to be ethical requires developing appropriate habits, that is, virtues. For the most part, habits are only acquired through practice. So, concrete action must complement the existential conversations. In 2014, the conversations are being complemented with specific practical interventions on campus and beyond. This is not the place to speak in detail about the programme, but it is worth highlighting that participants themselves are playing an active role in developing these activities.

Notwithstanding the shortcomings, there is plenty of anecdotal evidence that strongly suggests that the conversations were extremely effective in achieving the envisaged goals. I got a clear sense towards the end of 2014 that students were taking significantly greater responsibility for their own lives and their studies than they were prior to engaging in the conversations. They had started to consider ways in which what was discussed could be supplemented with concrete action.

One of the things that surprised me the most was the extent to which conversation participants started to take the lead, started to take possession of the space offered to them by the existential conversations and started quite spontaneously to think together about ways of improving what we had been doing throughout the year. In short, participants are starting to understand the importance of integrity and how integrity is inseparable from concrete action flowing from understanding.

A central aim of the existential conversations is to reflect upon and improve participants' abilities as leaders who are able caringly, effectively and in an informed manner to act for the sake of betterment. There is evidence to suggest that this aim was, at least to some extent, achieved. However, what is becoming increasingly clear through the process of conducting these conversations is that leadership qualities are best fostered indirectly. Clearly, given what has been discussed above, another way of characterising what was done in the existential conversations is to say that they aimed at promoting effective ethical agency, which is a predominant way of speaking about leadership in the literature, although the specific phrase is mine. The exponential growth in writings about leadership is a response to the urgent need to promote leadership that is both effective and ethical.[7] The same activities that foster effective epistemic agents are likely to also foster effective leaders.

Conclusion

If we understand, as many contributors to this collection do, that institutional cultures ground and are grounded in ways of being and perceiving, the academic project should be reconsidered. Academics should not simply be concerned with whatever disciplinary interests happen to capture their fancy, a pervasive tendency in the academy globally. Rather, they should also be concerned with how our ways of being and perceiving influence our interests and concerns and the character of our academic work. Minimally, the academic project is about increasing our understandings of reality, so academics need to be more concerned than they currently are with the existential background that informs academic work. This is as true in the humanities as it is in the natural sciences.[8]

Some could argue that academics cannot typically be expected to be concerned with ideological underpinnings, with the modes of being and perceiving that underlie their specific concerns, which are expressive of ideological commitments. They might argue that they are specialists and time and capacity for analysing such things is not available to all or even to most. I sympathise with this concern, but at the same time one needs to acknowledge to what extent the academic project is impoverished by dubious ideological underpinnings. So it is the responsibility of the academic community as a whole to make sure that their work is not distorted, that specific concerns are not informed by perverse modes of being and perceiving. The fact that it may seem that I am being too demanding on individual academics seems to underscore the extent to which academics should understand themselves as members of a community of thinkers, rather than as solitary travellers.

One widely held view, particularly but certainly not exclusively among those belonging to disciplines concerned primarily with reified universals, is that universities are static institutions, rather than historically contingent ones that are informed by the ideologies of the day, ideologies which are, in many ways, corrupt and have a distorting influence on academic work. This puts them in a particularly bad place to work for change and makes them susceptible to the negative influences that pervasive institutional cultures have on the academic project, institutional cultures that are largely a response to the ethos that defines a given time and place. The failure to see the impact that cultures have on academic work flows, in part, from an individualistic conception of the academic project, which in turn is informed by a naive understanding of human autonomy. The prototypical academic, at least in the humanities and social sciences, is seen in the eyes of those I am concerned to critique, as a solitary wonderer unaffected by climatic conditions. The prototypical figure may be slightly different in the applied natural sciences where teamwork is often the norm, but in this case the picture is that of a team of researchers unencumbered by historically contingent modes of being and perceiving.

Feminists and postcolonial theorists have been speaking about distortions in ways of being and perceiving for decades and, agreeing with Taylor's contribution to this volume, we need to pay very close attention to our disciplinary blind spots. We need to wonder, for instance, why it is that mainstream philosophy in South Africa, particularly but not exclusively during apartheid, was so single-mindedly focused on reified topics that rarely spoke to the surrounding horrors (this is arguably largely still the case, but it must also be said that there are important signs of change). Taylor tells us part of the story. And we could also appeal to the Eurocentrism and, relatedly, the difficulty that so many white South African have in recognising black people as fully human, so their concerns and perspectives, as can be expected, are at best uninteresting to them (see Minesh Dass's contribution to this volume, Chapter 4, for an eloquent and subtle characterisation of how this sort of blindness operates).

One feature that concerns me about ideology-blindness (or partial blindness) – blindness to the role our modes of being and perceiving play – is the effect that it has on the student population of my university and, more generally, of universities globally. Although my ideology-blind colleagues fail properly to see themselves as a product of their time and place and, particularly, to understand to what extent their research agendas are formed by contingencies that typically operate below the radar, they tend to have less difficulty identifying such distortions among the student population (expressed, I suggest, in the pervasive instrumentalist approach to learning, which in turn is an expression of a materialistic, status-driven and hedonistic consumer society).

That said, even ideology-insensitive academics tend to grasp – even if only imperfectly – the deleterious effect that the so-called publish-or-perish culture has had on the academic project. Despite this (largely imperfect) recognition, academics have bought into this with a vengeance, partly because academic survival hangs on it, partly because academics are often even more concerned with prestige than with understanding and partly because of the significant monetary incentives that towing the line of the times brings with it. Academics, as well as students, are deeply influenced by the ethos of our times and many tend to fail to grasp fully to what extent our agendas are set by the air of the times.

Bruce Janz, in this volume (Chapter 13), speaks of the corporatisation and bureaucratisation of the university. Lewis Gordon and Nigel Gibson, also in this volume (Chapters 8 and 9), speak of the neo-liberal university and largely agree with Janz's assessment, but possibly not with his recommendations. These authors, and all other authors in this collection, acknowledge that institutional cultures, however nebulous, often affect the academic project negatively in very deep ways.

The academic project, understood as a project aimed at increasing our understandings of the world, cannot be understood independently of understanding our ways of being and perceiving. We can either passively interpret reality through the ideological lenses we all have, or we can actively and critically engage with these lenses in order properly to understand our areas of concern and thus increase our understandings of the specific domains of inquiry that are nested in these ideological spaces. If I am right to understand the academic project in this way, both in terms of its teaching and research dimensions, then it follows that our standard practices must be re-evaluated. I further suggest that to critically engage in this way is also to aim to integrate the different aspect of our lives in such a way that we can be said, properly speaking, to be all there with ourselves. This is what it takes to be genuinely oriented towards the project of understanding. To be oriented in this way, I have suggested, is to be oriented towards the ethical, that is, to be oriented towards a mode of being and perceiving that is integrated and whole, where bad faith (and ignorance) have been significantly reduced. In order properly to be engaged in the project of understanding, we must be oriented, in the old Platonic fashion, but without metaphysical distractions, towards goodness.

I should add that this embodied directedness towards goodness – an orientation that includes thought, affect and behaviour – is what Plato thought was the mark of a genuine leader. I endorse this conception. Genuine academic work involves engaging not merely with narrow academic interests, but also with the space within which these interests are formed, to aim to improve our modes of being and perceiving so that we can liberate ourselves from subterfuge and act in ways that flow from understanding and influence understanding in a positive way. To do this is to act as world-transformers, as leaders who play a distinctive role in changing things for the better.

Notes
1. Some beliefs, such as racist beliefs, typically do not change as easily as more dispassionate beliefs, beliefs not accompanied by highly charged affective states. Generally, those beliefs that are most closely tied up with our modes of being and perceiving will tend to be more recalcitrant than others and to resist the subversive power of evidence.

2. For a helpful discussion on Gadamer's notion of prejudice, see Malpas, Arnswald and Kertscher (2002).
3. I should mention that the issues being discussed here are also central to Marxism, poststructuralism and feminism and to postcolonial and critical race theory.
4. I take up the issues I am currently dealing with here, but in a very different way, in Tabensky (2014).
5. Stanley Milgram's experiment, conducted in 1961 at Yale University, shows the extent to which people are influenced by figures of authority, even in high-stake situations where human life is potentially at risk. Most participants, despite their ethical commitments, were willing to administer what they thought were potentially lethal electric shocks to an actor pretending to be plugged into a device capable of administering such shocks because of the power exerted by the authority of a man pretending to be a scientist who was putting pressure on them to do as he commanded for the sake of completing an experiment, which the subjects believed was about memory and learning. The Stanford prison experiment, conducted by by Philip Zimbardo in 1971, shows the extent to which situational factors can influence behaviour in an extreme way. Stanford University students were placed in a mock prison situation. Some of them were asked to play the role of guards and others of prisoners. In the space of a few days, the experiment had to be called off. Prisoners were experiencing severe distress and guards – perfectly normal university students – were becoming increasingly more sadistic, showing the extent to which the roles that they were playing, even though they knew all along that they were enacting a prison situation, rather than actually being in one, can have a deep impact on behaviour. Finally, in 1973 Darley and Batson conducted the Good Samaritan experiment with the participation of Princeton University seminarians, which shows the extent to which being in a rush to achieve a particular goal can adversely impact the helping behaviour of people, even in the case of highly ethical individuals. The rush factor can trump our ability to act in accordance with our own deeply held ethical commitments.
6. I should mention that experiments such as these, particularly the Stanford Prison Experiment, have been used as evidence against virtue ethics. This critique of virtue ethics is known as the situationist critique. I disagree with this critique, although I do think virtue ethics needs to be revised in light of situationism. For a defence of virtue ethics against situationism, see Tabensky (2013).
7. For a brief summary of the literature, see Ciulla (2013).
8. For a groundbreaking study on how what I am arguing here applies to the natural sciences, see Kuhn (1962).

References

Arendt, H. [1963] 2006. *Eichmann in Jerusalem: A Report on the Banality of Evil*. London: Penguin Classics.
Ciulla, J.B. 2013. 'Leadership Ethics'. In *The International Encyclopaedia of Ethics*, ed. H. LaFollette, 2979–85. London: Wiley-Blackwell.
Fanon, F. 1963. *The Wretched of the Earth*. New York: Grove Press.
Freire P. [1970] 2005. *Pedagogy of the Oppressed*. New York: Continuum.
Gadamer, H.G. [1975] 2006. *Truth and Method*. London: Continuum.
Heidegger, M. [1927] 1996. *Being and Time: A Translaton of* Sein und Zeit. Albany: State University of New York Press.
Kuhn, T.S. 1962. *The Structure of Scientific Revolutions*. Chicago: University of Chicago Press.
Malpas, J., U. Arnswald and J. Kertscher. 2002. *Gadamer's Century: Essays in Honour of Hans-Georg Gadamer*. Cambridge: MIT Press.
McCumber, J. 2001. *Time in the Ditch: American Philosophy in the McCarthy Era*. Evanston: Northwestern University Press.
Rorty, A.O. 2001. 'How to Harden Your Heart'. In *The Many Faces of Evil*, ed. A.O. Rorty, 282–7. London: Routledge.
Tabensky, P.A. 2013. 'Virtue Ethics for Skin-Bags: An Ethics of Love for Vulnerable Creatures'. In *The Handbook of Virtue Ethics*, ed. S. van Hooft, 461–71. Durham: Acumen.
———. 2014. 'The Ethical Function of Research and Teaching'. *Educational Philosophy and Theory* 46 (1): 100–11.
Zimbardo, P. 2008. *The Lucifer Effect: Understanding How Good People Turn Evil*. New York: Random House.

12

Africanising Institutional Culture
What is Possible and Plausible

THADDEUS METZ

One central facet of the ideal of transformation in South African higher education institutions, at least for many self-described adherents to the idea, is Africanisation. Africanisation, in part, involves admitting African and other black students into academic programmes and hiring non-white staff as academics and managers. However, I do not investigate such practices in this chapter, since they have received more critical analysis and are, by and large, less contested than the other major part of Africanisation that I explore here. This concerns not which people are included in higher education institutions, but which norms are accepted. In this chapter, I expound and evaluate arguments for the view that higher education institutions have been and still are under a moral obligation to Africanise their institutional culture.

There is as yet in the literature no comprehensive discussion of whether, why and how to Africanise norms in higher education, that is, no thorough account of the different forms it could take, the competing rationales for them or their strengths and weaknesses. Such a critical and philosophical analysis, in the light of a wide array of written works, is what I aim to provide in this chapter. I distinguish between stronger and weaker versions of Africanisation with regard to institutional culture and maintain that there is good reason to think that a moderate version should have been adopted by South African higher education institutions and should still be.

I begin by describing what those who explicitly advocate 'Africanisation' with regard to academic norms have meant by that term, focusing principally on writings by those based in South Africa, including Catherine Odora Hoppers, Malegapuru William Makgoba,

Gessler Muxe Nkondo, Mogobe B. Ramose, Sipho Seepe and Lesiba Joe Teffo. Next, I analytically distinguish and critically evaluate five fundamental rationales that these and other thinkers have proffered for such Africanisation. In catchwords, these defences of Africanisation appeal to: relativism, democracy, redress, civilisation and identity. I point out that the sort of Africanisation that might be appropriate for South Africa differs radically, depending on which of the above rationales is accepted. I also provide a philosophical discussion of the major rationales, critically investigating which ones are most plausible and concluding that some arguments for a moderate sort of Africanisation merit serious consideration. Specifically, redress, civilisation and identity together make a strong philosophical case for much more Africanisation of institutional culture than there has been up to now, and they have implications for related epistemological and pedagogical struggles elsewhere in the world, particularly in the global South.[1] I conclude by summarising the findings and raising some practical implications of the most promising rationales for making academic norms substantially African, noting that the issue of how best to deal with prima facie impediments to Africanisation, such as academic freedom, merit thorough discussion in another forum.

What Africanisation is or, rather, could have been

I explain in some detail what I mean by 'Africanisation', as it, much like its companion term 'transformation', has been used in a variety of ways in South Africa. One reason for thoroughly exploring the sense of the term is to obtain clarity about what precisely is at stake in debates about Africanising institutional culture, but another is to dispatch objections based on an implausible understanding of what it involves.

Two misconstruals of 'Africanisation'

There are more than a few who would immediately reject Africanisation of institutional culture as an ideal, not on the grounds of liberalism, the usual suspect, but rather because it allegedly suggests essentialism. For some, to use labels such as 'African', 'sub-Saharan' and the like implies a fixed and distinct nature (see, for example, Parker 2003; Horsthemke and Enslin 2005). According to this perspective, when one calls something 'African', one is presuming that it is unique to, and exhaustive of, that part of the world, whereas it invariably not only can be found elsewhere, but also will not be found everywhere in it. Beyond the descriptive error, proponents of this line of thinking usually have a normative concern in the background, that in calling something 'African' one is cramping the ability of those who live in Africa to choose their own ways of life.

I have routinely encountered these concerns from social scientists in southern Africa, but I submit that my colleagues are the ones who are misusing language, not those who speak of things 'African'. When English-speakers use geographical terms to characterise a property, they usually do not mean to posit something fixed and distinct. The combination of markets, science and constitutionalism is, throughout the world, routinely called 'Western', although one will find it in Japan and Australasia and will fail to find it in the Amazon jungle. Baseball is 'American', though the Cubans are well known for playing it and many Americans prefer to play and watch football, basketball or even ice hockey. Maple trees and syrup are 'Canadian', but you will find plenty in Vermont and none, I presume, in the northernmost parts of Canada near the Arctic.

These and a myriad other examples suggest that geographical terms are aptly used when they pick out a feature that is *salient* in the given region and common there in a way it tends not to be elsewhere. Hence to call something 'African' or 'sub-Saharan' implies neither that it is to be found only below the Sahara Desert nor that it is everywhere in that locale. Again, these terms signify merely that something is particularly frequent or noticeable there, not necessarily something that is single or static (see Suttner 2010: 523–8). At least that is the way I elect to use them.

Hence, to speak of 'Africanisation' does not commit me to looking for features that make such a transformation utterly distinct from Western, Chinese or any other cultural processes. Instead, it means pointing out features characteristic of indigenous black peoples below the Sahara Desert and of contemporary ways of life that are or could be informed by their worldviews and practices. Africanisation might not be appropriate or justified, but not, I maintain, because it is essentially essentialist, even if a few of its self-described adherents appear to be (such as, it appears, Teffo 2000).

Here is another reason for rejecting Africanisation that can be dismissed for being grounded on a misconstrual of what it involves. Some might suggest that Africanisation is not to be taken seriously because it would require taking on *all* salient facets of sub-Saharan education or culture more generally, which would undercut any plausible understanding of a university's mission in a constitutional democracy. For example, it does appear that much of traditional African education was gendered, with the content of what one could learn determined by one's sex (Adeyinka and Ndwapi 2002: 19; Adeyemi and Adeyinka 2003: 432). Since a sexist approach to education has no place in contemporary South African society, Africanisation is to be rejected straightaway, so this sort of objection goes.[2]

However, virtually no self-described proponent of 'Africanisation' believes that it would require patently unjust or otherwise undesirable features of sub-Saharan ways of life to be taken on board. Instead, implicit in the discussion is usually the presumption that only the (particularly) attractive features of African norms should be adopted.

There are, of course, some Africanists who have romantic understandings of what pre-colonial life was like and who contend that anything undesirable was an importation from other cultures and so is not really African. The bad breath of ideology wafts from such people's mouths. However, one need not buy into the 'Myth of Merrie Africa' in order to make prima facie sense of Africanisation; one can grant that there have been both good and bad features of indigenous African ways of life and then maintain that what is meant by 'Africanisation' is a process of transforming universities so that more of the good ones are exhibited.

Africanising people versus Africanising place

I noted above that in using 'Africanisation' I am not fundamentally interested in the racial and ethnic composition of students and staff. As is well known, Africanisation, and transformation more broadly, have in practice over the past twenty years largely been reduced to the admissions, hirings and promotions of black people. One plausible explanation of why this reduction has occurred has been the government's drive for public accountability and university councils' and managers' interest in demonstrating their performance (Lange 2013). It is easy to measure the percentage of Africans in a classroom or workplace and hence to demand that quotas are filled and to demonstrate that they have been. It is much more difficult to quantify and hence publicise in sound bites, or tick off in a brief performance review meeting, the Africanisation of institutional culture that I explore in this chapter.[3] In spelling out what it would mean to Africanise a university's institutional culture below, I distinguish between content, extent and implementation.

Content

There are five central dimensions by which a university, which I take to be a representative higher education institution, could Africanise its functionings: curriculum, research, language, aesthetics and governance. I use the phrase 'institutional culture' to refer to all five elements.[4]

With respect to curriculum, are students being taught characteristically African perspectives and approaches, as well as texts written by Africans? Is a music department teaching indigenous forms? Is a philosophy department instructing sub-Saharan thinkers? Is a sociology department addressing African societies? Is a history department exploring unknowns about the past below the Sahara?

One might suspect that such questions are appropriate only for the humanities and social sciences, but it is worth considering what Africanisation could realistically mean in the contexts of the hard sciences and maths (see Seepe 2000). One prima facie attractive 'African' approach to maths might be not to do it in the abstract and in an isolated classroom, but rather in the context of, say, designing something that would benefit a village or township.[5]

Local readers will know that such pedagogical approaches have not been frequent over the past twenty years. The well-known 'racism report', commissioned by South Africa's minister of education and composed by Crain Soudien and several leading figures in higher education policy, briefly addresses the Africanisation of curricula and is bleak about progress made on this score (Soudien et al. 2008: 91–4, 117). In an overview of the report disseminated to the public, Soudien and his cohorts remark that 'the transformation of what is taught and learnt in institutions constitutes one of the most difficult challenges this sector is facing' (2009). The report's authors find, as did many other black scholars ten years prior (for example, see Jansen 1998: 109, 110–11), much instruction to be decontextualised, as well as not directly engaged with African perspectives.

Anecdotally, while it is clear to me that departments such as history, sociology and development studies routinely focus on sub-Saharan concerns, I doubt that many other disciplines systematically do. Certainly in my field of philosophy, African philosophy continues to be (nearly) entirely eclipsed by the presentation of Anglo-American and continental perspectives in most major departments. For all I can tell, it is not unique in that respect. To what extent do lecturers in psychology seriously explore collective conceptions of the self and relational perceptions of the world more prominent in Africa than in the West? How often do lecturers in political theory engage with sub-Saharan conceptions of democracy (on which, see below)? What percentage of class time do lecturers in journalism devote to addressing obligations that an ubuntu ethic might entail for reporters or a publishing firm? Having been a part of South African academe for more than ten years, I submit that rough answers to such questions are clear (which is not to say that systematic empirical inquiry into what is being taught and how would not be worthwhile). Note that Africanisation need not imply that such perspectives are correct, should be presented as such or should be the only ones critically discussed; in the first instance, it simply calls for not ignoring them.

Turning to research, the issue is whether African theoretical perspectives are being studied, used and advanced and African issues addressed. Questions paralleling those about the curriculum can be posed about research. One may reasonably surmise that Africanised scholarship has fared worse than that of teaching; after all, if instructors are generally not extending themselves to learn about and teach African approaches and issues, they surely are doing so even less when it comes to what they publish. Although there have been many conferences, centres and chairs established over the past twenty years devoted to issues of race, identity, justice and the like, which Soudien overviews (2011: 23–7), based on his familiarity with the research landscape in South African universities, he concludes: 'South African contributions, I suggest, are dominated by ideas of modernism and modernity. They have difficulty in working with knowledge forms and knowledge claims which fall outside the particular modernist imagination' (17; see also Suttner 2010: 525–6).

I submit that even modernist approaches could have been much more systematically applied to African contexts in revealing ways. For instance, one finds no thorough attempt to empirically ascertain what kernels of truth there might be in traditional medicine. Scientists in South Africa have a terrific opportunity to sift through indigenous peoples' knowledge of herbs and plants in search of those that are demonstrably efficacious (a point made by Vilakazi 1998: 73). Of course, some of this work is being done, but not in earnest and often it is being done by Big Pharma. For another respect in which traditional medicine begs for empirical study, consider what economists might learn from the fact that typical traditional healers do not demand payment from patients unless they are happy with the service they have been provided (Leonard 2009).

A third possible locus of Africanisation in higher education institutions is its mediums of communication, especially the languages that are spoken and written. The more students learn in an indigenous sub-Saharan language and the more university affairs are conducted in it, the more African the university's institutional culture, in one major respect. It is well known that an overwhelming majority of instruction at universities is conducted in English or Afrikaans. As the Council on Higher Education notes:

> Of the 21 universities, 16 use English as the language of tuition. In the other five institutions, English-medium tuition is steadily and often rapidly increasing alongside, and perhaps at the expense of, Afrikaans-medium tuition ... Of the universities that returned the questionnaire on which the survey was based, hardly any can be said to be promoting the

use of any African language as a Language of Tuition (2001: 4; see also Ministry of Education 2002: 7).

Since then, the use of English has increased substantially, including at the University of Johannesburg (formerly Rand Afrikaans University) and, to lesser degrees, at the universities of Pretoria and Stellenbosch. Since 2001, nothing notable has happened with regard to use of African languages, save for the University of KwaZulu-Natal's newly adopted policy of requiring all undergraduates to have learned some Zulu by the time they graduate and some very sporadic efforts at Rhodes University and the University of Limpopo (see Beukes 2014).

A fourth important dimension of Africanising institutional culture could concern aesthetic issues, by which I roughly mean those designed to touch the senses in ways that are expected to please others, to prompt reflection or to express oneself (and often all three). What kinds of music are played at university events? Which cultures inform the university's symbols in its advertising or its academic gowns? What sort of entertainment is there in a university's residences? Where have the rituals at a graduation ceremony come from? What kinds of food are served? What kinds of clothes may be expected to be worn? In a fairly notorious newspaper piece (Makgoba 2005), the previous vice chancellor at the University of KwaZulu-Natal discusses these facets in blunt terms:

> It should therefore become common sense that the white male soon learns to speak, write and spell in an African language; that he, like Johnny Clegg, learns to dance and sing like Ladysmith Black Mambazo. He should learn kwaito, dance like Lebo, dress like Madiba, enjoy eating 'smiley and walkies' and attend 'lekgotla' and socialise at our taverns.

To the extent that non-Africans participated in these ways of life – or indeed even Africans themselves did! – in a university setting, there would be a greater dimension of Africanisation of institutional culture.

While one occasionally encounters African colours and shapes in a university's symbols and indigenous songs or at least rhythms from university choirs, that is about all that readily comes to mind. The manners of dress at both formal and informal events, the types of food and drink largely sold in student centres and offered at events, the kinds of background music played at graduations and award ceremonies and the architecture in which one is housed on campus are little different from what I encountered when at a variety of academic institutions in the United States.

A fifth facet of academic life that admits Africanisation is the way that decisions are made and enforced. Who decides how a given department, faculty and university as a whole are run, how the decisions are made and how refusals to carry them out are dealt with? Are there salient decision-making processes in the sub-Saharan tradition that are attractive and should inform university practice? What sort of boundaries does a university have with respect to its neighbourhood and how are they secured?

Consider, for example, that African political philosophers have argued that pre-colonial sub-Saharan societies tended to make decisions consequent to some kind of consensus, either among all affected adults or among popularly appointed (male) elders, and furthermore that the search for unanimity is worth undertaking in contemporary, modern political settings (Wiredu 1996: 172–90; Ramose 1999: 135–52; Teffo 2004). More familiar, because of the influence of the Truth and Reconciliation Commission, is a characteristically sub-Saharan approach to conflict resolution, in which the aim is to reconcile offenders and victims (and their families) and not in the first instance to deter prospective offenders from misbehaving or to seek retribution in the form of an 'eye for an eye'.

Might an Africanised management be one that consults widely or at least with a group of elected senior academics or university representatives more generally, rather than making decisions unilaterally? Perhaps the idea of an institutional forum started out with such an aim, but the evidence is that it has not been realised (see Soudien et al. 2008: 108–9). Could an Africanised Senate be one that seeks unanimous agreement or at least a significant majority on key issues? Should a university's approach to student infraction typically involve a kind of sub-Saharan restorative justice, as opposed to penalties such as deregistration or expulsion? Unlike other facets of Africanising institutional culture, I am not aware of the extent to which any university in South Africa has tried out these approaches or any others grounded on salient African norms.

As other contributions to this volume have made clear, the phrase 'institutional culture' is vague. I submit that it is well understood as picking out all five of the elements of curriculum, research, language, aesthetics and governance. For the sake of this chapter, a university's institutional culture counts as more Africanised the more these five elements are imbued with features salient in the sub-Saharan tradition.

Extent

So far I have spelled out Africanising institutional culture as it concerns the content of what is or could be done at a university. Another issue is how much it should take place. According to some, radical views, there ought only to be Africanisation in South Africa's universities (or perhaps in a demographically representative cohort of them). Very few friends of Africanisation, even among the most vocal of them, favour that sort of approach.[6] Invariably, the suggestion is that Africanisation should proceed alongside other cultural approaches in a dialogue of mutual enrichment. However, there remains the issue of whether African norms should be the dominant ones and, if so, to what extent.

Implementation

More controversial is the issue of how the Africanisation of institutional culture ought to be promoted. Here, one can distinguish between the normative force that university leaders and members generally ascribe to Africanisation and the coercive force that should back it up.

In terms of normative force, managers, staff and students might think of Africanisation as either *permissible*, something that *may* morally be done, but that need not be; *praiseworthy*, something that *should* morally be done and, while not wrong not to do, would be ideal to do; or *required*, something that *must* morally be done and that would be wrong not to do. Most self-described adherents to Africanisation would favour the spread of the latter two kinds of judgements. Indeed, more than a few favour the view that Africanisation is an ethical necessity and would be delighted to see universities express the same.

Now, just because something is a moral requirement (or believed to be) does not necessarily mean it should be an enforceable requirement. That is, even if one supposes, for the sake of argument at this point, that academics and administrative staff have an ethical obligation to Africanise institutional culture, more argument would be needed to demonstrate that they should be forced to live up to that obligation. It might be, after all, that academics and other staff have a 'right to do wrong' as it is known in Anglo-American political philosophy; even if they would be wrong not to Africanise voluntarily, it could be that senior managers would *also* be wrong and perhaps even wrong, to a greater degree, to *make* them Africanise by withdrawing privileges, issuing threats and imposing penalties in response to failure to do so.

Hence, a separate issue with regard to the implementation of Africanisation is the mechanisms that are used to foster it. Here, it is useful to distinguish between policies that would merely *permit* Africanisation, that is, would not interfere with its realisation by members of a university; those that would *encourage* it, say, by seeking to come to an agreement about its promotion or by offering incentives; and those that would *require* it on pain of some kind of sanction. Resolving this issue raises tricky matters regarding institutional autonomy and academic freedom, which I briefly discuss in the conclusion of this chapter.

Strong, moderate and weak versions of Africanisation

In the light of the above analysis, it is useful to think of the Africanisation of institutional culture along a spectrum of possible manifestations. At one extreme would be a strong or robust form, according to which academic norms at South African higher education institutions should be only African along all the dimensions of curriculum, research, language, aesthetics and governance, they should be considered morally required, and ministers and managers should back them up with force.

At the other extreme would be a weak form of Africanisation, according to which it would be deemed permissible, but would not be encouraged by the powers that be. Africanisation with regard to curriculum, research, language, aesthetics and governance would be left to the haphazard and voluntary inclinations of particular individuals, managers and institutions. This more or less describes the status quo and what one expects to encounter in the near future.

In between these two poles would be a moderate form of Africanisation. Here, academic and administrative staff would deem it morally ideal or required to Africanise on their own, with line managers facilitating negotiations about, and providing praise, incentives and inspiration for, innovative and promising realisations of it. Universities would reflect carefully and systematically on how they might Africanise along all the dimensions of curriculum, research, language, aesthetics and governance, while minimising costs to other important values, including the need to pay attention to cultural norms springing from, say, Europe and Asia.

The moderate form has some intuitive appeal to me and I presume to most readers. However, my major aim in this chapter is to critically explore what *good arguments* there are for Africanising institutional culture and for which sort. In the end, I conclude that the most promising rationales are ones that entail a moderate form of Africanisation, one that would nonetheless mean substantial change for South African higher education institutions.

Exploring the rationales for Africanisation

Based on my familiarity with largely South African discussions of Africanisation in higher education, I distinguish five logically distinct reasons that have been given in favour of it and that are relevant to discussions of institutional culture. As mentioned in the introduction, I capture them under the headings of relativism, democracy, redress, civilisation and identity. My aim here is to specify these different rationales, bring out their implications and explore their plausibility or lack thereof. The five rationales progress in a developmental order, from what I consider the least promising to the most.

Relativism

Those who defend Africanisation on the grounds that it is a source of 'valid knowledges' and similar phrasings often veer into relativist conceptions of truth and justification, according to which a proposition is true or a policy is justified if and only if it is socially accepted. Relativism or constructivism, at its core, is the view that what makes something valid is that it is believed to be so by a given society. Since beliefs and practices differ from society to society, there is nothing universally valid, or at least nothing that is interesting or controversial. Instead, knowledge and culture generally is appropriate, relative to the context in which it originated and continues to be accepted, making African claims true in African societies, so the argument goes. Such a position is suggested by the following:

> People need to accept that there is no one unique truth which is fixed and found, but rather a diversity of valid, and even conflicting, versions of a world in the making (Venter 1997: 62).

> Africanisation ... holds that different foundations exist for the construction of pyramids of knowledge. It holds further that communication is possible between the various pyramids. It disclaims the view that any pyramid of knowledge is by its very nature eminently superior to all the others (Ramose 1998: vi).

> The assumptions which constructed Western thought, literature and traditions are not universal but are derived from special and discreet Western experiences prescribed by special historical levels of economic and industrial development. Implicit in this perspective is that standards are not universal but contextual (Lebakeng, Phalane and Dalindjebo 2006: 74).

In addition, the widely used phrase 'indigenous *knowledge* systems' (my emphasis) seems to imply that what is local is always already true and justified, as does being suspicious about 'hierarchies of knowledge' (for example, Odora Hoppers 2001: 81) and positing 'equally legitimate locations of human imagination' (Odora Hoppers 2000: 9).[7]

As is widely appreciated by epistemologists and other philosophers, but not yet sufficiently recognised by those in other fields, most who advance relativist conceptions of knowledge contradict themselves in doing so. The above authors are advancing controversial views that they know their readers might not already accept. They therefore are supposing that their thesis that there are equally valid competing perspectives is not *itself* merely relatively true and instead is a claim that is universally or objectively true, true regardless of whether a particular interlocutor or community recognises it or not.[8] Is it not a 'fixed and found' truth that there are a 'diversity of valid, and even conflicting, versions of a world in the making'? Is it not to argue from an 'eminently superior' standpoint that 'disclaims the view that any pyramid of knowledge is by its very nature eminently superior to all the others'? Is it not to appeal to a universal standard when making the claim that 'standards are not universal but contextual'? If the answers to these questions are 'yes', as they implicitly are, the content of the doctrine of relativism (or whatever doctrine is being expressed) is implied to be false in the very process of advancing it. For most epistemologists, this sort of contradiction or self-refutation is the kiss of death.[9]

Even if one were willing to maintain that relativist claims about knowledge can be justified merely relativistically, there would be the additional, second serious problem of specifying the relevant community's beliefs relative to which propositions are true. As Africanists themselves repeatedly point out, a large majority of the academic community in South Africa does not hold Africanist tenets. The logic of relativism therefore entails that any proposition in favour of Africanisation is false in relation to that community!

Third, and finally, suppose for the sake of argument that Afro-relativists were able to find a way to show that the academic community is not the relevant one that determines which beliefs are true and that it is instead the broader society that counts. Even so, such a relativist approach to knowledge would give majorities a 'dictatorship' about what counts as legitimate knowledge or appropriate culture more generally. Relativism logically implies that *minorities are necessarily incorrect* in a given context. So, even if from a global point of view there was no way to choose between Western and African epistemologies and cultures, when in an African context the Western or otherwise non-local would have to be considered false and something to be excluded from a university's institutional culture. This direct implication of relativism is not often appreciated by those who advance it and does not easily square with routine judgements – by most Africanists themselves – that both Western and African perspectives should be taught in South African institutions. If one believes that it is possible for majorities to be mistaken, that is, welcomes fallibilism about knowledge claims, one must reject relativism, on pain of incoherence.

These three objections lead me to conclude that some other basis for Africanising institutional culture should be sought out. Below I argue that there *are* some epistemic considerations that provide good reasons to Africanise a typical South African university. However, those factors involve neither the claim that contextuality determines validity, nor that one can always already know that propositions and practices arising out of a sub-Saharan context are true, justified or valid to a degree equal to those of any other context, nor that non-African perspectives should be left to non-Africans alone.

Democracy

Whereas a relativist approach to culture is roughly the view that what a majority believes about it makes it true and hence to be promoted, a democratic approach is the view that the culture to be promoted is what a majority prefers. Even if majorities do not construct validity as per the relativist, they could still be entitled to determine which objective and universal truths about what exists and how to act are to be transmitted and sought out. Along these lines, Vilakazi suggests: 'The largest experience in South Africa is the African experience, i.e., the experience of the African people, who form the overwhelming majority of the population of the society. Therefore, it is right and proper that this African experience should be the source of ideas and concepts' (1998: 79).[10]

The appeal to democratic values in support of Africanising South African universities has not been systematically spelt out, as far as I can tell from the literature. On the one hand, advocates of this rationale could have in mind certain formal, representative procedures. Perhaps they would say that since a majority of the population has voted for the African National Congress in presidential elections and since the president has chosen a minister of higher education and training who prefers Africanisation, Africanisation is justified. On the other hand, they might have a more informal, direct sense of how the majority should determine university norms. Maybe what a majority of South Africans want (or would say they want if asked) with respect to academic institutions is what should determine their nature, apart from the views of those whom they have elected. Either way, collective self-governance arguably demands infusing South African universities with African norms.

Upon reflection, this argument is readily seen to be a poor justification for Africanisation, in the sense of failing to give enough support to what Africanists themselves typically want when it comes to institutional culture.[11] Consider that appeal to democratic will supports Africanisation only so long as the majority's preferences (or those of whom they have elected) favour Africanisation. Majorities, however, can change their minds. It is not obvious that most of those in South Africa favour Africanisation, or would if they had to choose between it and socio-economic development and jobs for their children. From what I can tell, the poor and African majority sees tertiary education as a ticket to freedom from poverty and would be delighted if their children learned English well enough to participate in the global economy and bring home the bacon.

Of course, many friends of Africanisation maintain that development can truly take place only in conjunction with mining sub-Saharan perspectives. Here, they often point to the fact that what has made, say, Anglo-American universities strong is that they have drawn on the cultures in their territories. Perhaps something similar would be true of South African universities; maybe they will foster socio-economic improvement only when their institutional cultures are informed by African cultures. But maybe not. It might be that the sort of knowledge produced by Western universities is a function of a certain individualist culture exhibiting a distinct kind of rationalism, one that is competitive, unconventional and literate and that prizes instrumental efficiency and analytic experimentation, which has not been nearly as present in traditional sub-Saharan settings.[12]

In any event, the deep point is that an appeal to democratic will holds Africanisation hostage to the contingencies of what majorities want or choose. Suppose that a majority of South Africans did not prefer Africanisation. Imagine that colonisation cut so deep that all they wanted were Anglo-Americanisation en route to economic growth. Surely, Africanists would be inclined to think that the majority *should change its mind*. This judgement implicitly shows (again, as it did in the context of relativism above) that Africanists are ultimately committed to there being a mind-independent reason in favour of Africanisation, one that majorities should come to appreciate, even if they do not already.

The next three rationales for Africanisation that I explore below are more objective in this respect. Instead of appealing to what majorities believe or prefer to try to ground Africanisation, the following arguments invoke considerations that majorities ought to take into account, supposing they do not yet.

Redress

One influential argument for Africanisation appeals to ideals of liberation, emancipation, independence, freedom and similar concepts. The idea is that Africanisation is a proper response not so much to contemporary South African society's beliefs or preferences, but rather more to its history of apartheid, colonialism and related forms of oppression of Africans and black peoples generally. Such oppression was effected not only materially, in terms of the dispossession of land, and politically, with respect to lack of opportunities to vote, hold office and otherwise participate in governance, but also culturally. 'The colonial and apartheid orders were not simply political and military conquests and systems of governance, but knowledge projects' (Suttner 2010: 515–16). Characteristic African worldviews and ways of life were denigrated and excluded from consideration in many South African universities, part of a process of 'spiritual genocide' (Vilakazi 1998:

76), 'cultural violence' (Odora Hoppers 2000: 5), 'symbolic castration' (Odora Hoppers 2001: 74) and 'epistemicide' (Ramose 2004: 156; Lebakeng, Phalane and Dalindjebo 2006: 70).[13]

The present rationale for Africanisation is that promoting it in the context of a university's institutional culture is necessary to counteract epistemic injustice. Africanisation could serve this function in two distinct ways. First, it might compensate for harm that has already been done, serving a reparative measure, correcting epistemological and related oppression of the twentieth century. Second, though, it might serve as a defensive measure, analogous to the way that an innocent person would fight back against an aggressor. Supposing that teachers and researchers in South African higher education institutions are continuing to explicitly bad mouth, or, more often, conversationally imply, that African cultures are inherently inferior, Africanisation would be a way of protecting Africans from racism, arrogance and related harms.

It is worth considering whether Africanisation in South African universities would truly serve the function of paying back those wronged during the apartheid era or before then. On the face of it, only descendants of those wronged would be the ones to receive the recognition of African perspectives. In addition, it would be a relatively small handful of descendants getting something, namely, those lucky few able to attend an Africanised university. Some other form of epistemic compensation, effected outside of the academy and its expensive books and journals and directed toward the African public more generally, instead appears appropriate when it comes to those who were directly wronged by, say, not having been allowed to attend university at all during the apartheid era.

Suppose, for the sake of argument, however, that the university is at least one apt setting in which to adopt and explore sub-Saharan ways of life for purposes of compensation for historical epistemic injustice. Or suppose that a concern to prevent racism in the present, as opposed to compensate those wrongfully harmed in the past, is the relevant basis for Africanisation. Even so, the logic of the present argument cannot support the kind of Africanisation of institutional culture that most Africanists believe is appropriate.

Conceiving of Africanisation strictly in defensive and restitutive terms entails that it would no longer be justified if and when there were no longer such needs. Suppose that Africanisation proceeded for two or three decades or however long it would take to effect compensation and also imagine that after that time there were no longer any systematic attacks of the sort requiring a prophylactic. Africanisation would stop being justified by the present rationale. However, most adherents to Africanisation believe that it should be continued indefinitely, or at least for a much longer time than would likely be needed to end imperial dispositions on the part of South African academics and to make up for damage done. Hence, an additional rationale for Africanisation is needed that would support longer-term approaches to it, which the last two arguments promise to provide.

Civilisation

A fourth argument for Africanising the institutional cultures of South African universities appeals to what is these days often associated with talk of an 'African renaissance'. The basic idea is that sub-Saharan ways of life should be mined with the aims of revitalising African civilisation and thereby making a contribution to humanity's progress.

What do indigenous peoples know about the uses of certain plants and other aspects of the environment? What beliefs about the workings of nature do they have that are true and justified? How do they characteristically perceive reality and how might such perceptions inform more theoretical pursuits? What useful skills do they have to build upon and share? What kinds of local painting, sculpture, dance, music, literature and the like would those in other parts of the world appreciate and what new styles and genres might grow out of sub-Saharan soil? What values have traditional Africans tended to live by or extol that, upon reflection, are insufficiently acknowledged elsewhere? What myths, stories and proverbs might be revealing of the human condition or exhibit wisdom and so merit spread on this continent and others? In short, 'Africanisation seeks to provide a basis for originality and uniqueness that can contribute meaningfully to global knowledge and civilisation' (Makgoba 1998: 48).[14]

Unlike a relativist approach to culture, the present argument for Africanisation does not a priori suppose that Africans have equal amounts of knowledge to share when it comes to any given domain such as, say, mathematics or the workings of nature at a small-scale level. Instead, the current rationale urges those in universities to work to empirically establish what, if anything, sub-Saharan culture has in the domains of the good (values), the true (inquiry) and the beautiful (the arts) that would be of interest to those currently living below the Sahara Desert and to those living beyond it. In principle, such a search *could* come up empty-handed in a particular area. This might sound pessimistic, but it is a direct implication of the claim commonly made by Africanists themselves that those in the South African academic community, including the Africans, lack knowledge about African perspectives! After all, if we are ignorant of them, we are in no position to pronounce on their merit or lack thereof. This is therefore something to investigate over time.

However, since it is reasonable to suppose that any long-standing and widespread tradition has a substantial amount of insight and interesting expression, it is well worth an academic's time and other resources to explore the African one. That is the compelling argument for multiculturalism, and academics in South Africa have strong reason to mine the sub-Saharan intellectual tradition in particular, since they have the most ease of access to it and since, in comparison to many other civilisations, this one is grossly underexplored.

Note how the logic of the argument from civilisation differs from that of the argument from redress. Even if academics were no longer actively suppressing African perspectives and compensation for past suppression had been completely effected, the present rationale could continue to justify Africanisation as a way to enrich local culture and to develop Africa's opportunity to contribute to the civilising process of the human race. To use philosophical jargon, whereas the argument for redress is 'non-ideal', contending that Africanisation is justified merely in response to wrongdoing, the present rationale is 'ideal', maintaining that even in the (hypothetical) absence of any wrongdoing, Africanisation would still be justified as a way to promote something of value. In the latter context, one often encounters mention of Africa having a gift that it has yet to present to the world, a view expressed by Steve Biko (1971: 51).

The civilisational argument is strong and in my view provides some good reasons to Africanise. However, it also has limitations with regard to scope, by which I mean that it fails on its own to justify the range of Africanisation that is typically sought. Specifically, the present argument provides strong reason for academics to conduct research into sub-Saharan perspectives, to disseminate their findings and to teach them in the classroom. It naturally explains why curriculum content and research agendas should be substantially Africanised. However, it is weak when it comes to the other three potential dimensions of Africanising institutional culture.

First, in terms of language, while it is true that coming to grips with a particular African culture would be best facilitated by an intimate knowledge of its language, it does not follow that this language would need to be spoken on campus from day to day. I accept that teaching in an African language might well help to convey subtleties and more generally enrich the subject matter, but that presumes that South African students themselves have an intimate awareness of African languages, which is often not the case. Furthermore, to best understand Africa, it is not necessarily true that a given African language would include all of the most useful mental tools. It could be that routinely appealing to the words and the concepts associated with them found in English would (sometimes? usually?) be an ideal way to come to grips with a given sub-Saharan object. Consider, for example, scientific analysis of a plant's medicinal properties that have been appreciated by herbal healers, or an analytic treatment of a moral principle associated with an indigenous proverb.[15] Finally, even if using an African language were alone ideal when it comes to teaching and research, there would still, on grounds of civilisation, apparently be little reason, say, to greet people in the vernacular or to strive for the point at which one could realistically conduct a committee meeting in an indigenous language.

Second, when it comes to governance, the present considerations do not appear to recommend Africanisation. In so far as characteristically sub-Saharan modes of decision-making and responding to infraction should be approached by academics *on grounds of enhancing and disseminating African civilisation*, they should merely be objects of intellectual engagement, not ones of immediate practice. One might reply that a university could be an experimental site where African approaches are tested out. Perhaps. But they could just as well be tested out in other environments, where academics could study the results much more objectively.

Third, with respect to aesthetics, there appears to be little reason for a university to take on African artistic themes if the 'principle to be adopted is this: the unique African pattern of development into modernity should base itself, first and foremost, on the utilization of the resources provided by her civilization' (Vilakazi 1998: 71). Would it not be puffery to suggest that when a university adopts, say, a coat of arms inspired by local indigenous themes (abjuring any Latin phrases), it is thereby 'developing into modernity' or showing that Africa can 'make a meaningful contribution to universal human progress' (Ramose 1998: iv)? Some readers would be willing to say, 'It would be doing so, even if in a small way.' However, below I provide what I think is a more compelling reason for a South African university to feature African food, music, symbols, art and the like.

Identity

The fifth and last major rationale for Africanisation that one finds in the literature can be summed up by saying that Africanisation is necessary in order to fulfil 'the right to be an African', in Mogobe Ramose's pithy phrase (1998: vii).[16] This might seem to imply essentialism about what counts as 'African', but it need not. As per above, what is meant by 'African' and cognate terms is reasonably understood in terms of properties that are recurrently (not exhaustively, not exclusively) encountered below the Sahara Desert.

The ability to take on and express an African identity includes three central elements. First, it involves self-understanding on the part of those reared in sub-Saharan cultures and environments. This means not merely correcting incorrect beliefs about Africa, but also imparting true ones that are not yet held because of a lack of information. To understand who one is means obtaining a firm grasp of one's society, which has shaped one and will continue to do so. One must therefore become familiar with the values, norms, cultures and institutions of the community in which one lives. Understanding one's society means knowing how it arose, for to know who one is means knowing how one has arrived at the present and also what possibilities there are for the future.

These considerations in themselves provide good reason to Africanise the curriculum and to do so in the light of up-to-date and accurate research. In one of the first major books on Africanising the university, Joseph Ki-Zerbo remarks: 'Africanization of the curriculum is no more than conformity with the injunction, "know thyself"' (1973: 26). This consideration would apply not merely to those students fortunate enough to attend classes, but also, ideally, to people more generally, supposing academics took the time to disseminate their findings in ways accessible to the public.

There is some overlap, here, with the previous, civilisational argument, but there are important differences. The emphasis on cultivating identity is inward, directed toward Africans themselves, whereas a key part of the argument from civilisation involves an outward orientation of contributing to the world's order of higher achievements. In addition, a prescription for higher education institutions to enable people to become Africans does not involve merely the discovery and transmission of knowledge. Ki-Zerbo points out that Africanisation of the curriculum would serve a function beyond a cognitive one, namely, it would help when it comes to the emotional side of developing an African identity. He says that it 'is the first prerequisite for overcoming complexes and attaining self-development' (1973: 26). I presume that by 'complexes' Ki-Zerbo means negative emotions such as shame and self-hatred for being an African, as well as an absence of positive emotions such as pride and self-esteem. To truly exhibit an African identity requires feeling good at least about what is good about oneself and hence about one's society, history and future, as well as feeling confident to move forward to achieve one's goals.

There is probably a third core element of displaying an African identity beyond the cognitive and the emotive, namely, the active. To be an African means not only exhibiting certain states of mind, but also making certain decisions consequent to them. In this context, one sometimes finds the word 'authentic' invoked (for example, Teffo 2000), with the suggestion that for Africans to truly be themselves means making choices based on characteristically sub-Saharan values and norms and in the accurate awareness of local history and society. In the absence of such choices, the personality lacks integrity or wholeness and is instead incoherent and fragmented. Values and norms must be acted upon in order for one to become a real (African) person.

If South African universities had a duty to enable residents to choose to be Africans, a much larger scope of Africanisation would be defended relative to what the previous two arguments were able to underwrite. Recall that the redress argument entails that no Africanisation would be called for upon the end of racism and the achievement of compensation. However, it is plausible to suggest that public institutions, such as universities, would continue to have strong reasons to enable people to become Africans – indeed, so long as they continue to be set in an African environment. In addition, remember that the civilisation argument could not easily justify the Africanisation of language, aesthetics and governance at a university. However, considerations of identity easily do so; the more characteristically African ways of life that a university adopts, the more opportunity there is for students and staff to exhibit an African identity.

Notice that the present argument is 'ideal' in the philosophical sense that it does not essentially involve the claim that Africanisation is apt in response to wrongdoing. Instead, the heart of the claim is that, given a largely African context, public institutions have some substantial obligation to enable people to become Africans.

However, there are a variety of elements that are not African in our South African context. It is not only Africans who have a claim on South African universities to help them realise themselves; those from other cultural backgrounds living here do, too (see Suttner 2010: 518). So, while it would make sense for South African institutions to Africanise, the logic of the present argument does not entail that they should do this alone. They should also assist people to become Afrikaners, people of Indian descent and people of mixed heritage, if they should indeed enable people to become Africans.

Conclusion: How to Africanise

In the expository section above, I distinguished five dimensions along which Africanisation of institutional culture could take place: curriculum, research, language, aesthetics and governance. I also pointed out that a South African higher education institution could exclusively Africanise or do so alongside other enculturation policies. I further noted that the moral force ascribed to Africanisation could range from permissible, praiseworthy and required and, with respect to the use of coercion, managers could permit, encourage or mandate it. What has the evaluative section shown with regard to these different possible forms of Africanisation?

Recall that I found the arguments from relativism and democracy to be weak; majorities do not have deep epistemic or moral authority, at least when it comes to the knowledge that a university ought to seek out and the culture more generally it ought to adopt. Much more convincing, I contended, were the arguments from redress, civilisation and identity. It is plausible to think that the proper functions of a publicly funded university include: preventing racism and helping to make up for 'epistemicide', mining (South) African cultural heritage with an eye to revitalising African civilisation and providing the conditions that would enable people living in South Africa to adopt an African identity. Even if one doubts that these are ends that would justify the creation of a university in the first place, they are at least 'attendant' final ends that a university should adopt, upon having been created for other good reasons (see Metz 2009b: 181).

Supposing these are proper aims for a South African higher education institution, it follows that Africanisation should proceed along all five dimensions of institutional culture; there is strong reason to Africanise the curriculum, research, language, aesthetics and governance. Of course, to say that there is strong reason does not imply that it is the only reason or even that it is the strongest reason; further argument would be needed to establish something like that. However, at this stage it is reasonable to conclude that a university in South Africa ought to seek to Africanise as much as it can, while paying due regard to other important and competing values such as understanding of the physical world and human nature.

With regard to the extent to which enculturation ought to be African, the answer is clearly that it should not solely be. The arguments in favour of Africanisation do not justify such a strong form of it, at least in the light of the current diversity of South African society. The redress and civilisation arguments, however, do entail that, at least for a number of decades, Africanisation should receive the lion's share of attention.

Finally, with regard to implementation, one should conclude that Africanisation of institutional culture is a moral requirement, at least given the redress argument and probably the identity argument. I find it a bit harder to say that universities are *morally required* to develop African civilisation, although I naturally believe that it would be desirable for them to do so.

If Africanisation is indeed a moral requirement, may deans, deputy vice chancellors and ministers require it? This difficult question is left unanswered by the analysis in this chapter. To conclude, as I have, that academics and administrators ought to Africanise does not settle the issue of whether they should be forced to do so. Africanists often suggest that the reasons non-Africans will not Africanise is that they are racist and arrogant, but that is not the most common reason in my experience of white colleagues in South Africa. Insecurity and fear are more salient. In any event, the difficult question about the extent to which academic freedom and institutional autonomy are consistent with Africanisation and about how to make trade-offs among them where they are not must wait for another occasion.[17]

Notes

1. For discussion of how higher education should avoid and respond to oppression of aboriginal peoples in New Zealand and the Americas, see, for example, Andreotti, Ahenakew and Cooper (2011) and De Oliveira Andreotti (2012). In this chapter, I focus on issues of Africanisation in particular, paying close attention to what self-described 'Africanists' say about it. Such is plausibly required to give the concept of Africanisation its due, particularly given how large the literature on it is and how distinct the experiences and perspectives of sub-Saharans are likely to be.

2. For similar objections, but different sorts of responses to them, see Makgoba (1998: 51) and Seepe (1998: 63–4).
3. Hence by 'Africanisation' I mean precisely the opposite of what Prah (2004) does. By the way, I recognise that if some kind of Africanisation of norms were appropriate, promoting it would probably require some substantial presence of African people. However, it also (nearly) goes without saying that merely hiring African people would be unlikely to ensure Africanisation with regard to norms. Both points are by now banalities in Africanist analyses of higher education.
4. For a thoughtful sociological analysis of the way the phrase 'institutional culture' gets used in South Africa, see Higgins (2007).
5. I lack the space to defend the 'Africanness' of such an approach, but refer the reader to Adeyinka and Ndwapi (2002) and Adeyemi and Adeyinka (2003), who discuss the salient communal and utilitarian dimensions of traditional African education.
6. But see Lebakeng, Phalane and Dalindjebo (2006: 77), who do advocate 'jettisoning' Western perspectives and Murove and Mazibuko who compare Eurocentric standpoints to HIV, a virus that must be eradicated (2008: 104–5), and to a ghost that must be exorcised (108). Compare Van Wyk and Higgs (2004: 201).
7. For additional apparent flirtations with relativism, see Higgs (2006); Nabudere (2006: 20); Murove and Mazibuko (2008: 110).
8. In the South African context, this inconsistency has been noted by Horsthemke (2004: 584) and by Horsthemke and Enslin (2008: 214–15).
9. For a thoughtful intellectual from South Africa willing to tolerate this sort of contradiction, see Cilliers (2005). Note, by the way, that if the answers to the above questions are 'no', there is no point in having published these works and no reason for someone who does not already accept their views to do so, for they are, *ex hypothesi*, true merely relative to a given, local context. Hence, another sort of contradiction would be involved in having published them.
10. For closely related views, see Makgoba (1998: 46, 51); Makgoba (2005); Seepe (1998: 64, 65, 68); Dowling and Seepe (2003: 44–5); Makgoba and Seepe (2004: 30, 41); Prah (2004: 103).
11. For additional criticisms of an appeal to majority will to ground knowledge-production, see Metz (2009a: 523, 528, 529–33).
12. See the sociological discussion of 'rationalisation' in the work of Max Weber and the 'uncoupling of the system from the lifeworld' in that of Jürgen Habermas.
13. See also Makgoba (1998: 46–7, 51–2, 58); Nkondo (1998: 33–4); Seepe (1998: 64); Vilakazi (1998: 76); Goduka (2000: 80); Odora Hoppers (2000); Teffo (2000: 106); Lebakeng (2004).

14. See also Ramose (1998: iv);Vilakazi (1998: 69–80); Goduka (2000: 80); Odora Hoppers (2000: 6–7);Teffo (2000).
15. To be a bit cheeky, I note that Africanists have invariably published in English. Is part of that because they have found English to be particularly useful when discussing the case for Africanisation?
16. For similar considerations, see Makgoba (1998: 49, 52);Vilakazi (1998: 85–7); Goduka (2000: 80); Odora Hoppers (2000: 7); Seepe (2000: 134); Teffo (2000); Makgoba and Seepe (2004: 23–7).
17. See Metz (2011: 50–5) for some prima facie reason to be hopeful about their compatibility. For those who clearly favour substantially sacrificing other, 'liberal' values for the sake of Africanisation, see Murove and Mazibuko (2008).

References

Adeyemi, M.B. and A.A. Adeyinka. 2003. 'The Principles and Content of African Traditional Education'. *Educational Philosophy and Theory* 35 (4): 425–40.

Adeyinka, A.A. and G. Ndwapi. 2002. 'Education and Morality in Africa'. *Pastoral Care in Education* 20 (2): 17–23.

Andreotti, V., C. Ahenakew and G. Cooper. 2011. 'Epistemological Pluralism: Challenges for Higher Education'. *AlterNative Journal* 7 (1): 40–50.

Beukes, A-M. 2014. 'Challenges for South Africa's Medium-Sized Indigenous Languages in Higher Education and Research Environments'. In *Lingua Academica: Language Policy in Higher Education*, ed. F.X. Vila and V. Bretxa, 121–37. Bristol: Multilingual Matters.

Biko, S. 1971. 'Some African Cultural Concepts'. Reprinted in *I Write What I Like*, 44–53. Johannesburg: Picador Africa, 2004.

Cilliers, P. 2005. 'Complexity, Deconstruction and Relativism'. *Theory, Culture and Society* 22 (5): 255–67.

Council on Higher Education. 2001. 'Language Policy Framework for South African Higher Education'. http://www.info.gov.za/otherdocs/2001/langframe.pdf.

De Oliveira Andreotti, V. 2012. 'Education, Knowledge and the Righting of Wrongs'. *Other Education* 1 (1): 19–31.

Dowling, D. and S. Seepe. 2003. 'Towards a Responsive Curriculum'. In *A Tale of Three Countries: Social Sciences Curriculum Transformations in Southern Africa*, ed. P. Naudé and N. Cloete, 41–53. Lansdowne: Juta.

Goduka, I. 2000. 'African/Indigenous Philosophies: Legitimizing Spiritually Centred Wisdoms within the Academy'. In *African Voices in Education*, ed. P. Higgs, N.C.G. Vakalisa, T.V. Mda and N.T. Assie-Lumumba, 63–83. Lansdowne: Juta.

Higgins, J. 2007. 'Institutional Culture as Keyword'. In *Review of Higher Education in South Africa*, 97–122. Pretoria: Council on Higher Education.

Higgs, P. 2006. 'In Defence of Local Knowledge'. *Indilinga* 5 (1): 1–11.

Horsthemke, K. 2004. 'Knowledge, Education and the Limits of Africanisation'. *Journal of Philosophy of Education* 38 (4): 571–87.

Horsthemke, K. and P. Enslin. 2005. 'Is There a Distinctly and Uniquely African Philosophy of Education?' In *African(a) Philosophy of Education*, ed. Y. Waghid and B. van Wyk, 54–75. Stellenbosch: Department of Education Policy Studies, Stellenbosch University.

———. 2008. 'African Philosophy of Education: The Price of Unchallengeability'. *Studies in Philosophy and Education* 28 (3): 209–22.

Jansen, J. 1998. 'But Our Natives Are Different! Race, Knowledge and Power in the Academy'. *Social Dynamics* 24 (2): 106–16.

Ki-Zerbo, J. 1973. 'Africanization of Higher Education Curriculum'. In *Creating the African University*, ed. T.M. Yesufu, 20–6. Ibadan: Oxford University Press.

Lange, L. 2013. 'Transformation by Numbers Skims the Surface of Tertiary Realities'. *Mail & Guardian*, 6–12 September, 50–1.

Lebakeng, T. 2004. 'Towards a Relevant Higher Education Epistemology'. In *Towards an African Identity of Higher Education*, ed. S. Seepe, 109–19. Pretoria: Vista University and Skotaville Media.

Lebakeng, T., M.M. Phalane and N. Dalindjebo. 2006. 'Epistemicide, Institutional Cultures and the Imperative for the Africanisation of Universities in South Africa'. *Alternation* 13 (1): 70–87.

Leonard, K.L. 2009. 'African Traditional Healers: Are They as Good at Economics as They Are at Medicine?' In *African Ethics: An Anthology of Comparative and Applied Ethics*, ed. M.F. Murove, 178–87. Pietermaritzburg: University of KwaZulu-Natal Press.

Makgoba, M.W. 1998. 'South African Universities in Transformation: An Opportunity to Africanise Education'. In *Black Perspective(s) on Tertiary Institutional Transformation*, ed. S. Seepe, 42–62. Florida Hills: Vivlia Publishers and the University of Venda.

———. 2005. 'Wrath of the Dethroned White Male'. *Mail & Guardian*, 25 March. http://mg.co.za/print/2005-03-25-wrath-of-dethroned-white-males.

Makgoba, M.W. and S. Seepe. 2004. 'Knowledge and Identity: An African Vision of Higher Education Transformation'. In *Towards an African Identity of Higher Education*, ed. S. Seepe, 13–57. Pretoria: Vista University and Skotaville Media.

Metz, T. 2009a. 'Higher Education, Knowledge for its Own Sake, and an African Moral Theory'. *Studies in Philosophy and Education* 28 (6): 517–36.

———. 2009b. 'The Final Ends of Higher Education in Light of an African Moral Theory'. *Journal of Philosophy of Education* 43 (2): 179–201.

———. 2011. 'Accountability in Higher Education: A Comprehensive Analytical Framework'. *Theory and Research in Education* 9 (1): 41–58.
Ministry of Education. 2002. 'Language Policy for Higher Education'. http://www.info.gov.za/otherdocs/2002/langpolicy.pdf.
Murove, M.F. and F. Mazibuko. 2008. 'Academic Freedom Discourse in Post-Colonial Africa: A Quest for Transformation and Appropriation of Relevant Knowledge in Higher Education'. *Africa Insight* 38 (2): 101–14.
Nabudere, D. 2006. 'Towards an Afrokology of Knowledge Production and African Regeneration'. *International Journal of African Renaissance Studies* 1 (1): 7–32.
Nkondo, G.M. 1998. 'Developing a Philosophy of Education for South Africa in Our Time'. In *Black Perspective(s) on Tertiary Institutional Transformation*, ed. S. Seepe, 31–41. Florida Hills: Vivlia Publishers and the University of Venda.
Odora Hoppers, C. 2000. 'African Voices in Education'. In *African Voices in Education*, ed. P. Higgs, N.C.G. Vakalisa, T.V. Mda and N.T. Assie-Lumumba, 1–11. Lansdowne: Juta.
———. 2001. 'Indigenous Knowledge Systems and Academic Institutions in South Africa'. *Perspectives in Education* 19 (1): 73–85.
Parker, B. 2003. 'Back on the Chain Gang: Some Difficulties in Developing a (South) African Philosophy of Education'. *Journal of Education* 30 (1): 23–40.
Prah, K.K. 2004. 'Africanism and Africanisation'. In *Towards an African Identity of Higher Education*, ed. S. Seepe, 93–108. Pretoria: Vista University and Skotaville Media.
Ramose, M. 1998. 'Foreword'. In *Black Perspective(s) on Tertiary Institutional Transformation*, ed. S. Seepe iv–vii. Florida Hills: Vivlia Publishers and the University of Venda.
———. 1999. *African Philosophy through Ubuntu*. Harare: Mond Books Publishers.
———. 2004. 'In Search of an African Philosophy of Education'. *South African Journal of Higher Education* 18 (3): 138–60.
Seepe, S. 1998. 'Towards an Afrocentric Understanding'. In *Black Perspective(s) on Tertiary Institutional Transformation*, ed. S. Seepe, 63–8. Florida Hills: Vivlia Publishers and the University of Venda.
———. 2000. 'Africanization of Knowledge'. In *African Voices in Education*, ed. P. Higgs, N.C.G. Vakalisa, T.V. Mda and N.T. Assie-Lumumba, 118–38. Lansdowne: Juta.
Soudien, C. 2011. 'The Arythmic Pulse of Transformation in South African Higher Education'. *Alternation* 18 (2): 15–34.
Soudien, C., W. Michaels, S. Mthembi-Mahanyele, M. Nkomo, G. Nyanda, N. Nyoka, S. Seepe, O. Shisana and C. Villa-Vicencio. 2008. 'Report of the Ministerial Committee on Transformation and Social Cohesion and the Elimination of Discrimination in Public Higher Education Institutions'. http://us-cdn.creamer media.co.za/assets/articles/attachments/21831_racismreport.pdf.

———. 2009. 'Is "Racism" Pervasive in Our Universities?' *Politicsweb*, 18 May. http://www.politicsweb.co.za/politicsweb/view/politicsweb/en/page71656?oid=129308&sn=Detail.
Suttner, R. 2010. '"Africanisation", African Identities and Emancipation in Contemporary South Africa'. *Social Dynamics* 36 (3): 515–30.
Teffo, L.J. 2000. 'Africanist Thinking: An Invitation to Authenticity'. In *African Voices in Education*, ed. P. Higgs, N.C.G. Vakalisa, T.V. Mda and N.T. Assie-Lumumba, 103–17. Lansdowne: Juta.
———. 2004. 'Democracy, Kingship, and Consensus: A South African Perspective'. In *A Companion to African Philosophy*, ed. K. Wiredu, 443–49. Malden: Blackwell.
Van Wyk, B. and P. Higgs. 2004. 'Towards an African Philosophy of Higher Education'. *South African Journal of Higher Education* 18 (3): 196–210.
Venter, E. 1997. 'Philosophy of Education in a New South Africa'. *South African Journal of Higher Education* 11 (1): 57–64.
Vilakazi, H.W. 1998. 'Education Policy for a Democratic Society'. In *Black Perspective(s) on Tertiary Institutional Transformation*, ed. S. Seepe, 69–90. Florida Hills: Vivlia Publishers and the University of Venda.
Wiredu, K. 1996. *Cultural Universals and Particulars: An African Perspective*. Bloomington: Indiana University Press.

13

Instrumentalisation in Universities and the Creative Potential of Race

BRUCE B. JANZ

When discussing race and higher education, in South Africa or elsewhere, the default discussion has tended to be over the nature and extent of historical racial inequities and how to rectify them. The university has been seen as a potential solution or response to social inequality and lack of opportunity for black students, the incipient continuation of racist beliefs and the lack of inspiring role models in society. The university, and education in general, so the argument goes, should be at the vanguard of social progress. It has been complicit in the racism in society, of course, and so the first task would be to put its own house in order by becoming truly representative of its culture, by giving full access to all and promoting a curriculum that is progressive. Beyond this, though, we imagine the university to be an engine of social change, where a new kind of leader is trained, where injustices throughout society are called out and condemned and where an equitable and harmonious society is modelled. In other words, if race is the lingering problem, the university is a potential solution.

What if, though, instead of regarding race as the problem and education as the solution, we thought of university education as the problem and race, or rather the history of survival and flourishing in racially oppressed and cramped situations, as a potential solution? How might the university be a problem? I argue here that universities around the world have moved ever further towards a model of instrumentalisation. The common response to this move is to re-assert the liberal arts vision of the university, but despite numerous attempts to reverse it, instrumentalisation proceeds apace. Thinking of the university as a problem does not only mean looking at its failed potential on issues of race, but also its transformation into an instrument of neo-liberal politics in two ways – by responding to external mandates and marketplace metaphors (this I call corporatisation) and by transforming itself internally by framing all problems as problems of implementation and accountability (this I call bureaucratisation). The turned question, then, is this: what can we learn from the history of flourishing and creativity in racially oppressed situations that might address the university's move toward instrumentalisation? Exploring this question is the goal of this chapter.

In what follows, I wish to use a Deleuzian approach to race to suggest some useful directions in higher education during an age of instrumentalisation. Universities in an age of instrumentalisation, I argue, are constrained, controlled and cramped spaces. The myriad ways that race has become manifest in South Africa and elsewhere can be described using concepts such as becoming, otherness and emergence. Race has a history of marginalisation and brutality, but also of survival and creativity. Survival is possible only because of creativity, which allows those who are deterritorialised to reterritorialise. The fact that race can become a creative space does not justify the brutal forces that produce inequality and injustice in the first place, nor does it suggest that we should not look for solutions to racial inequality. But this does not change the fact that creativity still exists within racially restricted and cramped circumstances.

Clearly the oppression of apartheid and racial oppression in general are far more serious than instrumentalisation in universities. However, much can be learned from the ways in which race has been creative, by providing concepts, experiences and affects that open up the university to ways of thinking and being that cannot be easily codified in disciplinary structures or methods. Small examples of this already exist – race studies and gender studies emerged because no single discipline was adequate to address the shifting and heterogeneous experience of some people and groups. The rise of these programmes provided space for this kind of inquiry and also simultaneously challenged disciplinary approaches that tended to reduce questions in these areas to ones that could be answered using already existing methods and theories. These areas served to deterritorialise disciplines, that is, they eroded a disciplinary geography and opened its borders to methods from other areas. But there is nothing in these areas that guarantees the space will be creative – these could just as well be absorbed into an instrumentalised university. They are, rather, the evidence of past struggles, even as they continue to open up inquiry in various ways.

And so, there are traces of past deterritorialisations still remaining in universities. This chapter explores other ways in which the negotiations and knowledge learned in the context of the lived experience of race might creatively destabilise university structures and help to resist the move toward instrumentalisation. My argument here is that there is much to be learned from those who suffered racial discrimination, not only in the forms of resistance that they mounted or in the triumphalist stories we can tell now about how everything turned out, but also in the recognition that life was still to be lived even in the circumstances of oppression and that creativity was still possible. The instrumentalised university is a dying university and its attempts to make itself relevant to the corporate or political world need to be met, not with an equal and opposing vision of the classical liberal arts university, but with moments of creativity within the cramped space that presents itself.

Instrumentalisation and universities

As universities worldwide move towards a corporate model of knowledge-production based on instruments of accountability and competitive metrics, there is a sense that the classic model of the university is slipping away. Universities are increasingly seen by governments and the public as agents for the solution to social problems such as poverty, racial inequality and lack of opportunity. They are also seen as economic drivers, either through the kind of training they provide or because of the products, patents or innovations they make possible.

While these may be laudable goals in the abstract, this amounts to an instrumentalisation of the university that is difficult to rationalise with the traditional role of the university as a site for the creation of knowledge in all its forms. If the goal of the pursuit of knowledge for its own sake and the ideals of a liberal education leading to informed citizens were both maintained, it might even be that these goals could all be met. There is, of course, nothing that says an institution must remain fixed in one role or that it cannot meet multiple goals at the same time. The problem is that instrumentalisation tends to lead to an either/or situation, in which the imperatives of a corporate or social agenda supersede and undermine the imperatives of an educational agenda. There ends up being a centripetal pressure towards rationalisation of resources within an instrumentalised setting. Publically funded education is particularly susceptible to these forces, as it is in some sense subject to political governance (at least some of its funding comes from people who need to be re-elected). Universities find themselves in a new situation, one in which they are being asked to fulfil economic and social imperatives imposed from outside themselves, to the exclusion of any others.

When I use the term 'instrumentalisation' in connection with universities, I mean to include two processes: corporatisation and bureaucratisation. Corporatisation is the overlay of the metaphor of corporate governance and processes on the university. This includes (among many other features) a focus on outcomes defined in quantifiable terms such as graduation rates, student credit hour production and so forth; the use of the metaphor of the marketplace as a model for internal university relationships and an orientation toward 'practicality' as defined externally (an example of this can be seen in Trani and Holsworth 2010). In addition, it includes using priorities set in the private sector as the priorities for public higher education. The phenomenon of corporatisation in universities has been well documented over the past ten years, in books by Derek Bok (2003), Mark Bousquet (2008), Frank Donoghue (2008), Martha Nussbaum (2010), Gaye Tuchman (2009) and Trevor Hussey and Patrick Smith (2010) and in edited volumes by Mike Molesworth, Richard Scullion and Elizabeth Nixon (2011) and also by Benjamin Johnson, Patrick Kavanagh and Kevin Mattson (2003), among many others. These volumes focus mainly on universities in North America and the United Kingdom, but the phenomenon has also been noted in Africa (Habib, Morrow and Bentley 2008; Barchiesi 2009; for an extended treatment, see Bentley, Habib and Morrow 2006).

Bureaucratisation, sometimes also known as 'managerialism', is the move towards treating all problems as problems of implementation and procedure. It is the assumption that all problems can be addressed by a procedure. This is a phenomenon perhaps less documented, but which grows out of an emphasis on accountability and assessment within universities. Even when accountability is said to spring from the disciplines themselves, defining their own assessment tools, the structure of that accountability is often defined externally, so that results can be compared across the board. As a consequence, assessment tools rooted in positivist social science tend to be used, which can miss the core of disciplinary training, particularly in the humanities and arts. Bureaucratisation is like the move towards corporatisation in that it also prizes rationalisation, although the goal for bureaucratisation is less often the maximisation of production and more often the protection of the university against threats such as lawsuits, lost revenue or further government or accrediting body intervention. The result of this focus is a burgeoning administrative sector within the university, sometimes in tandem with a reduction in teaching staff, and the resultant rationalisation of procedures for oversight and surveillance.

Both aspects of instrumentalisation assume a kind of totalising picture of higher education and this totalisation infuses all aspects of both internal and external language about the university. Students become at once 'customers' and 'products'; families, governments and businesses become 'stakeholders'; faculties become 'service personnel' and more than ever are hired in the short term to teach specific courses, like independent contractors; administrators become 'managers', having control over all aspects of the operation of the enterprise, treating those who have expertise in (for instance) curricular areas as advisers, rather than as centrally invested in the design of the educational experience.

Instrumentalisation manifests itself somewhat differently in different places, depending on factors such as the history of styles of university governance and funding, the history of the relationship between the university and the state and the histories of the participating people and groups. It can range from framing higher education's value as predominantly being an engine of economic growth and job-creation to more subtle forms of instrumentalisation that come out of the pressure of decreasing resources available to universities to serve larger and more diverse populations and the concomitant need to focus on the maximisation of those resources prior to any questions about any other function that is more difficult to operationalise. It comes in the form of increasing class sizes and escalating administrative staff, at the same time as more administrative work is passed to departments and individuals to do. Each of these elements reasserts the model of the university as factory, not as lab, atelier, seminar room or performance space.

One temptation when thinking about instrumentalisation is to see it as a form of modernisation, which would tend towards rendering subjects as anonymous cogs in a machine called 'education'. We may then think that resisting this instrumentalisation is a process of resubjectifying the members of the university community, that is, bringing them back to individuality after their having been turned into elements in a corporatised and bureaucratised system. The reality is, though, that it is more likely that the restrictions and 'cramped' forms of life that result from instrumentalisation allow a kind of shared creation. Just as the strictures of racial oppression produce a kind of solidarity, mediated and sustained through literature and forms of expression that create something new, resistance to instrumentalisation in the university setting may be an engine of creativity, rather than merely of frustration.

Most responses to the instrumentalised university try to construct a system of meaning as powerful as that driven by the market and by bureaucratised systems. The liberal arts, we argue, are still necessary to produce the informed and active citizen. Art and beauty, we say, are still necessary in a world of bottom lines and outcomes. There is another register of meaning beyond the instrumental. But these defences of the traditional university ring hollow. They certainly do little to convince anyone to support activities that do not immediately lead to jobs or that do not clearly produce transferrable skills or cannot be operationalised and tested. And it is perhaps no wonder, since the battle is being fought in the marketplace, in the very place that instrumentalisation is meant to succeed. It is, in Gilles Deleuze's terms, a molar system (in other words, a massive dominant or state-like system that has much invested in its own stability and structures – Deleuze and Guattari 1987: 213ff.) and the attempt to meet it with the memory of the classic university and its virtues is an attempt to meet one molar system with another.

It is noteworthy that examples of successful racial resistance have not followed the path of pitting race against race, trying to substitute one system of supremacy with another. What we see, especially in South Africa, is a combination of reactions, some overt, some political and some subtle and nuanced, to respond to a molar system that cannot be met on its own terms.

Instrumentalisation is a linguistic phenomenon. It changes the language of the university into one of efficiency and outcomes. This language changes the institutions within the university. Because it is linguistic, the response is also linguistic. As we think about the strategies of racial flourishing, we should be looking to the linguistic strategies primarily. How is it, in other words, that in the face of an overwhelming linguistic paradigm (what we might call a 'major' language), those who do not easily fit within its structures find ways to live and move? They use, following Deleuze and Félix Guattari (1986), a 'minor' language and, with it, a minor literature. This does not refer to an unimportant language, or even a marginal language, but rather a language that undermines and reappropriates the major language, to show its gaps and oversights.

Instrumentalisation often uses the language of becoming, in the sense of changing university structures to something more resembling a marketplace. The image is often of a university stuck in the past, while other institutions of society have moved forwards. The move to more accountability is claimed to be a kind of becoming, an emergence into a new order. The problem with this frame is that it gets the move backwards. The language of instrumentalisation, and the resulting effects within the university, is one of the last moves towards bringing an institution of society fully into the marketplace. It is not about becoming, in other words, but about being, about an essence that already exists in society and that is seen as necessary in the university as well.

It is rather the minoritarian move, the ones resisting instrumentalisation who find themselves becoming. They necessarily must use the language of outcomes, assessment, accountability and so forth. They must live within university structures that deliberately miss that which cannot be quantified and measured in human learning. Just as racial resistance often found ways to use the elements of the majoritarian world against itself, finding its cracks even as it used them to bring the marginalised together so, too, effective resistance to instrumentalisation will find cracks, creating something new without owning the system in which it exists.

Minor literature, race and universities

What is a minor literature? Deleuze and Guattari (1986: 16) address this question in their work on Franz Kafka: 'A minor literature doesn't come from a minor language; it is rather that which a minority constructs within a major language.' It is, in other words, a set of creative options that are expressed within a 'cramped' space. It has several characteristics. First, in a minor literature, 'language is affected with a high coefficient of deterritorialisation'. In other words, if we think about the major language as having staked claim to a territory, minor literature unseats its pretensions of ownership and mastery over that space. We can see this in classic African works such as Ngũgĩ wa Thiong'o's treatments of post- and neocolonial Kenya, in Okot p'Bitek's song forms (for example, *Song of Lawino*) and so forth. These are works that do not simply yearn for an imagined (although not imaginary) past, but create a community with contemporary actions that inevitably draw on the molar structures.

Second, in minor literatures, 'everything is political' (Deleuze and Guattari 1986: 17). In major literatures, it is possible to imagine that there are areas that are not affected by politics, areas of individual concern. In minor literatures, the 'cramped space forces each individual intrigue to connect immediately to politics'. And third, in a minor literature, 'everything takes on a collective value', since the cramped space left for action within the major territory forces those who act in that space to recognise the place (the community, the situation) out of which that literature emerges. The collectivity is not a Marxist-style class consciousness, but an assemblage of those who are able to grasp the minoritarian frame due to sharing the limited space afforded by the major language.

> The minor, then, is a creativity of minorities: those who find their movements and expressions 'cramped' on all sides such that they cannot in any conventional sense be said to have carved out a delineated social space of their 'own' where they could be called 'a people'. Without an autonomous delineated sphere, the site of minor politics becomes the wealth of social forces that traverse minorities and cramp movement into identity. It is from their very cramped and complex situations that politics emerges – no longer as a process of facilitating and bolstering identity, or 'becoming-conscious', but as a process of innovation, of experimentation, and of the complication of life, in which forms of community, techniques of practice, ethical demeanours, styles, knowledges, and cultural forms are composed (Thoburn 2003: 8).

Racial resistance under apartheid and other forms of domination often took the form of minoritarian literature. And, without suggesting that the molar structures of the instrumentalised university are at all like the apartheid government and other racist regimes in the severity and brutality they visit upon people, there is one abstract feature that is similar – both those governments and the instrumentalised university stand as majoritarian languages, territorialising as much as they can. In this sense, those who find themselves in a cramped position have a choice – they can either take the route of trying to establish a competing territorial claim and setting up a situation of war, one molar structure against another, or they can proceed as minoritarian, deterritorialising the space that the major language has claimed for itself, undermining it and showing how the assemblage of those who do not fit into the major language nevertheless have the ability to create something new. None of this means that either those under racial oppression or those in the instrumentalised university need to accept the inevitability of those regimes. What it does mean is that creativity can happen along the way and that creativity will have as much of a part in eventually changing the major language as anything else.

This is what those in the university who are unwilling to simply accept instrumentalisation can learn from those who have gone through the brutally cramped space of racial marginalisation. To extend Arun Saldanha's argument, there can be a 'thousand tiny races'. 'Race,' he says,

> should not be eliminated but *proliferated*, its many energies directed at multiplying racial differences so as to render them joyfully cacophonic ... What is needed is an affirmation of race's creativity and virtuality: what race *can be*. Race need not be about order and oppression, it can be wild, far-from-equilibrium, liberatory (Saldanha 2006: 21).

It is the molecularisation of race, the ability to see the small differences as creative moments, even as they are rationalised by the majoritarian literature into a single category, or a small number of categories, more easily dealt with on its own terms. Deleuze and Guattari (1987: 379) take up the issue of race:

> The race-tribe exists only at the level of an oppressed race, and in the name of the oppression it suffers: there is no race but inferior, minoritarian; there is no dominant race; a race is defined not by its purity but rather by the impurity conferred upon it by a system of domination.

If the instrumentalised university is molar, or majoritarian, the form of resistance that Nicholas Thoburn derives from Deleuze and Guattari's work on Kafka is about a politics for a time when 'the people are missing' (2003: 16). And if race is minoritarian, the missing people can, in fact, form a creative response.

The use of 'race', rather than another concept such as 'culture' is important in this context because this is the basis for the difference between the molar and the minor. Cultural artefacts certainly arise from racialised activity in a minor literature (literature is, after all, a cultural construct itself), but the driving difference during apartheid was not simply culture, but race. It was race that created cramped spaces and that enabled a certain kind of Deleuzian intensity, or creative tension, that allowed specific cultural forms to manifest themselves. For the purposes of this chapter, it is this frission that is instructive. It is not the only possible one, of course.

Race and creativity

There are plenty of examples in which those oppressed under apartheid resisted a variety of strictures within universities. But this is not exactly what I have in mind when I think about strategies of resistance within race. I am thinking of more basic strategies of racial survival and flourishing. I am thinking of the ways in which subjects live in the concrete world. As Achille Mbembe (2001: 17) puts it:

> In Africa today, the subject who accomplishes the age and validates it, who lives and espouses his/her contemporaneousness – that is, what is 'distinctive' or 'particular' to his/her present real world – is first a subject who has an experience of 'living in the concrete world.' She/he is a subject of experience and a validating subject, not only in the sense that she/he is a conscious existence or has a perceptive consciousness of things, but to the extent that his/her 'living in the concrete world' involves, and is evaluated by, his/her eyes, ears, mouth – in short, his/her flesh, his/her body. What are these modes of validation of conscious existence? Which are capable of being re-actualised? What is the share of arbitrariness in that re-actualisation? And to what particular figures of reason and violence does that arbitrariness refer?

Reactualising the self in this concrete world, this material and embodied place, is what Mbembe is interested in. Mbembe's *On the Postcolony* imagines a vulgar, cramped, violent space that faces inhabitants of African countries today, a space where flourishing seems all but impossible. And so, we might be surprised by the last sentences of the book:

What is certain is that, when we are confronted by such a work of art, Nietzsche's words regarding Greek tragedy are appropriate: 'We must first learn to enjoy as complete men.' Now, what is learning to enjoy as complete men – and women – unless it is a way of living and existing in uncertainty, chance, irreality, even absurdity (Mbembe 2001: 242).

Is it possible to learn to 'enjoy as complete men' and women in such a place? If we imagine that the injustices must be overcome first, that the majoritarian literature will be overthrown, then no. And yet, Mbembe sees life in this space. He is, in fact, arguing for life in 'irreality', not unreality, but a virtual life in a cramped space. 'Virtual' here does not mean imaginary, utopian or immaterial, but emergent from existing conditions, autopoietic and contingent. It is a life that can be enjoyed because, I would maintain, it is a spontaneous creation.

In 'African Modes of Self-Writing', Mbembe considers some dead ends that he terms 'instrumentalism' (used in a different sense than I am using it here) and 'nativism', which claim to reassert African subjectivities, but which in fact totalise African experience by only considering slavery, colonisation and apartheid as relevant factors in the dissipation and recovery of the subject. Mbembe's (2002: 242) alternative is as follows:

> Against the arguments of critics who have equated identity with race and geography, I show how current African imaginations of the self are born out of disparate but often intersecting practices, the goal of which is not only to settle factual and moral disputes about the world but also to open the way for *self-styling*.

The question, in other words, is not about resistance to the conditions that produced tragic results for African subjectivity, but about the imagination that makes subjectivity possible, given the history of the place. It is the privileging of victimhood over subjecthood (Mbembe 2002: 245).

> African identity does not exist as a substance. It is constituted, in varying forms, through a series of practices, notably *practices of the self* ... These forms and idioms are mobile, reversible, and unstable. Given this element of play, they cannot be reduced to purely biological order based on blood, race, or geography (Mbembe 2002: 272).

Mbembe's point is that opposing a molar identity of colonialism or apartheid with another molar identity of 'Africanity', established through a process such as instrumentalism or nativism, will doom African thought to conceive of politics as the recovery of an essential but lost identity, rather than the construction of an identity responsive to the contemporary world (for more on this, see Janz 2012). As with his conclusion to *On the Postcolony*, he is calling for the creation of a life in circumstances where the majoritarian literature will not be overturned.

Another example of molecular creativity connected to race is Sophiatown, the township destroyed in the 1950s by the apartheid government. Sophiatown has been compared to the Harlem Renaissance and for good reason. There was incredible creativity, in a variety of ways. Many great writers lived and worked there. There was freedom, but in a sense it was a freedom that was claimed. It did not last, of course – the state apparatus of apartheid saw to that. And yet, it was a place where there was a particular kind of freedom, the kind that did not simply answer the molar presence of apartheid, but which allowed for multiple lines of flight, multiple ways of using the materials of the world at the time for new creative acts. Father Trevor Huddleston gave a young boy a trumpet and, even though Sophiatown was destroyed, that young boy, Hugh Masekela, got his start. Others found a way to experiment, to try things, in the midst of a situation that was anything but free. Can Themba (1959: 53) captures the moment, shortly after the loss of Sophiatown:

> Somewhere here, and among a thousand more individualistic things, is the magic of Sophiatown. It is different and itself. You don't just find your place here, you make it and you find yourself. There's a tang about it. You might now and then have

to give way to others making their ways of life by methods not in the book. But you can't be bored. You have the right to listen to the latest jazz records at Ah Sing's over the road. You can walk a Coloured girl of an evening down to the Odin Cinema, and no questions asked. You can try out Rhugubar's curry with your bare fingers without embarrassment. All this with no sense of heresy. Indeed, I've shown quite a few white people 'the little Paris of the Transvaal' – but only a few were Afrikaners.

The place must not be romanticised – the crime rate was high and it was a difficult life for those who lived there. But it was also a place where difference produced new ideas, where rich rubbed elbows with poor. It was a long time before apartheid fell and things got worse before they got better, but the construction of identity happened here in a way that informed and sustained those who came later. Sophiatown's *Drum* magazine showed life under apartheid as it was, while training a host of writers and photographers. Most importantly, it was a place where racial difference existed, but was turned to creative purpose, instead of destructive purpose as in the rest of South Africa at the time. It was a cramped space and yet it led to cultural and intellectual creativity.

Part of the mark of the power of Sophiatown is that it continues to exist in the public imagination, through books, musicals and art. What would it mean to reinstate the spirit of Sophiatown? It would not mean that the place should be reconstructed and recaptured in any literal way. It is reinstated by being re-enacted, remembered and seen as a moment in the imagination of blackness during apartheid. This is not romanticisation, it is repetition, in the manner that we can see in the work of Søren Kierkegaard, Martin Heidegger and Hans-Georg Gadamer. It cannot be duplicated, but it can be repeated by finding ways to bring to the surface its creative and life-giving nature. This is the essence of minoritarian literature – it is creativity in a cramped space and that creativity is carried forward through difference.

Another example of racial responses to cramped situations is the song and performance form known as *isicathamiya*. This musical form emerged with the rise of apartheid among isiZulu speakers (Gunner 2006) and its early a cappella forms were particularly popular at a local level from the 1930s onwards. While today it stands in the shadow of other musical forms such as kwaito among young people, what is important is that it can be seen as a minoritarian literature in its place and time. Liz Gunner (2006: 90) explains its role:

> The space of the song becomes a means of participating in the public sphere and passing on messages to the powerful: about the lack of jobs, about child rape, about women abuse, but also about hope for the future, '*ikusasa lethu*' (our tomorrow). It also provides a means of unlocking memory and the past, because the genre allows for memory and is through its very continuity – its elastic and flexible continuity – a means of keeping open a window to the past in a fast-paced world that is both intensely local and also clearly very global.

Notably, this music is not about answering back to racial oppression, but rather is about living in the space that is available. This is done in the content of the songs, but also in the performative space that *isicathamiya* operates. The group competitions are a form of struggle, but more than that, they 'propose an alternative ideal social order' (McNeill 2011: 158). Fraser NcNeill continues:

> They attempt to fuse the negative structural relationships of their immediate environment with positive meaning by replicating its competitive logic on a smaller and more manageable scale in *isicathamiya* performances and competitions. Exponents of the genre thus attempt to return coherence into a world shattered beyond their control by singing critically about the alienation of migrant life ... Performance thus constitutes the search for an autonomous social and political sphere, a created space able to connect notions of the past and the present, and through which new ideas are spun and contested.

The performance is another example of a minoritarian literature, a creative act in a cramped space. It is not only the fact of the music itself, but also the space created through the competitions and performances that allow the creation of subjectivity in the midst of the overwhelming economic logic present in both apartheid and post-apartheid South Africa.

A final example is the history of *négritude*. *Négritude* is usually thought as an essentialist racial strategy, designed to answer back to European racial essentialism by positing an alternative form of Africanity, equal but different from European rationality. Put in these terms, it is anything but minoritarian. And yet, it is worth considering the possibility that *négritude*'s power has been misunderstood, that too much emphasis has been placed on its interpretation as essentialist, while not enough attention has been given to the ways in which it used majoritarian forms to produce something new in the moment, for the moment. A 2010 issue of the journal *Third Text* raises the question of the misunderstanding of *négritude*. The argument in this issue, as expressed in its call for papers, was to rectify the mistaken interpretation of *négritude*, which was an 'over-privileging of racialist, ethno-artistic contents [that] seemed to have suppressed many of Negritude's rich sociopolitical insights' (Araeen 2010: 171). The authors who responded to this issue tend not to interpret *négritude* through the actions of Léopold Sédar Senghor while he was president of Senegal, or the later 'failure' of *négritude* (as if it was meant as a blueprint for the future), but through the creative moment that the movement afforded at a time when that was needed.

Négritude is not the positing of another molar essence, a black alternative to white rationality, but the imagination of a blackness-to-come. A majoritarian point of view sees it as a model of itself, another form of rationality equal but different to its own. But this misses the force of it. Its transgressive force is in its performance, its sometimes overblown rhetoric, its way of turning molar European assumptions on their head, playing with them, finding space for a new literature within them. Aimé Césaire, Senghor and others captured a moment and perhaps the greatest compliment one could give to its minoritarian status was that it could not be turned into a credible political philosophy or theory of identity.

These examples, and more that could be given, give evidence of ways of turning racial marginalisation into moments of creativity. Those moments may not have had an immediate effect – Sophiatown, for instance, was bulldozed and *négritude* did not produce any change in state structures – but the creative life of those moments lived in later developments. The point was not to overcome, but to survive as human beings. Overcoming is also a worthy goal, but surviving has to come first.

Instrumentalisation and creativity in universities

The argument so far has been that universities are characterised by instrumentalisation, manifest in the form of corporatisation and bureaucratisation. This is what I have termed a 'majoritarian' literature, a totalising language that attempts to bring all life under its purview. The instrumentalised university is a cramped form of academic life. It exists in a time hemmed in by external imperatives for knowledge-production and internal structures that must be met in advance of any creative activity. For Deleuze, the molecular response draws on the existing semiotics of the molar. It does not merely subvert, but produces a line of flight that is not anticipated within the molar structure. It makes language rich again, after it has been forced into a cramped mode.

As previously suggested, the problem with many arguments against the instrumentalised university is that they come in the form of presenting a contrasting molar identity, the 'classical liberal arts university', as an alternative. Intellectually, this makes good sense, just as pitting 'Black' against 'White' or 'Indigenous' against 'Colonial' makes good intellectual sense. The problem is, as Mbembe and others have pointed out, in our material reality these battles seldom come out in favour of justice for the marginalised. 'White' can always find ways to reinscribe itself; 'Colonial' can always find new ways to dominate. The market always wins and, as Karl Marx suggested, everything can be commodified.

Does this leave us in despair? Is there then no point in fighting against injustice? Far from it. It leaves us in the position to recognise the ways in which racially oppressed groups have found ways to turn a molar identity against itself, to write minoritarian literature. Deleuze thought that all the world's great literature was minoritarian and the reasons are clear. It is the cramped space that produces the conditions of creativity. It was the cramped space of Sophiatown that could invigorate *Drum*; without it, there would only be the *South African Panorama* of the 1950s. The daring ideas produced daring writing, photographs and an entire orientation toward creativity in *Drum*, whereas *South African Panorama*, as the voice of the apartheid state, could produce little more than propaganda, packaged in a banal manner. Instead of *Drum*'s vision of a creative, molecular future, *South African Panorama* reinscribed the white molar fantasy, with non-white races happy in their subservience. One could hardly imagine great literature or images in *Panorama*, whereas these became a regular feature in *Drum*.

A similar move is needed, I would argue, as we conceive the history and future of higher education, in Africa and around the world. The instrumentalised university has achieved dominance in most public education. Appeals to the liberal arts tradition have tended to fall on deaf ears. Why is that? There are several reasons. It is difficult to operationalise or monetise liberal arts education. It is difficult to draw direct lines between it and countable social goods (despite the studies that show the importance of the creative class to economic health and prosperity). But there is a more fundamental reason – the classical liberal arts have been positioned as a combatant with instrumentalisation, a majoritarian foe against another majoritarian foe. While it is conceivable that liberal higher education might once have been like this (and that is debatable), as the twentieth century ended, the dominant voices in education were the instrumental ones, not the classical liberal ones. This suggests that the strategy of positioning liberal education as a kind of bygone empire of education may hold emotional appeal, but little else, just as thinking about the lost grandeur of racial achievement may allow an emotional connection to a place, but does not hold forth the hope of articulating and creating a new space, given the material realities of the present and future. What is needed instead is for liberal education to think of itself more like a minor literature, rather than a lost classic.

How can the creative tradition in the university be considered a minor literature? Is it not the case, after all, that we are talking about the classical liberal arts tradition that is being pushed aside by instrumentalisation? I would like to frame the issue differently than seeing this as a struggle between the liberal arts and market-based and bureaucratised universities. Many of the contemporary arguments against the instrumentalised university do so against the backdrop of the good old days and what has been lost from the tradition of 'real' education. It is worth noting, though, that the defences of the liberal university are mainly from the twentieth century (John Henry Cardinal Newman's *The Idea of a University* notwithstanding). In other words, they arise along with the advent of corporate and industrial models in both the private and governmental world. The 'classic' university is articulated as such only when it is perceived to be under threat. As with the concept of 'tradition', it arises for a specific set of historical reasons and is understood as a stable object standing against a real threat (for more on tradition, see 'Tradition in the Periphery' in Janz 2009).

In other words, the conscious imagination of the classical liberal arts university is relatively recent. Of course, descriptions of the liberal arts in the university go back to the foundation of universities themselves in the Middle Ages, but those were descriptions of modes of operating, rather than molar entities pitted against other molar entities. The point here is this: arguing from the classic nature of the university has not had much success for a good reason – that classic nature never really existed in the first place. What existed were patterns and flows of knowledge-creation and -transmission (and as Newman makes clear, the transmission of universal knowledge was far more important than the production of new knowledge). Those could become ossified (as happened with the Aristotelean curriculum until the nineteenth century), but that was only an increasingly thick shell of custom and form around the timeless knowledge that was the focus of most universities. With the rise of disciplinarity in the late nineteenth century, we begin to have an emphasis on the production of knowledge.

Where are the interdisciplinary points of creation, the places where the university is not only productive, but also creative? Are there any left? Where are the spaces that regimes of knowledge can play off against grant-driven, state-sanctioned research? Is there a place where those disciplines suspected of resisting instrumentalisation can go to maintain their identities? Where is the university's Sophiatown?

It is interesting to look at proposals for reform in the face of instrumentalisation. Sometimes, what is seen as creativity in higher education is more or less an attempt to maximise student outcomes and success, in terms recognisable by instrumentalised logic. These 'transformations' of the university do not address any of the issues raised here. At other times, they involved dialogue amongst those marginalised, implementing transformative pedagogical strategies, adopting technologies of various sorts that will ensure access and so forth (for instance, see the proposals in Walker and Nixon 2003). These are perfectly acceptable strategies, but if my argument to this point is correct, these efforts will continue to be frustrated, due to operating in the cramped space of instrumentalisation. What is apparent from the examples given of minoritarian literature in cramped racial spaces is that the space that is gained comes through finding ways to use the molar system against itself, to use its language to show forth the cracks.

One prospect for a minoritarian literature within the university is a form of interdisciplinarity, specifically knowledge that occurs at the boundaries of existing methodological approaches and resists essentialised categories. One strategy in a racially complex environment is to cross boundaries and understand multiple languages and worlds in order to survive. The survivors of racial oppression often do so as polyglot, hybridised subjects, able to operate at different registers and in different dialects. This adaptability is, in fact, seen as a virtue within universities, even though the structures of universities mitigate against its full engagement. The skills of racial survival can make common cause with other aspects of the university that are valued and that undermine instrumentalisation.

Interdisciplinarity is often seen as an advanced mode of production in the university, an additive strategy that can leverage aspects of disciplines to solve a difficult problem. To this extent, it is simply another aspect of the instrumentalised university. But we can imagine a form of interdisciplinarity that does not simply serve external imperatives or rationalise resources, but creates space for those left behind in the move towards instrumentalisation. Disciplines currently are the place of knowledge-production and -transfer and are founded on sets of methods that can reliably produce that knowledge. What is needed is a kind of anti-disciplinarity, where methods are not combined to produce a greater effect, but where those disciplinary methods show the scope and limits of each other. Such a relationship would likely garner few grants, but it would be a new creative space, because it would be a space in which questions would be asked that could not be asked from within the discipline itself. It would be a space in which STEM disciplines (science, technology, engineering, mathematics) would not merely be touted as the engine of economic growth (as the molar system would continue to do), but rather as part of a flow of questions that includes non-STEM areas.

Another form of disruptive, creative space is a different way of breaking down the reliance of disciplines on the methods they have honed over the years. Disciplines currently foster a culture of expertise, and necessarily so, as advanced knowledge requires a great deal of technical knowledge. What is becoming apparent, though, is that it is possible to bring non-experts into aspects of the creative process. Sciences have started to use crowd-sourced data collection and analysis. History has begun to be conducted by amateurs, as well as professionals, in the form of public history and oral history projects. These amateurs are not simply informants, but in some cases are a motivated public (for example, see Trewhela 2010). This has had several effects. In some cases, it has actually advanced understanding in ways that would not have been possible otherwise. Foldit, for instance, the online game that was developed by scientists to aid in finding solutions for protein folding, has uncovered strategies for folding that had stumped scientists for years. Another effect, though, is that this presents a model for collaboration between scientists and another expert community, of gamers, which directs the scientists to think about their objects of study differently.

This can be seen as simply an advanced mode of production and, in the case of Foldit, perhaps it is. A minoritarian literature does not reject the possibility of production; it just does not hold this as its primary goal. The general idea of collaboration between expert communities that are not all academic could easily be seen as spaces in which the experts are pushed out of their comfort zone. Creativity is virtual in this case – it cannot be programmed, although the ground may be laid for it by setting up a tension between communities that can generate new questions. And, the tendency of disciplines will always be to regularise and absorb discoveries of this sort, so creativity will be virtual in that sense as well.

A third space that could be opened in an instrumentalised setting is international collaboration, in particular North-South or South-South collaboration. Sverker Sörlin and Hebe Vessuri (2007: 2) distinguish between the knowledge economy and the knowledge society. Knowledge economies have a 'democratic deficit':

> Knowledge-based economies are growing all around us, but they do so without always acknowledging the democratic, ethical, and normative dimensions of science and scientific institutions. The knowledge economy is market-driven and performs according to a market ideology, which stands in a problematic but not necessarily conflicting relation to the norms and ideas of the knowledge society.

For universities to be driven primarily by the knowledge economy is to fail to recognise the democratic and normative dimensions of their own pursuits. These deficits cannot be fixed merely with codes of conduct or faculty governance, as important as these are. And they cannot be addressed merely by realising that they are an issue, because the external imperatives will always render them secondary concerns. So, a more creative space can be opened only when institutions willingly place themselves in dialogue with other institutions outside of the immediate knowledge economy they inhabit. Of course, in a global world, ultimately all economies are interrelated. But we are not yet at that point and the difference between national discourses of knowledge, which are able to raise questions unavailable within one's own context, can provide some of the creative space that instrumentalisation undermines.

Interdisciplinarity of the sort that I describe here, putting academics and non-academics in creative tension, as well as international collaboration, can open spaces for creativity in an instrumentalised space that has all but squeezed out the potential for creativity. None of these strategies is necessarily stable on a long-term basis – as mentioned, it is the tendency of disciplines to absorb creativity and transform it into productivity (which is not the same thing) and it is the tendency of instrumentalised universities to regularise and frame any creative act in such a manner that it can be marketed (at least to its alumni, if not through patents and copyrights). Just as with the examples earlier, such as Sophiatown, the moment of creativity is ephemeral, but crucial. The point is this: just as racially cramped spaces afforded some creative moments that can be seen as minoritarian so, too, can the cramped nature of instrumentalisation afford the basis for a minoritarian literature within the university, where creativity has a chance of happening.

References

Araeen, R. 2010. 'Preface: Why "beyond" Negritude?' *Third Text* 24 (2) (March): 167–76.

Barchiesi, F. 2009. 'Lean and Very Mean: Restructuring the University in South Africa'. In *Toward a Global Autonomous University*, ed. The Edu-Factory Collective, 66–71. New York: Autonomedia.

Bentley, K., A. Habib and S. Morrow. 2006. *Academic Freedom, Institutional Autonomy and the Corporatised University in Contemporary South Africa.* Pretoria: Council on Higher Education. http://www.cshe.uwc.ac.za/docs/2007/BentleyHabibMorrow.pdf.

Bok, D. 2003. *Universities in the Marketplace: The Commercialization of Higher Education.* Princeton: Princeton University Press.

Bousquet, M. 2008. *How the University Works: Higher Education and the Low-Wage Nation.* New York: New York University Press.

Deleuze, G. and F. Guattari. 1986. *Kafka: Toward a Minor Literature.* Minneapolis: University of Minnesota Press.

———. 1987. *A Thousand Plateaus: Capitalism and Schizophrenia.* Minneapolis: University of Minnesota Press.

Donoghue, F. 2008. *The Last Professors: The Twilight of the Humanities in the Corporate University.* New York: Fordham University Press.

Gunner, L. 2006. 'Zulu Choral Music: Performing Identities in a New State'. *Research in African Literatures* 37 (2) (Summer): 83–97.

Habib, A., S. Morrow and K. Bentley. 2008. 'Academic Freedom, Institutional Autonomy and the Corporatised University in Contemporary South Africa'. *Social Dynamics* 34 (2): 140–55.

Hussey, T. and P. Smith. 2010. *The Trouble with Higher Education: A Critical Examination of Our Universities*. Oxford: Routledge.

Janz, B. 2009. *Philosophy in an African Place*. Lanham: Lexington Books.

———. 2012. 'Forget Deleuze'. In *Postcolonial Literatures and Deleuze: Colonial Pasts, Differential Futures*, ed. L. Burns and B.M. Kaiser, 21–36. London: Palgrave MacMillan.

Johnson, B., P. Kavanagh and K. Mattson, eds. 2003. *Steal This University: The Rise of the Corporate University and the American Labour Movement*. Oxford: Routledge.

Mbembe, A. 2001. *On the Postcolony*. Berkeley: University of California Press.

———. 2002. 'African Modes of Self-Writing'. *Public Culture* 14 (1): 239–73.

McNeill, F. 2011. *AIDS, Politics and Music in South Africa*. Cambridge: Cambridge University Press.

Molesworth, M., R. Scullion and E. Nixon, eds. 2011. *The Marketisation of Higher Education and the Student as Consumer*. Oxford: Routledge.

Nussbaum, M. 2010. *Not For Profit: Why Democracy Needs the Humanities*. Princeton: Princeton University Press.

Saldanha, A. 2006. 'Reontologising Race: The Machinic Geography of Phenotype'. *Environment and Planning D: Society and Space* 24 (9): 9–24.

Sörlin, S. and H. Vessuri, eds. 2007. *Knowledge Society vs. Knowledge Economy: Knowledge, Power, and Politics*. New York: Palgrave MacMillan.

Themba, C. 1959. 'Requiem for Sophiatown'. *Africa South* 3: 3.

Thoburn, N. 2003. *Deleuze, Marx and Politics*. London: Routledge.

Trani, E. and R.D. Holsworth. 2010. *The Indispensible University: Higher Education, Economic Development, and the Knowledge Economy*. Lanham: Rowman and Littlefield.

Trewhela, P. 2010. *Inside Quatro: Uncovering the Exile History of the ANC and SWAPO*. Reprint edition. Johannesburg: Jacana Media.

Tuchman, G. 2009. *Wannabe U: Inside the Corporate University*. Chicago: University of Chicago Press.

Walker, M. and J. Nixon, eds. 2003. *Reclaiming Universities from a Runaway World*. Buckingham: Open University Press.

Postscript

PEDRO TABENSKY and SALLY MATTHEWS

We would like to bring this collection to a close with a brief postscript, proposing a way forward for future research, based on a common thread found either implicitly or explicitly in most, if not all, contributions to this collection.

Our aim in putting this book together is practical. We believe the contemporary South African academic community has the rare opportunity – compared to global counterparts – of being in a position to recreate itself. The end of apartheid loosened recalcitrant structures, creating a unique space for engaging in transformative epistemic projects. Although this book does not provide a specific list of concrete recommendations, we hope that the ideas that have been developed here can inspire further debate and help to guide policy decisions.

We know that this book has not done enough to guide in a particular way, but this was never our intention, although many potential lines of flight have been explored. Before a blueprint for action can be provided, we need to understand the almost intangible, but potentially (and actually) caustic problem of untransformed institutional culture.

The transformation of the tertiary sector entails precisely a transformation of institutional cultures. A proper understanding of transformation therefore requires that we understand what institutional culture is. One of the primary motivators of this book is a sense of how little we actually understand the problem of institutional culture. Often sweeping generalisations are used to describe the culture of certain institutions, but these seldom enlighten. It is frequently said that traditionally white institutions in South Africa are racist, for instance.

We do not deny that this is the case, to a greater or lesser degree; however, we need to properly understand how it is that racism plays itself out in promoting particular institutional cultures. How does racism embed itself in the cultures of institutions of higher learning?

In this postscript, we provide a brief account of the nature of institutional culture that, complementing what has been discussed in the rest of this book, will hopefully help us to understand just how complex transformative projects are.

To claim that the problem of institutional culture is both intangible and corrosive is to suggest that the problem is akin to the questions that motivated Sigmund Freud's journey into the subconscious. Indeed, dare we say, to address the problem of institutional culture is largely to address the problem of what could be characterised as the institutional subconscious?

This may seem like an outlandish suggestion on first inspection, but the uncanny appearance of the suggestion will dissipate once we connect the present concerns with institutional culture with insights from feminism and critical race theory, both deeply influenced by psychoanalysis or, indeed, once we consider frequently used descriptions of the South African situation, which speak of our country as being pyschologically broken or psychically distorted. The insidiousness of racism and sexism stems mostly from the intractability of the problems, which is largely a function of the work of the subconscious in constituting and perpetuating racist and sexist injustice. Racists and sexists rarely admit to being so, not so much because they are being dishonest in a straightforward sense, but chiefly because they are being psychically disingenuous. We would be very ill-equipped indeed to address racist injustice, for instance, if we assume that its prototypical manifestation is overt racism. And when some proclaim their allegiance to some form or other of supremacy, one wonders what strange undercurrents motivate such proclamations. Indeed, one wonders, in the first instance, whether the proclaimer is sane.

Reason seems singularly ill-equipped to deal with these recalcitrant trends and, more often than not, helps to further entrench prejudice when it papers over cracks that would otherwise be visible. Reason is ill-equipped precisely because the region of the mind responsible for prejudice is resistant to the domain of reason. Prejudice, paraphrasing

Jean-Paul Sartre (1976), is a passion, that is, it is not so much guided by reason and a desire to make sense of the world but, rather, by needs that are better explained through psychoanalysis than through an appeal to theoretical commitments. Passions require therapy, rather than merely good argument. Therapy, in part, requires rational conversation, but it requires more than this, as Frantz Fanon knew all too well, which is why this insightful psychoanalyst understood that what Algeria needed – affected as it was by a deeply corrosive culture – was therapy of a very special sort. We may disagree with his specific revolutionary therapy, but we cannot fail to appreciate the insight that reason on its own is not going to bring racism to an end. What we need are changes in social and psychological structures, structures that feed on each other, thus constituting a recalcitrant feedback loop.

To think of the problem in this way is helpful, for it points to the idea that what is going to help us realise the goals of producing thriving institutions of higher learning is less intellectual work than it is therapy. The reader may think that we may be taking the analogy with psychoanalysis a little too far here, but we believe that this is not so. What we are pointing to here, and what most contributions to this collection in one way or another have grappled with, is the idea that institutional culture operates largely at the level of the invisible, or in the twilight zone between visible and invisible, detectable and undetectable – detectable in the sense that institutional behaviour flows from it, but undetectable in the sense that the underlying motivations require the subtle observational abilities of what could be characterised as an institutional psychotherapist.

We are not suggesting that it should be professional psychologists who are championing transformation. But we are inviting members of the South African academic community to reflect on their condition in ways that are analogous to the psychoanalytic method. Freud discovered the subconscious when he observed that overt behaviour and commitment could not be fully explained without appealing to recalcitrant motivational structures that are largely hidden from sight. If we are right to assume that the problem of institutional culture should indeed be understood in this way, we suggest that the epistemic project itself needs to be reconsidered, a topic we will turn to shortly.

Institutional culture is the character of an institution. By character here, we mean something akin to the character of a person. Most of what constitutes the character of a person operates beneath the radar, informing the texture of a life or, in the case that interests us, the texture of an institution. And it must, by virtue of the fact that it is a character, be recalcitrant, for characters are what define individuals in the first place, and institutions derivatively, rather than being incidental features of them.

There are aspects of character, personal or institutional, that are clearly observable. Those are the aspects that attentive outsiders can detect with relative ease. But overt aspects are part of a greater whole that is largely under the bonnet. Many people who come to Rhodes University for the first time, for instance, tend to see it as quaint and welcoming, as vibrant and dynamic, and so on. But closer scrutiny reveals traces of darker undercurrents and such traces are extremely difficult to interpret, although their effects on certain populations – particularly those who were previously excluded from attending Rhodes – is powerfully felt in the flesh, but often not properly understood, even by those who experience them.

The characters of persons only change, and only gradually and to a limited extent, after much personal work aimed at transforming patterns of thought and affect. They do not change by mere acts of will and veiled forces that are rarely properly understood starkly delimit how much they can change. Taking a leaf from Aristotle, at least one thing that is required for our characters to start to change is habituation. But, taking a leaf from Karl Marx, shifts in structural conditions are also required. We are deeply susceptible to adopting views that stem from our specific locatedness in social space and much systematic and attentive work on the self is required for us to be able to resist structural pressures.

Much the same applies to the character of institutions. What does all this say about the intellectual project as it is currently conceived of? What does the recalcitrance of institutional culture tell us about epistemic projects in general? We believe that it points us towards an understanding of epistemic projects that departs from the mainstream. The mainstream view embodies the old prejudice that the intellect floats free from individual psychology and structural conditions. Reason, the largely covert prejudice goes, is too pure to be tainted by the mind outside the pure space of reasons (whatever that may be) and our locatedness in social space. Pure reason, the view goes, is largely untainted by those things that result in characters and institutional cultures being deeply recalcitrant. Part of what needs to be understood is that the intellectual project does not, in fact, float free of other aspects of the mind and its embeddedness in social space. It follows, then, that part of what intellectuals must do, *qua* intellectuals focused as they should be on understanding, is to work on the elusive features of the space within which they operate so that genuine academic freedom (from distortion) can be achieved.

The texture of our thinking, the sensibilities with which we approach our intellectual concerns, our intellectual tastes and preferences are all guided by our locatedness in social space and, relatedly, by our locatedness in academic space. Our styles of academic being, one could say, are a function of location. What matters to us, and in what ways it matters, is a function of our socio-historical subconscious.

The academic project, properly understood, can no longer be understood as separate from the characters of the institutions that sustain and nurture them. It follows that academics genuinely committed to the epistemic project should pay close attention to the largely unseen substratum upon which the life of the intellect rests.

Reference
Sartre, Jean-Paul. [1944] 1976. *Anti-Semite and Jew*. New York: Schocken Books.

Contributors

Minesh Dass is a lecturer in the English Department at Rhodes University. He has recently completed a PhD on representations of home and hospitality in post-transitional South African literature. His other areas of interest include American literature, poststructuralism and postmodernism.

Natalie Donaldson holds a Master's of Social Science degree and is a full-time lecturer in the Department of Psychology at Rhodes University. Her research interests fall under the general field of critical studies in race, gender and/or sexuality. Specifically, her focus is on how various social institutions construct race, gender and/or sexuality in the South African context.

Nigel C. Gibson is the director of the Honours programme at Emerson College in Boston and honorary research fellow at the School of Development Studies at the University of KwaZulu-Natal. He is author of *Fanon: The Postcolonial Imagination*, which won the 2009 Caribbean Philosophy Frantz Fanon Prize and was translated into Arabic in 2013. His most recent books are *Fanonian Practices in South Africa* and *Living Fanon*, which he edited to mark the fiftieth anniversary of Fanon's death.

Lewis R. Gordon is professor of philosophy, Africana studies and Judaic studies at the University of Connecticut at Storrs; Europhilosophy visiting professor at Toulouse University; Nelson Mandela visiting professor of Politics and International Studies at Rhodes University and chair of the Frantz Fanon and Nicolás Guillén awards committees of the Caribbean Philosophical Association. He is the author of numerous award-winning books and articles. Visit his website at http://lewisrgordon.com.

Amanda Hlengwa lectures at the Centre for Higher Education, Research, Teaching and Learning (CHERTL) at Rhodes University. She has worked in the field of higher education as an academic developer for nine years. Her interest in the relationship between disciplinary knowledge and curricula formed the basis of her PhD, which focused on the possibilities of service-learning as pedagogical tool that brings community engagement into the curriculum.

Bruce Janz is professor of humanities in the Department of Philosophy at the University of Central Florida. He is also graduate faculty with the Texts and Technologies PhD programme and director of the Center for Humanities and Digital Research. He is the author of *Philosophy in an African Place*, along with articles and papers on African philosophy, contemporary European philosophy, postcolonialism, studies in place and space, digital humanities, cultural and visual studies, and the history of mysticism.

Sally Matthews is a senior lecturer in the Department of Political and International Studies at Rhodes University, where she teaches comparative politics and African studies. Her recent publications have been on the topics of development theory, the politics of poverty and privilege, and race in contemporary South Africa.

Thaddeus Metz is research professor of philosophy at the University of Johannesburg. He is the author of more than 100 publications on an array of topics in moral, political and legal philosophy. Some recent works include: 'A Theory of National Reconciliation' (in *Theorizing Transitional Justice*), 'Dignity in the Ubuntu Tradition' (in *Cambridge Handbook of Human Dignity*) and 'African Values, Human Rights and Group Rights' (in *African Legal Theory and Contemporary Problems*).

Thando Njovane is a Flanagan scholar and a PhD candidate at the University of York in the United Kingdom. She has a first-class

Master's degree from Rhodes University, where she also worked in the English Department and in the Vice-Chancellorate. Her publications include peer-reviewed articles on Mia Couto, Uwem Akpan and trauma fiction.

Pedro Tabensky is the director of the newly formed Allan Gray Centre for Leadership Ethics (AGCLE), nested in the Department of Philosophy at Rhodes University. A central aim of the AGCLE is to help to transform the South African tertiary education sector. He is the author of *Happiness: Personhood, Community, Purpose* and several articles and book chapters. Tabensky is also the editor of and contributor to *Judging and Understanding* and *The Positive Function of Evil*.

Paul C. Taylor teaches philosophy at Pennsylvania State University, where he also heads the Department of African-American Studies and directs the programme on Philosophy after Apartheid. He has provided commentary on race and politics for newspapers and radio shows on four continents and has lectured at universities from Cape Town to Cornell. He is the author of *Race: A Philosophical Introduction* and is currently working on a book entitled *Black is Beautiful: A Philosophy of Black Aesthetics*.

Samantha Vice wrote this chapter while an associate professor of philosophy at Rhodes University. She has recently accepted a position as a professor at the University of the Witwatersrand. She is the co-editor of three collections – *Ethics at the Cinema* (with Ward Jones), *The Moral Life* (with Nafsika Athanassoulis) and a special issue of the journal *Philosophical Papers* on ageing and ethics (with Tom Martin) – and has published papers on various topics in ethics, social philosophy and aesthetics.

Louise Vincent is professor of political studies at Rhodes University in South Africa. Her research is principally in the field of the politics of the body. This interest expresses itself in a variety of projects in which she attempts to read the 'political' through a corporeal lens.

Index

Abahlali baseMjondolo, Durban shackdwellers movement 190–1
able-bodiedness 47
abolitionism 194
academic freedom 140–2, 243
academic intellectual communities 205
academic project
  contemporary global 228
  as leadership project 223
  open-endedness and limitless 110
academics 60, 67
  black 74, 76–7, 85–6, 89
  female 132
  professional and personal life 53
  white 73, 78, 85–7
access challenges 103
accountability 3, 277
accounting ethics 230
  teaching 229–33
aesthetics 246, 251, 252–3, 263, 266
affirmative action 15, 161–4, 168–9, 176
  debates 9, 177
  effort to eliminate 170
  legitimacy as social remedy 163
  opponents 171
Africana philosophy 217
Africanisation 10, 13, 242–3, 266–7
  curricula 246–7
  institutional culture 252
  misconstruals of 243–5
  moral force ascribed to 266
  strong, moderate, weak versions 252–3
Africanisation rationales 253
  civilisation 253, 260–3
  democracy 253, 256–8
  identity 253, 263–5
  redress 253, 258–60
  relativism 253, 254–6
Africanised management 250
Africanised scholarship 247–8
Africanising people versus place 245–6
  content 246–51
  extent 251
  implementation 251–2
African National Congress 257
African political philosophers 250
Afrikaners 265
Afro-relativists 255–6
agency 34, 54, 66
  and experience 52
  or hope 226
  of the material 36–8
AIDS 175
Ake, Claude 187
  'Social Science as Imperialism' 187

Algeria 212, 299
  independence 198
Algerian Revolution 185–6
alienating and racist rhetoric 127
alienation experience 46, 57, 128
Allan Gray Centre for Leadership
  Ethics 233
American Bar Association 167
American Philosophical Association
  205, 206–7
American Revolution 194
analytic and continental thought 214
Andrew W. Mellon Foundation 148
anecdotes 13
Anglo-American
  political philosophy 252
  universities 257
Anglo-Americanisation 258
Anglo-analytic mode of decoloniality
  217
Anglo-analytic philosophy 207, 210,
  211–14, 217
Anglo-analytic professional
  philosophers 204
Anglo-analytic world 205–6
anti-affirmative action arguments
  170, 173–4
anti-black racism 176
anti-black society 170
anti-colonial intellectuals 196
anti-gay sentiments and stereotypes
  137
apartheid 45, 117, 129, 147, 203, 284,
  297
  era and black people 76, 90
  government 158
  history 258
  legacies 35, 116
  legislation 131
  practices 22
  social inequalities 131
  transition from 13

Arendt, Hannah 234
Aristotelean curriculum 291
Aristotle 229, 230, 233, 300
Armstrong, Lance 234
arts 168, 291
  classical liberal 290
  assimilationist approach 7
Australasia 244
Australia 171, 205

bad faith (self-deceit) 233
  and ignorance 239
  language of denialism 169
Basic Conditions of Employment
  Act 138
becoming, otherness, emergence
  concepts 274
being
  collective modes 227
  at home 5, 45
  in one's element 6, 47–55, 66
  and perceiving modes 221–39
  relational 52–3
  styles of 227
belonging, sense of 53
Biko, Steve 195, 262
Black Consciousness conception 173
black identity politics 31
blackness 117
black South Africans
  academics 8
  admissions, hirings, promotions
    246
  African, coloured, Indian 118
  biologisation and dehumanisation
    192
  exceptional 121
  exclusion and suffering 163
  females 117, 122, 145
  fighting against exclusion 89–90
  incarceration of 173–4
  middle class 167, 177

population statistics 147
staff appointments 73
with white accents 124–5
black trade union movements 195
book reviews 212
Boxill, Bernard 163
Blacks and Social Justice 163
Brazil and *favelas* 177
Brecht, Bertolt 33
British Philosophical Association 205
Brown University study of race and domicile 177
brutality of revolutionary violence 197
bureaucratisation 238, 274, 276, 289
also known as managerialism 277

call for utility 110
Cambodia 214
Cambridge University 205
Canada 171
Cape Town as slave colony 157
capital
  cultural 151
  white racial 176
career choices 234
Centre for Higher Education, Research, Teaching and Learning (CHERTL) 2, 101
Césaire, Aimé 288
China 166
civil engagement 184
civilisation 243, 253, 260–3
  enhancing and disseminating 263
class 27, 47, 59, 72, 157
  discrimination 3
  divisions 189
  hypocritical concerns 177
classical liberal arts 290, 291
classification, opposing poles of 102–3
Cold War context 214–15
collective effort 226

collective memories 46
work 33–4, 42
collegial system 57
Collini, Stefan 109–11, 113
What Are Universities For? 109
Colombia 177
colonial anthropological practice 188–9
colonial attitude and repression of blackness 127
colonial culture, inherited 126
colonial domination 187
colonialism 129, 172–3, 188
  history 258
  modern 213–14
  and postcolonial period 35
colonial regimes 147
  tolerated violence and injustice 172
colonial societies 13
colonisation 284
colour-blindness *see under* race
commonality 42
communication mediums 248
community
  academic 237
  critical 30
  learning 30
  practical, of inquiry 30–1
  townships and informal settlements 189
  values, norms, cultures, institutions 264
compensation 265
conscientisation programme 195
conscious capitalism 184
consciousness
  changes in 222, 225–6
  critical engagement with 224
  historical 224
consciousness-raising process 31–3
  in group context 32

Constitution, South African 3, 130–1, 139, 142, 147, 159, 161
  same-sex sexualities protection 131
consumption, right to 159
contemporary global university 228
continuity 26
Cooper, Anna Julia 177
  'What Are We Worth?' 177
corporatisation 185, 238, 274, 276, 289
corruption 234
  and delivery failures 189
  garden-variety individual 208–9
  see also institutional corruption
countercultural academic environment 223
counternarratives 26–7, 41–2
courage, lack of 64
creativity 274–5, 278, 282
  cultural and intellectual 286
  instrumentalised space 295
crime 173, 175
criminalisation of black populations 174
critical analysis and understanding 31
critical race theory 211, 298
'Critical Reflections on Three Popular Tropes in the Study of Whiteness' (L.R. Gordon) 165
Cubans 244
cultural artefacts 282–3
cultural heritage, mining 266
cultural investment 177
cultural transformation 218
culture(s)
  academic 222
  elements of 211
  historical 222
  transformed 47
  see also under sub-Sahara
curriculum 246, 247, 251, 252–3, 266
  content 262

issues 204
market-driven status quo 232

debates 46, 55, 58
decoloniality 217
decolonial mode of inquiry 217
decolonial theorists 217
dehumanisation, systematic 186
Deleuze, Gilles 290
Deleuzian approach to race 274
Deleuzian intensity, creative tension 283
democracy 243, 253, 256–8, 266
democratic values 256–7
denialism 119, 123
  bad faith language of 169
  of persisting racism 170
Derrida, Jacques 7, 103–6, 109, 125
deterritorialisations 274–5
development
  programmes 8
  and service delivery 189
disabilities 17, 72
  physical or mental 161
disadvantage, socio-economic and educational 117
disaffirmative action 168
disciplinary decadence 196
disciplinary expertise 229
disciplinary inquiry 205
disciplinary procedures 78
  racist incidents 88
discourses 23–4
discrimination 15, 25, 26, 27, 90, 131, 132, 139, 142, 143, 144, 161, 234
  invidious on grounds of social identity 216
  racial 3, 75–6, 160, 275
  reverse 169, 170, 173
  unfair 139–43
diversity 9, 22, 145
  sexual 130
  sexual and gender 138

Index

dominance
  forms of 24
  reproduction of 38
  white 87
domination 281
  contemporary forms of racial 80–1
  elimination of racial 91
drama as engagement with racism 90
Drum, magazine 286, 290
Du Bois, W.E.B. 87
Dummert, Michael 215

economic privation 59
Edmond J. Safra Research Lab, Harvard University 208
education 159–60, 165, 178
  access to 160–1
  humanistic 160
  liberal 275–6, 290
  liberatory mission 197
  limiting 158
  physical 168
  publically funded 276
  sexist approach to 245
  traditional African 245
'Education White Paper 3: A Programme for the Transformation of Higher Education' 3, 131
egalitarianism, ambient 217
Eichmann, Adolf 234
Eliot, T.S. 122–3
elitism 195
emancipation ideals 258
empirical self-inventory 218
employees of universities, professional and personal lives 60
employment equity programmes 73
enculturation 267
English 205
  non-first-language speakers 127
  study of literature 192

enlightenment 230
  secularisation 192
enslavement 160, 172
entanglement 117, 123
environment
  and character 54
  developing 54
epistemic cultures 9–10, 204, 218–19
epistemicide 259, 266
  cognitive side of genocide 175
epistemic injustice 259
  compensation for historical 259
epistemic projects 300, 301
epistemic puritanism 224, 226
epistemological change 204
epistemological struggles 243
epochal ethos 226
equality
  and democratisation goals 160
  economic and social 193–4
  historical racial 273
  and non-racialism notions 119–20
  racial 55, 72, 79, 82, 130–1
equity
  focus 130
  statistics 150
Eradicating Unfair Discrimination and Harassment policy 140
essentialism 243, 245, 263
essentialist and biological discourses 134–5
Ethembeni informal settlement 190–1
ethical conduct as living and equal relationship 188
ethical conversion 230
ethical life 232
ethical-psychological lives 233
ethics 106, 229–33
Ethics, journal 212
ethos 55, 58
  challenges of institutions 49

insight, persistence, research,
self-knowledge 228
and motivations 65
uniting 67
eulogies project for students 230–3
Eurocentric resources and frames 217
Eurocentrism 186–7, 238
Europe 168, 186
concept of humanism 192
European and American models 63
European traditions 64–5
exclusion 25, 26, 122
policies to address 14–15
Existential Conversations, pilot
project 233–6
existential philosophy 195
experience 33–4
exploitation 160

fairness 55
familist ideology 135
Fanon, Frantz 9, 31, 160, 172–3,
185–99, 212, 225, 299
Black Skin, White Masks 198–9
'Colonial Wars and Mental
Liberation' 190
critique of colonised intellectual
185
A Dying Colonialism 197
preface by Jean-Paul Sartre 128
revolutionary therapy 299
The Wretched of the Earth 128, 185,
190, 193, 197
feeling at home 47–55
feminism 31, 298
feminist(s) 237
and queer theory 211
methodology in social sciences 30
feminist theory 217
force
coersive 251
normative 251–2

Ford Foundation 2
Forster, E.M. 102, 105
A Passage to India 102
freedom
academic 140–2, 243, 267, 301
and equality 193
of expression 142
ideals 258
struggles 196–7
French Revolution 192, 193, 194
declaration of liberty, fraternity,
equality 192
rights of man 192, 193
Freud, Sigmund 298, 299
funding, international 148

Gadamer, Hans-Georg 226, 286
Truth and Method 224
gender 8, 17, 27, 47, 59, 72, 129, 130,
132, 213
Imbizo on 139
transformation 131–2, 139
ghettoisation 218
global neo-liberal capitalist context 185
goodness 239
Good Samaritan experiment 234
governance 251, 252–3, 262–3, 266
Grahamstown
local history 124–5
Race and Higher Education
roundtable 161–2, 164
Gramsci, Antonio 160
praxis of philosophy 196
Greco-Roman pedestal 172, 185–6
group(s)
process 30
shared setting 32–3
under-represented 148, 207–8
guiding ideal 64

habits 229
habituation 300

Index

Haiti 214
  Saint-Domingue struggle for freedom 192
Haitian Revolution 194–5
harassment 143
hate speech 142
Heidegger, Martin 221, 286
  Being and Nothingness 224
heteronormative gendered practices 138
heteronormative parenting structures
  definition of partner 136
  maternity and paternity benefits 137
  primary caregiver 136
heteronormative values and morals 139
heteronormativity 14, 15, 130, 133, 134, 137, 144, 153
heterosexist notions of gender and sexuality 132
heterosexual individuals and couples 135, 139
hierarchy 57
higher education
  apartheid-era sector 73
  corporatisation, marketisation, instrumentalisation 185
  economic growth and job-creation 277–8
  and gender and sexuality 130–3
  institutional culture 74–5
  race in South African context 73–4
  transformation in South Africa 218–19
higher education institutions 2, 17, 45, 90
  black-led project of transformation 91
  'multiversities' 203
  patriarchal and heteronormative 132
  professional citizenship production 138
  race and white privilege 74–8, 83–7
  transformation 47
Higher Education Management System (HEMIS) statistics 147
Higher Education South Africa (HESA) 74, 148
  report 77
historical legacy 225
history 224–5
  public and oral projects 293
  unfolding 226
HIV/AIDS 135
'home for all' at Rhodes University 144
homophobia 3, 132, 134
hospitality 100–1
  conditional, conventional 104–5, 109
  ethical imperative of infinite 109
  limited 104–5, 125, 126
  unlimited 112
hospitality, unconditional/absolute 109
  ethical demand for 112
  ethical imperative of 11–12, 104
  principle and paradox 102–5
Huddleston, Father Trevor 285
human agency, limits of 226
human credit rating 164
human freedom 193, 195
humanism
  bourgeois 194
  oppositional and critical 185
  radical 197, 198
humanities
  critique of education 185, 186
  radical 190, 192–5, 196, 199
human kindness and dignity 187
human resources 208

human rights and transformation 131
human welfare and rehumanisation 187
human worth question 195
humiliation 123

identity 28–9, 243, 248, 253, 263–5
  African 263–4
  expression of 53
  'other' 132
  post-apartheid South Africa 1
  theory 288
ideology-blindness 238
immigration, metaphysical 172
Immorality Act 131
inclusion 204
  and anti-homophobia discourses 133–9
inclusivity strategies 134
independence ideals 258
India, slums in 177
Indian descent, people of 265
indigenous peoples 172, 244–5, 260
  knowledge of herbs and plants 248
individualism 175–6
individual misbehaviour 209
inequality 25, 27, 189
  gender and sexuality 130–1, 133
  racial 275
  reproduction of 38
inhospitable social conditions 126
injustice 284
  correcting 129
  racial 172
  racially motivated against others 120
  racist and sexist 298
  reproduction of 38
  stories and reproduction of 27–35
  struggles against racial 11
institutional autonomy 267
institutional climate surveys 75
institutional corruption 204, 208–10

institutional cultures 1–7, 12–13, 16–17, 21–4, 45–55, 116, 153, 227, 246, 297–8, 300
  change 218
  discursive dimension 5
  ethical obligation to Africanise 252
  as homely or alienating 46
  materiality of 35–42
  narrating 23–5
  narrative understanding of workings 38
  in post-apartheid spaces 204
  reference to race and whiteness 27
  transformation 47, 72, 88, 203
  transformational debates 46
  untransformed 2
institutional environments, contemporary 22
institutional history 63
institutional identities 24–5
institutionalisation of literary education 192
institutional membership 25
institutional psychotherapist 299
institutional reform 103
institutional subconscious 298
institutional transformation 1
  related to race 72
institutions
  material dimension 5
  physical features 5
  'whiteness' of 6
instrumentalisation 291
  and creativity in universities 289–95
  of higher education 13–14
  linguistic phenomenon 279
  model 273–4
  at universities 11, 273–80, 290
instrumentalism 284
integrity 234, 235
  breakdown 233
  life of 233

intellectual alienation 189
intellectual deficiency 175
intellectual history 65
intellectual practice modes 205
intellectual project 300
intellectual virtues, lack of 64
intellectual work 223
interaction styles 46
interdisciplinarity 292–3, 295
and anti-disciplinarity 293
international collaboration 294–5
North-South or South-South 294
interpersonal relations 117
inter-racial contact in South Africa 116–17
intolerance feeds off tolerance 120
intra-action 23

Jamaica 213
Japan 166, 244
Jaspers, Karl 172
The Question of German Guilt 172
Johnson, James Weldon 166
'Black National Anthem' 167
'Lift Every Voice and Sing' 167
justice 79, 163, 248
conception of 65
global 212–13
lack of 64
racial 79

Kafka, Franz 280, 282
Kierkegaard, Søren 286
King, Martin Luther 173
knowledge 223, 275–6, 292
contingent 110
discovery and transmission 264
economy 294
hierarchies 254
and identities 131
indigenous systems 254
national discourses 294

open-ended pursuit of 109–13
production of new 291
relativist claims about 255
society 294
transmission 48
valid 254
Western universities 257–8
'know thyself' injunction 264
Kresge Foundation 148
Kristeva, Julia 28–9

labour 157, 160
cheap force 158, 159
global capacity 159
Labour Relations Act 138
land
dispossession 258
and resources acquisitions 162
language 125, 127, 128, 214, 244, 246, 248, 251, 252–3, 266, 289
African 262
of becoming 279
indigenous 262
of instrumentalisation 279
second-language speakers 127
law professions 168
leadership 16, 42, 66, 236
glass ceilings 166
virtue and academic project 233–6
legal and ethical sanctions 207
lesbian couples 138
lesbian, gay, bisexual, transgendered, intersex, asexual and queer (LGBTIAQ) 132
organisation (OutRhodes) 133
Levinas, Emmanuel 7
liberal arts 278, 291
liberation 198
defeat of movement 186
ideals 258
second struggle 198
struggle 189, 197

Lincoln, Abraham 167
literature 192
　whiteness 83
　white privilege 72, 91
　see also major literatures;
　　minoritarian literature; minor
　　literature

Madagascar 157
majoritarian languages 281, 288
major literatures 280–1
Makana Municipality water crisis
　190–1
Mamdani, Mahmood 158
　Citizen and Subject 158
Mandela, Nelson 162, 168, 176
　statue in Trafalgar Square 39–40
marginalisation, racial 282, 289
market forces 60
markets, science, constitutionalism 244
Marx, Karl 289, 300
Marxists 214
masculinity politics 33
Masekela, Hugh 285
Mashinini, Emma 198
　Strikes Have Followed Me All My Life
　198
massacre of miners at Marikana 197
material artefacts 35
material-discursive idea 23
materiality 42
　of institutional culture 35–42
Mbembe, Achille 283, 289
　'African Modes of Self-Writing'
　284–5
　On the Postcolony 283–5
mediocrity
　racial hegemonic 164–5
　presumed 165
　white 165
metaphors *see under* being
micro cultures 26

Middle Ages 291
migration, forced 160
Milgram experiment 234
minoritarian literature 286, 288, 290,
　293–4
　in cramped racial spaces 292
　minor literature 291
　race and universities 280–3
mixed heritage, people of 265
modernist approaches 248
modes of practice 211
molar system 11, 14, 279, 292
molecular creativity 285
molecularisation of race 282
money-related conflicts of interest
　209
morality 35
moral point of values 64–5
multiculturalism 261
music 249, 287–8
　cappella forms 287
　indigenous songs or rhythms
　　249–50
　isicathamiya, song and performance
　　286–7
　jazz 168
　kwaito 287
privatisation of education 168
university choirs 250
myths, stories, proverbs 260

narratives 5, 12, 29, 36
　approach 24
　dominance 27
　of excellence 26
　logic of 225
　role of 129
　see also molar system
national liberation and nationalism
　186
national ressentiment 171
nativism 284, 285

Index

Nazi criminals 234
negative emotions for being African 264
négritude 289
   essentialist racial strategy 288
   history of 288
neo-classical economics 232
neo-colonial present 187
neo-conservatism 174–8
neo-liberal and neo-conservative market fundamentalist demands 161
neo-liberal capitalism 184–5, 189
neo-liberal critics 176
neoliberalism 174–8
New Left Marxism, France 195
Newman, John Henry Cardinal 291
   The Idea of a University 291
noble savage concept 121, 127–8
non-discrimination 59
non-first-language speakers of English 127
non-normative genders and/or sexualities 130
non-violence expectations 173
normative social practices 163
norms 47, 264, 265
   somatic 28, 39

Obama, Barack 162, 176
'on-the-ground' heterosexism and prejudice 140
opportunity
   for black students 273
   lack of 275
oppression 16, 42, 126, 143, 144, 275
   colonialism and apartheid legacy 116
   and exclusion 81
   mental scars of 198
   survivors of racial 292
organisational culture 4

orientation programme 100
'other', situation of being 77–8
otherness 274
overcoming and surviving 289

Parental Leave and Benefits policy 134–6, 138, 139
participatory action research 30–1
'past discrimination' expression 169
patents and copyrights 295
pathologies, psychological disorders, traumas 197
patriarchy 153
   and Empire 215
p'Biket, Okot 280
   Song of Lawino 280
pedagogical appoaches 246
pedagogical practices 116, 227
pedagogical struggles 243
philosophers, analytic 224
Philosophical Society of South Africa 205, 206
philosophy
   African 247
   African-American political 252
   after apartheid 217
   analytic 205
   Anglo-American political 252
   Anglo-analytic 207, 210, 211–14, 217
   anglophone 205
   corrupted 210–11
   decolonial analytic 216–19
   and English quarrel 214
   as institution 204–8
   Latino/a 217
   political 46, 58, 288
   post-colonial analytic 211–16, 217
   professional 204–5
   transformation 208
   United States and South Africa 206

Philosophy and Public Affairs, journal 212
philosophy department appointments
 African-Americans 206
 women 206
Plato 229, 233, 239
policies 134
 and ethos 61
 and practice gap 128–9
 and procedures 78, 90
 against racism 88, 90
political debate about multiculturalism 59
political shootings 197
politics of recognition 59
post-apartheid South Africa 1, 159, 190, 216, 225
 pathology of politeness 117
 society 203
post-colonial duties 212
post-colonial environments 174
post-colonialism 213
post-colonial society as political society 198
post-colonial theory/theorists 217, 237–8
 or scholarship 214
post-colonial university 187
Postgraduate Diploma in Higher Education (PGDHE) 149
postmodernism 213
post-racial and post-apartheid world 177–8
post-racialism as racial project 217
post-segregational settings 79–84
post-segregationist societies 79, 81, 82, 88, 91
post-transitional South Africa 123
poverty 175, 275
power 41, 116, 117
 and authority relationship 123
 behind power 166

elite academic institution 32
hegemonic structure of colony 124
structures 128
pre-colonial life 245
prejudgement 224
prejudice 118, 126, 131, 132, 142, 143, 144, 224, 225, 226, 298–9, 300
 covert 301
 racial 77
pressures, social, economic, political 65
Pride Week 142
 banner on StudentZone website 142
Princeton University 205
privatisation 176
privilege
 conception 165
 racial and hierarchy reformulation 217–18
 see also white privilege
privileging of victimhood over subjecthood 284
productivity 295
 and flourishing 66
professionalism 3
professional organisations 205
professional philosophy as an institution 210
Programme for Accelerated Development (PAD) 148–54
 reflections on 150
 research time for academics 149
proletarianisation of people of African descent 157
psychoanalysis 298, 299
psychological health 198
Public Arts Committee, Westminster Council 39–40
public funds for private interests 175
 welfare for the rich 175
publish-or-perish culture 238

qualifications 173
   debate 161–71
   narrative 164
queer individuals 145
   equality in relation to 139
   genders and sexualities 137–8
   prejudice against 134
   staff and students 133, 142, 144

race 4, 16–17, 47, 59, 117, 129, 130, 157, 161, 248
   and creativity 283–9
   disguised as colour-blindness 82, 119, 120
   marginalisation and brutality history 274
   politics on campus, Grahamstown 234
   and power in academy 8, 116
   survival and creativity history 274
   theory 217
   and transformation 75
race-neutral approaches 82
racial essentialist stereotypes 121
racialisation, South African 157
racism 6, 15, 72, 76, 82, 87, 118, 132, 169, 259, 298, 298
   American 157
   'black-on-black' 2
   claims 78
   contemporary forms 77, 88–9
   covert 128
   experience of black academics 77
   histories 160
   at institutional levels 177
   overt 298
   policies to address 14–15
   preventing 266
   report (minister of education) 246–7
racist beliefs 80, 273
racist incidents, explicitly 86–7

racist laws, repeal of 79
radical humanities model 14
radicality 192–3
Rawls, John 65
   A Theory of Justice 215
Reagan, Ronald 175
reason 301
Reclaiming the Human Sciences and Humanities through African Perspectives (Lauer and Anyidoho) 187
redress 10, 243, 253, 258–60, 261
   and social equity principles 147
reform proposals 292
regulative ideal 61
relativism 253, 254–6, 266
   implication of 256
   logic of 255
religion 47, 59, 161
research 110, 189, 246, 247, 251, 252–3, 266, 297
   agendas 262
   grant-driven, state-sanctioned 292
   medical, and interest conflicts 209
   open-ended 111
   pharmaceutical and industry funding 209
   World Bank and funding sources 187
researchers, non-financial interests of 209
resistance 284
   apartheid 281
   countercultural points of 10
   racial 279
   to resistance 175
responsibility 172–4
   ideas of 106
   political and legal 172
   social 172
revitalising African civilisation 260

Rhodes University 1–2, 6–8, 90,
    147–8, 227, 249, 300
  annual postgraduate conference
    paper 140–1
  black experience 127
  challenges 105–9
  community engagement
    programme 107–9
  Cycle of Knowledge poetry group
    108
  Department of Accounting 232
  Department of Philosophy 233
  disadvantages of black students 117
  heteronormativity problem 130–45
  Ntsika Secondary School reading
    group 108
  parental leave policy 8
  personal experience of discomfort
    99–101
  presentation on transformation
    85–7
  Stephen Bantu Biko Building 1
  strategies and policies 131–2
  vision and mission statement 47–8,
    133, 143, 185, 187
  'where leaders learn' logo 199
Rhodes University Equity Policy
    120–1, 128
rural/urban divide 162
Russell, Bertrand 215

safe bets 148–9, 150–4
  advantages to employing 152
  element of surprise 153
  fitting description of 151–3
  notion 119
same-sex couples 139
  egalitarian parenting structures 136
  legislation to adopt and parent
    children 135–6
same-sex sexualities 131
sanctions 159

Sartre, Jean-Paul 128, 299, *see also
    under* Fanon, Frantz
savagery and civilisation arguments 214
sciences 168
Scholastic period 222
self-commodification 185
self-conceptions 211
self-critique 215, 217
self-development, value of 10
self-esteem and basic dignity 165
self-excavation aversion 215
self-knowledge 210
self-serving greed 228
self-understanding, value of 10
Senghor, Léopold Sédar 288
sense-making and identity-
    constructing tools 25
sensibilities and interests 227
sex 129, 161
sexism 3, 132, 169, 298
sexual harassment 132
sexuality 8, 17, 27, 72, 130, 132
Sexual Offences Act 131
sexual orientation 132
sexual transformation 139
shelter 165
slavery 166, 171, 194, 284
  racialised and colonialism 174
slave trade, mass extinction of 192
social activism 189
social consciousness 199
social entrepreneurship 184
social ethics 215
social exclusion 153
social inequality 273
socialised individual 199
socialists 214
social justice for black people 163
social practices of exclusion and
    systemic violence 157–8
social psychological experiments 234
social relations 31, 116

Index

social reproduction 5, 25–7
social science 35
social status and affluence, self-serving desire for 10
social structures 34
social theory 42
society
   socially and politically transformed 47
   transitional or transforming 54–5
   uncivil 174
socio-economic inequality 198
socio-historical conditions 226–7
socio-historical subconscious 301
somatic norm 28, 39
Sophiatown 285–6, 289, 290, 295
   compared to Harlem Renaissance 285
   see also Drum, magazine
Soudien Committee report 73–4
South Africa 171, 175, 205
   crime and insecurity 173
   1994 elections 159
   shacks 177
South African Department of Higher Education and Training 147
South African Institute of Chartered Accountants 232
South African Journal of Higher Education 3
South African Panorama, voice of apartheid state 290
South African Students' Organisation (SASO) 195
   creation of 'formation schools' 195
space-clearing 213
spaces 58–9, 89, 126, 199
   academic 107
   individual needs 66–7
   invaders 39
specialisation 228
spiritual genocide 258–9

stability 65–6
staff orientation programme 111
standards 26
Stanford prison experiment 234
Stangl, Franz 234
Stanton College Preparatory School, Florida 167
STEM (science, technology, engineering, mathematics) disciplines 293
   non-STEM areas 293
stereotyping 90, 118
stock stories of excellence 26–7, *see also* story stock
stories 5, 16, 24–5
   institutional 26
   public telling of 41–2
story stock 29–30
   dominant narratives of institution 30
storytelling 16
   collective 32
strangeness, repressed 28
Student Representative Council (SRC) 1–2
subconscious 298, *see also* Freud, Sigmund
subjectivity 34–5, 38, 284
sub-Sahara
   conflict resolution approach 250
   cultures 261, 262
   education or culture 245, 261
   intellectual tradition 261
   perspectives 257
   restorative justice 250–1
   values and norms 265
   ways of life 259, 260
success as wealth and social standing 228
supremacist projects 214
supremacy 298
survival skills 292

symbolic castration 259
symbolism 35
symbols of universities 249–50
systemic heterosexism and
    heteronormativity 134

teaching 229–30
    accounting ethics 229–33
    pedagogical experiments 227–9
technical knowledge 293
tertiary institutions 45, 203
Thatcher, Margaret 175, 184
theodicy 196
theoretical sociology 205
Thinking Africa edition, *Mail &
    Guardian* 164
Thiong'o, Ngũgĩ wa 280
Third Text, journal 288
thought and action, relationship
    between 223
thrownness 221–2
    thrown into the world 225
tolerance 120, 218
    and inclusion, limits of 14
    in liberalism 119
    role of 118
total way of life (an ethos) 227
townships and informal settlements
    190
traditional healers 248
traditionally marginalised people 59,
    see also marginalisation, racial
traditionally under-represented groups
    206
traditional medicine 248
traditions, articulation and stability
    61–7
transformation 4, 7, 12, 17, 35, 41, 49,
    50, 90, 130
    agenda 204, 219
    agents 15–16
    challenges 55–61

complexity 2–3
    of discrete spaces 56
    in higher education 2
    initiatives for change 131
    of institutional cultures 297
    lack of 13
    racial 131–2
    of tertiary sector 297
transformative epistemic projects 297
transparency 3
trauma 198
Truth and Reconciliation Commission
    250
truthfulness, lack of 64

understanding 224, 228, 239
    ancients 228
    modes 227
    nature of 222
    non-puritanical 226
    quests for 12, 225
    of understanding 227
unemployment and structural
    pauperisation 198
Unfair Discrimination and
    Harassment policy 132
United Kingdom 158–9, 161, 205,
    213
United States 158–9, 60, 161, 169,
    173–5, 205
    anti-affirmative action group
        169–70
    civil rights movements 82
    ghettos and reservations 177
    Leiter Reports 206
    white immigrants 171
unity 42
universal knowledge transmission 291
universities
    classic 291
    as countercultural institutions 229
    elite, privileged space 199

environment 46
governance and funding 277
historically advantaged 61
instruction in English or Afrikaans 248–9
as instruments for success 228
management style 204
market-based and bureaucratised 291
mission statements 47–8, 52
neo-liberal 238
post-apartheid 188–9
rethinking 187
social inclusion 204
and state relationship 277
University of Cape Town 205
'Institutional Climate Survey Report' 75
racial discrimination 75
University of the Free State 129
racist incidents 129
University of Johannesburg 106, 249
University of KwaZulu-Natal 249
University of Limpopo 249
University of Natal 195
University of Stellenbosch 129, 249
racist incidents 129
University of Pretoria 249
University of Texas, Austin 169–71
University of the Witwatersrand 90, 106
perceptions of racism 75, 78
unjust justice and just injustice 163
utilitarianism 111

values 46, 47, 58, 60–1, 134, 140
articulation of as moral task 64–5
commitments 53
of cultures 62–3
of experience and impact of absence 54
and goals 48, 53

promoted by apartheid 3
traditional Africans 260
verbal toyi-toying 118
victimisation 143
violence 25, 117, 120, 139, 143, 173
of colonial racism 192
cultural 259
objective 125
of the state 189
subjective and objective 125
systemic and symbolic 125, 192
verbal 121
violent crime 173
violent geographies of fast capitalism 189
virtue 216, 228–9, 235
generally rather than intellectual 223
theory 217
virtuous living 223–4, 233
vocational colleges 110
vulnerability, production of 169

ways of being 22, 211
ways of life 46
African 258–9
indigenous Africans 245
sub-Saharan 259, 260
white females 169
whitely habits 80, 90
environments and development of 89
of privilege 87
white males 169
white minority 158
whiteness 22
critique 47
culture of 27
literature on 83
privileged over blackness 117, 118–19
white normativity and privilege 176

white people
  need to be race-cognisant 82–3
  numerical minority 89–90
white privilege 6, 80–2, 83, 90–1
  habits 80, 83
  as invisible knapsack 83–6
  literature on 72, 91
  tackling indirectly 87–90
  variety of list 84
white supremacism 79, 81
white supremacy 158, 166, 215
  inertial racism of white
    predominance 79
  reigning public philosophy 79
  social investment in 164
  and white privilege 79–80
women 206
  of colour, inclusion of 166
  young 8
worldviews 224–5
  African 258–9
  of institutions 5

xenophobia 3
Xhosa
  initiation practices 127–8
  traditional rituals 128

Zuma, Jacob 190